The International Brand Valuation Manual

A Complete Overview and Analysis of Brand Valuation Techniques, Methodologies and Applications

Gabriela Salinas

A John Wiley & Sons, Ltd., Publication

Registered office
John Wiley & Sons Ltd, The Atrium, Southern Gate, Chichester, West Sussex, PO19 8SQ, United Kingdom

For details of our global editorial offices, for customer services and for information about how to apply for permission to reuse the copyright material in this book please see our website at www.wiley.com.

Revised and updated from the original Spanish edition *Valoracion de Marcas: Revision de enfoques, metodologias y proveedores* published in 2007 by Ediciones Duesto, Barcelona.

The right of the author to be identified as the author of this work has been asserted in accordance with the Copyright, Designs and Patents Act 1988.

Reprinted March 2011

Library of Congress Cataloging-in-Publication Data

Salinas, Gabriela.
  The international brand valuation manual : a complete overview and analysis of brand valuation techniques and methodologies and their application / by Gabriela Salinas.
    p. cm.
  Includes bibliographical references and index.
  ISBN 978-0-470-74031-6 (cloth)
1. Branding (Marketing)   2. Brand name products.   3. Valuation.   I. Title.
  HF5415.1255.S35 2009
  657'.7–dc22

                                                                2009004184

A catalogue record for this book is available from the British Library.

Set in 11 on 16 pt Trump Medieval by SNP Best-set Typesetter Ltd., Hong Kong
Printed in Great Britain by TJ International Ltd, Padstow, Cornwall

To the memory of Ethan
and all my loved ones . . .

Contents

LIST OF FIGURES AND TABLES   xiii
FOREWORD   xix
ACKNOWLEDGEMENTS   xxiv
INTRODUCTION   xxvi

1   **THE CONCEPT AND RELEVANCE OF BRAND**   1
   1.1   THE CONCEPT OF BRAND   1
      1.1.1   *The accounting perspective*   2
          1.1.1.1   *The brand as an intangible asset*   2
          1.1.1.2   *Non-recognizable intangible assets: Internally generated brands*   4
          1.1.1.3   *Trademark, brand and branded business*   5
      1.1.2   *The economic perspective*   7
          1.1.2.1   *Economic vs. accounting criteria*   7
      1.1.3   *The management perspective*   8
          1.1.3.1   *Brand and corporate reputation*   8
          1.1.3.2   *Brand and visual identity*   11
      1.1.4   *Brand, intangible assets and intellectual capital – Everyday vocabulary and conflated terms*   12
          1.1.4.1   *Brand equity and intangible assets*   12
          1.1.4.2   *Brand, intangible assets and intellectual capital*   14

1.2   BRAND VALUE   18
     1.2.1   *What is brand value?*   18
     1.2.2   *How do brands create value?*   19
1.3   THE GROWING IMPORTANCE OF THE ECONOMIC
VALUE OF BRAND   20
     1.3.1   *Business evidence*   20
     1.3.2   *Social evidence*   22
     1.3.3   *Economic evidence*   22
     1.3.4   *Normative and institutional evidence*   24
     1.3.5   *Academic evidence*   30
1.4   CONCLUSIONS   31

**2   THE ORIGIN AND EVOLUTION OF VALUATION
METHODS   33**
2.1   THE ORIGIN AND EVOLUTION OF VALUATION
METHODS   33
     2.1.1   *Origins: The series of acquisitions in
the 1980s*   33
     2.1.2   *The first brand valuation: Rank Hovis
McDougall*   35
     2.1.3   *The accounting conflict generated by brand
capitalization*   36
     2.1.4   *Rapid development and applications*   37
     2.1.5   *Who values brands today?*   38
     2.1.6   *How do corporations use this tool?*   40
     2.1.7   *How do investment analysts use this
information?*   41
     2.1.8   *How do other players use this information?*   43
2.2   CONCLUSIONS   45

3   BRAND VALUATION METHOD AND PROCESS   47
3.1   BRAND VALUATION PROCESS   47
     3.1.1   *What is brand valuation?*   48
     3.1.2   *The current debate: Why bother with
brand valuation?*   48
     3.1.3   *The purpose of brand valuation*   50
         3.1.3.1   *Brand management*   51
         3.1.3.2   *Accounting purposes*   52
         3.1.3.3   *Internal or external transaction
purposes*   52
     3.1.4   *Defining the scope of valuation and the
concept of brand*   54

| | 3.1.5 | Choosing an appropriate methodology | 54 |
| 3.2 | CONCLUSIONS | | 56 |

4 GENERAL APPROACHES TO BRAND VALUATION | | | **57**
4.1	COST APPROACH		58
4.2	MARKET APPROACH		61
4.3	INCOME APPROACH		63
	4.3.1	Price premium	65
	4.3.2	Royalty savings	70
	4.3.3	Demand drivers/brand strength analysis	82
	4.3.4	Comparison of gross margin with that of relevant competitors	89
	4.3.5	Comparison of operating profit with that of relevant competitors	91
	4.3.6	Comparison with theoretical profits of a generic product	92
	4.3.7	Cash flow or income differences with a benchmark company ("subtraction approach")	94
	4.3.8	Present value of incremental cash flow (the company's value "with" and "without" brand)	95
	4.3.9	Free cash flow (FCF) less required return on other non-brand-related assets	96
	4.3.10	Excess earnings	96
	4.3.11	Company valuation less value of net tangible assets	102
	4.3.12	Real options	103

5 BRAND VALUATION METHODS AND PROVIDERS | | | **109**
5.1	ABSOLUTEBRAND		110
5.2	AUS CONSULTANTS		112
5.3	BBDO		117
	5.3.1	Brand Equity Evaluation System (BEES)	118
	5.3.2	Brand Equity Evaluator®	121
	5.3.3	"Brand Equity Valuation for Accounting" (BEVA)	126
5.4	BRANDIENT		129
	5.4.1	Brandient's model based on demand driver analysis	129
	5.4.2	Brandient's model based on royalty savings	131

5.5	BRANDECONOMICS	132
5.6	BRAND FINANCE	144
	5.6.1 Royalty savings	145
	5.6.2 Earnings split	147
5.7	BRANDMETRICS	151
5.8	BRAND RATING	158
5.9	CONSOR	164
	5.9.1 Royalty savings model based on Valmatrix® analysis	165
	5.9.2 ValCALC® model (excess earnings)	167
	5.9.3 $BVE_Q{}^{TM}$ model (core brand value plus the value of incremental efficiencies)	168
	5.9.4 Residual approach (market cap less the value of tangible assets)	170
5.10	DAMODARAN'S VALUATION MODEL	171
5.11	FINANCIAL WORLD	174
5.12	FUTUREBRAND	179
5.13	GFK-PWC-SATTLER: ADVANCED BRAND VALUATION MODEL	184
5.14	HERP'S MODEL	192
5.15	HIROSE MODEL	193
5.16	HOULIHAN ADVISORS	207
5.17	INTANGIBLE BUSINESS	209
5.18	INTERBRAND	215
	5.18.1 Interbrand's multiplier model ("Annuity" model)	216
	5.18.2 Interbrand's discounted cash flow model	222
5.19	KERN'S X-TIMES MODEL	232
5.20	LEV'S INTANGIBLES SCOREBOARD	234
5.21	MILLWARD BROWN OPTIMOR	236
5.22	MOTAMENI AND SHAHROKHI'S GLOBAL BRAND EQUITY VALUATION MODEL	250
5.23	PROPHET	257
5.24	REPENN'S BRAND VALUATION MODEL (SYSTEM REPENN)	260
5.25	SANDER'S HEDONIC BRAND VALUATION METHOD	262
5.26	SATTLER'S MODEL	265
5.27	SEMION	267
5.28	SIMON AND SULLIVAN'S STOCK PRICE MOVEMENTS MODEL	270
5.29	THE NIELSEN COMPANY: BRAND BALANCE SHEET AND BRAND PERFORMANCE	274

	5.29.1	*The Nielsen Company: Brand Balance Sheet*	275
	5.29.2	*The Nielsen Company's Brand Performance*	277
5.30		TROUT & PARTNERS	281
5.31		VILLAFAÑE & ASSOCIATES' COMPETITIVE EQUILIBRIUM MODEL	284
5.32		OTHER BRAND VALUATION PROVIDERS AND MODELS	289
5.33		CONCLUSIONS	293

6 A TAXONOMY OF BRAND VALUATION METHODS   **295**

6.1		BY USE OF FINANCIAL OR NON-FINANCIAL INDICATORS	295
6.2		BY APPLICATION OR POSSIBLE OBJECTIVES	296
6.3		CLASSIFICATION PROPOSED BY BBDO	297
6.4		CLASSIFICATIONS BASED ON MIXED CRITERIA	299
6.5		BY INTENDED UNIVERSALITY OF THE CALCULATED VALUE	300
6.6		BY ITS NATURE OR ORIGIN (ACADEMIC VS. COMMERCIAL)	301
6.7		BY APPROACH EMPLOYED (COST, MARKET AND INCOME)	303
6.8		BY METHOD OF DETERMINING THE PROPORTION OF INCOME OR REVENUES ATTRIBUTABLE TO BRAND	307
	6.8.1	*Demand driver analysis*	309
	6.8.2	*Ratio of loyal consumers to total consumers*	309
	6.8.3	*Price premium*	309
	6.8.4	*Excess earnings*	309
	6.8.5	*Royalty rates*	312
	6.8.6	*Operating profits comparison*	312
	6.8.7	*Comparison with theoretical earnings yielded by a generic product*	316
	6.8.8	*Comparison of the cash flows of branded and unbranded companies*	316
	6.8.9	*Difference in price to sales ratios*	316
	6.8.10	*Economies of scale*	316
	6.8.11	*Differences in cash flow with a benchmark company*	316
	6.8.12	*CVH (Conjoint Value Hierarchy)*	318
	6.8.13	*Free cash flow less required return on assets other than brand*	319
	6.8.14	*Arbitrary constant coefficients*	319

		6.8.15	Competitive equilibrium analysis	319
		6.8.16	Equations based on accounting data	321
	6.9	By method of "representing brand risk"		321
		6.9.1	Comparison of models by representation of brand risk	321
		6.9.2	Classification by representation of brand risk	322
	6.10	By method of "representing the brand's growth and useful life"		327
		6.10.1	Classification by representation of the brand's useful life and long-term growth	330
7	**THE CURRENT SITUATION**			**331**
	7.1	General trends in brand valuation		331
		7.1.1	Proliferation of proprietary methods and brand valuation firms	333
		7.1.2	Lack of understanding and credibility among brand valuation users	335
		7.1.3	Commercial and academic concentration in Anglo-Saxon countries	337
		7.1.4	Increasing professionalism in the sector and sophistication of brand valuation techniques	338
		7.1.5	Growing convergence between marketing specialists and corporate finance experts	338
		7.1.6	Widespread use of certain models among practitioners	339
		7.1.7	Financial validity vs. widespread usage of models among practitioners	341
		7.1.8	Worlds apart: the academic and practitioners' realms	343
		7.1.9	The third world: "black box" methods	343
		7.1.10	Vast inconsistency in the application of various brand valuation techniques	344
		7.1.11	Differences in implementation	345
		7.1.12	Diversity and divergence of results yielded by different methods	346
		7.1.13	Determining useful life	347
		7.1.14	Determining discount rates	348
	7.2	Common errors and misconceptions in brand and intangible asset valuation		350
		7.2.1	Conceptual errors	350

		7.2.2	*Errors in management*	*356*
		7.2.3	*Errors in interpretation*	*358*
	7.3	Conclusions		359

8 IS CORPORATE BRAND VALUATION POSSIBLE? — **363**

	8.1	What is "corporate brand," and is it the same as "corporate reputation?"	364
	8.2	Why value corporate brands?	365
	8.3	Methodological options proposed for corporate brand valuation	366
	8.4	Models based on the concept that "corporate brand or reputation" adds value to product brands	369

		8.4.1	*Association-Affinity Model*	*369*
		8.4.2	*Critique*	*372*
		8.4.3	*Model based on demand analysis*	*373*
		8.4.4	*Critique*	*374*

	8.5	Model based on the company value's sensitivity to variations in "corporate brand or reputation" value	376

		8.5.1	*Assumptions*	*376*
		8.5.2	*Empirical development*	*379*
		8.5.3	*Theoretical model*	*381*
		8.5.4	*Critique*	*386*

	8.6	CoreBrand's model for measuring the percentage of market capitalization attributable to corporate brand	388

		8.6.1	*Brand Power^{TM} Analysis*	*389*
		8.6.2	*ROI Analysis*	*390*
		8.6.3	*Brand Equity Valuation Model*	*390*
		8.6.4	*Stock performance forecast*	*391*
		8.6.5	*Critique*	*392*

	8.7	Conclusions		395

9 THE FUTURE OF BRAND VALUATION — **397**

	9.1	The prospect of methodological consensus: Standardization vs. affinity of applications and methods	397
	9.2	Future trends in the supply and demand of brand valuation services	399
	9.3	Accounting users: financial officers' discomfort	402

9.4   MARKETING SPECIALISTS: USING VALUATION
       PRUDENTLY AND FOUNDING A NEW LANGUAGE
       COMPATIBLE WITH FINANCE   403
9.5   REGULATORS: BEHIND THE SCENES, BUT WITH GREAT
       CONFIDENCE   404

REFERENCES   **406**
INDEX   **414**

List of
Figures and Tables

Figures

Figure 1.1	Corporate brand as reputation	9
Figure 1.2	Different perspectives on the meaning of *brand equity*	14
Figure 1.3	Intellectual capital model for Skandia	17
Figure 1.4	Relationship between intellectual capital and brand	17
Figure 1.5	Evidence of the growing importance of intangible assets and brands	20
Figure 1.6	Which institution is the most trusted?	22
Figure 1.7	Market value breakdown for selected indices	23
Figure 1.8	S&P 500 book-to-market ratio, 1982 to 2003	24
Figure 1.9	Rise in investments in intangible assets in the US as percentage of GDP	25
Figure 2.1	Goodwill as percentage of the acquisition price in M&A transactions in the 1980s	34
Figure 2.2	Number of valuation methods developed annually from 1962	39
Figure 2.3	Elements of intellectual property, according to capital market players	44
Figure 3.1	Evolution of the number of brand league tables published since 2000	49
Figure 3.2	Transactional purposes: internal and external transactions	52
Figure 4.1	"Bundle of Brand Rights" theory	77

Figure 4.2	Analysis of the brand's contribution, treating brand as an independent attribute that influences the perception of the other attributes	84
Figure 4.3	Analysis of the brand's contribution, treating brand as an independent variable that does not influence the perception of other attributes	85
Figure 4.4	Revenue Ruling 68-609	99
Figure 4.5	Valuation in conformity with Revenue Ruling 68-609	99
Figure 4.6	Tree diagram used in real options analysis	106
Figure 5.1	BEES® model	120
Figure 5.2	BEE® model	122
Figure 5.3	The BBDO Five-level Model®	124
Figure 5.4	BBDO and Ernst & Young's BEVA model	128
Figure 5.5	General components of the BrandEconomics model	133
Figure 5.6	The role of EVA in the BrandEconomics model	135
Figure 5.7	Relationship between brand health and financial performance based on BAV and EVA Databases	136
Figure 5.8	The four pillars of brand health	137
Figure 5.9	The "Power Grid" of brand health	138
Figure 5.10	Impact matrix of BAV vs. intangible value	140
Figure 5.11	BrandEconomics® brand valuation model	143
Figure 5.12	Royalty savings Brand Finance valuation model	146
Figure 5.13	"Earnings split" Brand Finance valuation model	148
Figure 5.14	Four components of the BrandMetrics brand valuation model	152
Figure 5.15	Dilution percentages by sector	154
Figure 5.16	BrandMetrics brand valuation calculation: brand profit "curve"	156
Figure 5.17	Icon value-added iceberg	159
Figure 5.18	Brand Rating brand valuation model	162
Figure 5.19	Consor valuation model	167
Figure 5.20	Analysis of brand contribution	181
Figure 5.21	FutureBrand methodology	183
Figure 5.22	Revenue effect attributable to brand	186
Figure 5.23	Importance of risk drivers	189
Figure 5.24	Model for measuring brand equity GfK – PricewaterhouseCoopers – Sattler	191
Figure 5.25	HVA Asset taxonomy	207
Figure 5.26	Intangible Business model	210
Figure 5.27	Determination of the royalty rate	212
Figure 5.28	Interbrand's alternative brand valuation models	215
Figure 5.29	"S-curve" and the determination of brand multiplier in the Interbrand model	220
Figure 5.30	Kern's model	233
Figure 5.31	Millward Brown Optimor: three components of brand valuation	237

Figure 5.32	Calculation of brand contribution with the BrandDynamics™ Pyramid	241
Figure 5.33	Regional variations in brand strength: brand contribution metric for Nokia	242
Figure 5.34	BrandDynamics™ Pyramid	246
Figure 5.35	Voltage™ and changes in market share	248
Figure 5.36	Application of the Global Brand Equity model	256
Figure 5.37	Prophet brand valuation process	258
Figure 5.38	Saleable value according to System Repenn	261
Figure 5.39	Sander's Hedonic brand valuation method	264
Figure 5.40	Principal elements of Sattler's Model	266
Figure 5.41	Semion brand value outline	269
Figure 5.42	Brand Balance Sheet brand value criteria	276
Figure 5.43	Modules of The Nielsen Company's "Brand Balance Sheet" model	277
Figure 5.44	Brand Monitor: "Brand Performance" brand value criteria	278
Figure 5.45	Modules of The Nielsen Company's "Brand Performance" model	280
Figure 5.46	Villafañe Competitive Equilibrium Model	285
Figure 6.1	Myers' brand valuation model classification	296
Figure 6.2	Classification of models by applications	297
Figure 6.3	Characteristics of different categories of brand valuation models according to BBDO	298
Figure 6.4	Classification of models according to BBDO	298
Figure 6.5	Roos' brand valuation model classification	301
Figure 6.6	Academic, commercial and hybrid methodologies	302
Figure 6.7	Classification of brand valuation methodologies by approach	304
Figure 6.8	Distribution of methods by valuation approach	305
Figure 6.9	Classification of brand valuation models by method of determining the proportion of earnings or revenue attributable to brand	307
Figure 6.10	Providers and principal methods of calculating brand contribution to income	308
Figure 6.11	Classification by representation of risk	327
Figure 6.12	Classification by representation of useful life and expected long-term growth	330
Figure 7.1	Distribution by provider type	335
Figure 7.2	Reasons for not carrying out a brand valuation (sample: 79 companies)	336
Figure 7.3	Distribution of brand valuation models by country	337
Figure 7.4	Methods most commonly used by practitioners	340
Figure 7.5	Validity vs. widespread commercial usage	342
Figure 7.6	The worlds of academics and practitioners	343

Figure 7.7   The degree of consistency of various techniques used to determine profits or income attributable to brand   345

Figure 7.8   Comparison of 2004 brand valuation estimates for Microsoft and GE calculated by Predictiv, Interbrand and Corebrand (in US$ billion)   346

Figure 7.9   Comparison of 2005 brand valuation estimates for Toyota, Samsung and Apple calculated by Interbrand, Millward Brown Optimor and Vivaldi Partners (in US$ billion)   347

Figure 8.1   Brand contribution analysis   374

Figure 8.2   Reputation-beta relationship   380

Figure 8.3   Reputation-required return relationship   382

Figure 8.4   Impact of corporate brand by industry   391

Figure 8.5   CoreBrand corporate brand valuation model   392

Figure 8.6   Comparison of CoreBrand's corporate brand value estimates and Interbrand's product brand value estimates   395

Tables

Table 4.1   Example of residual development cost   60

Table 4.2   Royalty savings method – Valuation of trademark   72

Table 4.3   "Reasons-to-buy" analysis   83

Table 4.4   Allocating income among assets   101

Table 5.1   AbsoluteBrand model   110

Table 5.2   AUS Consultants model   112

Table 5.3   Trademark valuation based on free cash flows less the required return on other non-brand-related assets ("DCF-based technique")   114

Table 5.4   BBDO model   117

Table 5.5   Brandient model   129

Table 5.6   BrandEconomics model   132

Table 5.7   Brand Finance model   144

Table 5.8   BrandMetrics model   151

Table 5.9   Brand Rating model   158

Table 5.10   Consor model   164

Table 5.11   Damodaran model   171

Table 5.12   Financial World model   174

Table 5.13   Financial World valuation methodology – Gillette brand value estimate (1995)   178

Table 5.14   FutureBrand model   179

Table 5.15   Benchmarking analysis   182

Table 5.16   GfK-PwC-Sattler model   184

Table 5.17   ABV Valuation model   190

Table 5.18	Herp's model	192
Table 5.19	Hirose model	194
Table 5.20	Original example presented in the "Hirose Report"	202
Table 5.21	Modified example for a company with sustained growth	204
Table 5.22	Houlihan Advisors model	207
Table 5.23	Houlihan Valuation Advisors brand value calculation ($000 USD)	208
Table 5.24	Intangible Business model	209
Table 5.25	Intangible Business model components	211
Table 5.26	Analysis of relative brand strength: selecting a benchmark	211
Table 5.27	Analysis of relative brand strength: calculation of the BSA Index	212
Table 5.28	Market analysis in the Intangible Business model	213
Table 5.29	Application of the Intangible Business model	214
Table 5.30	Interbrand model	215
Table 5.31	Brand strength analysis in the Interbrand model	219
Table 5.32	Brand value calculation in the Interbrand model	220
Table 5.33	Brand strength specific attributes or evaluation criteria by factor	228
Table 5.34	Relationship between Brand Strength Index, Multiples and Discount Rates in the Interbrand model	229
Table 5.35	Kern's x-times model	232
Table 5.36	Intangibles Scoreboard model	234
Table 5.37	Millward Brown Optimor model	236
Table 5.38	Application of Millward Brown Optimor brand valuation methodology	244
Table 5.39	Motameni and Shahrokhi model	250
Table 5.40	Prophet model	257
Table 5.41	System Repenn	260
Table 5.42	Sander's Hedonic brand valuation method	262
Table 5.43	Sattler's model	265
Table 5.44	Semion model	267
Table 5.45	Simon and Sullivan model	270
Table 5.46	The Nielsen Company model	274
Table 5.47	Trout & Partners model	281
Table 5.48	Villafañe & Associates model	284
Table 6.1	Different methods of demand driver analysis for the determination of brand profits	310
Table 6.2	Millward Brown Optimor's method of determining income attributable to brand	312
Table 6.3	Methods of calculating brand profits based on price premium	313
Table 6.4	Variations of the excess earnings method used to determine brand earnings	314

Table 6.5   Methods of calculating brand earnings through royalty
            relief   315
Table 6.6   Methods of calculating brand earnings compared with
            theoretical earnings of a generic product   317
Table 6.7   Methods of calculating brand cash flow through com-
            parison with theoretical cash flow of a generic product 318
Table 6.8   Methods of calculating brand profits through differ-
            ences in price/sales ratios   318
Table 6.9   Methods that apply CVH to calculate profits attributa-
            ble to brand   319
Table 6.10 Methods of calculating brand profit as free cash flow
            less return on assets other than brand   320
Table 6.11 Methods based on arbitrary constant coefficients   320
Table 6.12 Equations based on accounting data   322
Table 6.13 Classification of methods by their approach to "brand
            risk"   323
Table 6.14 Classification by method of representing long-term
            brand growth and useful life   328
Table 8.1   Corporate brand contribution and association   370
Table 8.2   Corporate brand contribution calculation   375
Table 8.3   Selected portfolios   379
Table 8.4   Results of the beta vs. reputation regression   381
Table 8.5   Simulation for a hypothetical case   384
Table 8.6   CoreBrand's estimation of "Brand Equity Values"   393

Foreword by David Haigh, Chief Executive Officer, Brand Finance PLC

I first met Gabi Salinas in late 2003 when she was working at Futurebrand in New York. I was struck by her passion for the subject of brand valuation and her already extensive knowledge of brand valuation techniques, which were proliferating rapidly at the time.

Gabi has an enquiring and analytical mind with an amazing capacity for hard work. Her approach is logical and academically rigorous. She always wants to open the bonnet of any brand valuation approach and see how the engine works. She is then remarkably good at explaining in words of one syllable what she has found. Some approaches turn out to be Ladas while others are Rolls Royces.

I naturally took the first opportunity to recruit Gabi into Brand Finance. She joined us in early 2004, as Managing Director of Brand Finance Iberia. We have worked on many technical and brand strategy projects together and I miss the enjoyable debates we used to have about brand contribution, brand drivers analysis, brand values and what it all means. She left Brand Finance in early 2008 to join Deloitte as global brand manager to apply her wide ranging knowledge of brands and branding to the Deloitte corporate brand. Brand Finance's loss is Deloitte's gain.

During Gabi's time with Brand Finance I encouraged and supported her desire to understand more about the increasingly complex world of brand valuation. Brand Finance joined the Institute of Intangibles in Spain, which is one of the leading institutions to explore all aspects of intangible assets, including their valuation. Gabi was invited to research the many available brand valuation techniques, which provided a good opportunity to further her academic work.

She later teamed up with Tim Ambler, associate Professor of Marketing at the London Business School, to compile a taxonomy of brand valuation methodologies.

Gabi used her time well, compiling an incredibly thorough inventory of the major, and many of the minor, approaches to brand valuation. This book is the product of her labors and is an invaluable summary of the many and varied brand valuation approaches which have been developed in the last 20 years.

Since brand valuation first hit the headlines in 1988, when Interbrand valued Hovis as part of RHM's takeover defence against GFW, an industry has been created. I jointly ran

Interbrand's brand valuation practice until leaving in 1996. At that time there were very few commercial providers of brand valuation services. The Big 4 accounting firms regarded the subject as a black art and generally avoided it. Management consultancies and market research firms were not interested. Internal valuation teams did not aspire to value brands. How things have changed. Now everyone seems to be at it. This is exciting because it means our work has been recognized as something worthwhile. But it is also frightening given the confusion and contradiction which prevail.

Gabi's excellent work is therefore extremely timely. It indicates just how many providers have sprung up and how many alternative methods are out there, both academic and commercial. It meets the highest standards of academic rigor in cataloging, sourcing and critiquing all approaches featured in the book.

Caveat emptor is the underlying subtext of Gabi's magnum opus. She has objectively and clearly elaborated how each of the different approaches works, with an explanation of the steps in conducting each one and the pros and cons. Her work can be used as a 'What Car?' guide to what is available in the global market for brand valuation.

She has also discussed in helpful terms how the next 20 years might see brand valuation techniques move away from fragmented proprietary techniques towards a consensus over the approaches and methods used by all brand valuation practitioners. In fact her work highlights the need for a global standard-setting body to help this process along.

This may become more pressing in the next few years as demands grow for companies to value all their intangible assets, including brands, on an annual basis, rather than just on acquisition. The Australian accounting standards body recently released a discussion paper calling for just such a move. This approach challenges the "prudence concept" and the "historical cost convention" most accountants so admire. It may never get anywhere. But then that is what accountants were saying about brand valuation 20 years ago and look where we are today!

If this trend becomes irresistible it is crucial that intangible asset and brand valuation techniques are consistent, robust and widely accepted. What is at stake is the credibility of the newly created brand valuation industry with its growing audience of users and consumers, from tax authorities, courts, auditors, bankers and investors to management and their Boards of Directors.

As Gabi rightly points out there is a pressing need for harmonization of terms, assumptions, approaches and methods of brand valuation. In fact, the International Standards Organization has commissioned a global committee to develop an ISO Global Standard for brand valuation which will hopefully be released in 2010. Gabi and I both sit on that committee and it is gratifying to see that brand valuation practitioners are now working together to limit the differences which Gabi has illustrated so well in this book.

I am sure that for academics, students and practitioners in the field of brand valuation this will be a "must read" book and a "must have" technical reference manual. For those managers interested in acquiring a detailed technical knowledge of the subject before embarking on a brand valuation study, this will be an invaluable source of reference. It makes the task of briefing a brand valuation professional infinitely simpler. I commend it to anyone with a serious interest in the subject. It is extremely easy to read, reflect on and absorb. 20 years experience is now summarized in one easy reference book.

Acknowledgements

I would firstly like to thank my translator, Emily Toder, for the infinite patience, professionalism and enthusiasm she showed throughout the preparation and editing of this work.

I would also like to thank Marta Lorenzo, Global IFRS Offering Services at Deloitte, for her assistance with several concepts included in Chapter 1.

Special thanks to Carlos Martínez Onaindia, from the Global Brand Development Team at Deloitte, who has contributed a great deal to the design of the cover for this book.

David Haigh, CEO of Brand Finance plc, has provided invaluable comments that have vastly improved the presentation of different ideas throughout the book. I will be forever indebted to the wonderful professionals at Brand Finance who fostered the perfect environment for learning, challenging, and discovery.

At Deloitte, I found the perfect environment for continuous growth and development. Heartfelt thanks to all my colleagues and superiors for encouraging me to always be "one step ahead."

Several colleagues have been kind enough to comment on previous works that have served as the framework for this manuscript. I would like to thank Tim Ambler from London Business School, Roger Sinclair from BrandMetrics, Luis Miguel Bernardos, Eva Toledo, Elise Fournier, Karla Anguiano and Carla Jaquez for this attention.

Claire Plimmer and her associates at Wiley have been very supportive and patient during the editing process. It has been a pleasure to work with such a professional team.

Last but not least, special thanks to Paul, Elena and José for being there, and for offering never-ending patience and support at every step along the way. And finally to Issy, a little miracle who has changed my life marvelously …

Introduction

When I first began working in the field of brand valuation, with a division at one of the world's biggest ad agencies, I longed for some sort of manual that could guide me through various methods and intelligently explore their respective advantages and disadvantages. That sentiment is what prompted a long intellectual journey through which I have come to know the work of many authors, mostly North American and British, in search of clear, "black and white" references to valuation methodologies and the possible errors contained therein. In 2001, I came upon *Company Valuation* by Professor Pablo Fernández, a wide-ranging work on company valuation, with an extraordinary profound, sincere, clear and detailed treatment of brand valuation. Later on I had the great fortune to meet Pablo Fernández, and it was he who, in 2004, encouraged me to begin working on this book, on which I have now spent four and a half years.

In 2005, on the cusp of the new accounting standards that would impose the estimation of the Fair Value of Intangible Assets (the brand among them), greatly exposing the vast lack of consensus surrounding the various methods of determining this value, the Institute for the Analysis of Intangibles decided to fund research on brand valuation methods as part of a broader investigation into intangible resource and other asset valuation. I had the great honor of collaborating with the Institute on a module of this project, which entailed reviewing and evaluating different methodologies as a preliminary step towards proposing a reasonable and agreed-upon valuation methodology. With the support of the Institute, I was able to complete and augment the research I'd begun in 2004, upon which this book is based.

This work thoroughly and extensively reviews and critiques the principal brand valuation methods, and accurately depicts the current state of the brand valuation industry, with the objective of establishing criteria for the classification and assessment of the various existing models.

Many scholars and experienced professionals in the field may already be very familiar with the methodologies discussed. The novelty of this book does not lie in the presentation of innovative or different methodologies, but rather in the description, analysis and exhaustive critique of all the methodologies that have been developed to date, as well as the review of major trends in the theory and practice of brand valuation today. The goal – and I hope I have met it – was to produce a reliable reference book for "one-stop" consultations, that could efficiently and meaningfully introduce all valuation professionals to the various methods developed and practised all over the world. It is crucial that specialists be familiar with their options before advising clients on which methodology to employ, or adopting one themselves.

The nine chapters of this book address the different issues surrounding current and historic brand valuation methodologies and models. Chapter 1 reviews the concept of "brand" and its relevance in today's world from economic, accounting and business perspectives. Reviewing the variable interpretations of this term is fundamental for understanding later chapters, and being comfortable with the premises on which valuation methods are based. Chapter 2 discusses the origin and evolution of brand valuation techniques. Chapter 3 outlines the principal elements and components of brand valuation models. Chapter 4 carefully explores general approaches to brand valuation and lays the groundwork for the index of proprietary models reviewed in Chapter 5. Chapter 6 presents various proposals for classifying those models, discusses the relevant criteria for their classification and proposes new criteria; these are then referenced in the analysis of trends, convergence and divergence of brand valuation methods examined in Chapter 7. Chapter 8 introduces corporate brand valuation, a new issue in the field that has awoken great interest in the wake of the "corporate reputation" craze. Chapter 8 also examines the differences between the concepts of corporate reputation and corporate brand, and reviews several models developed for their valuation, analyzing their respective advantages and disadvantages. Finally, Chapter 9 presents various questions and predictions for the future of brand valuation.

1

The Concept and Relevance of Brand

IN THIS CHAPTER, WE WILL EXAMINE VARIOUS CONCEPTS OF the term *brand* and discuss its economic value. Before analyzing different methodologies, we will need to clearly define brand and *the economic value of brands*, as well as explore how these relate to the associated concepts of corporate reputation, intellectual capital and intangible assets.

We shall also look at the economic significance that these notions have acquired in recent decades, both on a national and a global level, and discuss the various accounting, legal, institutional and business developments that have resulted from this growing importance.

1.1 The concept of brand

Before valuing any asset, we must first define it. This is particularly essential when dealing with brands. The word *brand* is used quite frequently and has consequentially assumed multiple and at times very different meanings. Defining an asset before valuing it helps limit the scope of the valuation model to be applied. Therefore, familiarity with the various concepts of brand, as well as a good understanding of the circumstances in which each concept is relevant, is absolutely essential for any valuation expert.

In this section, we will review three concepts of *brand* based on accounting, economic and management-oriented perspectives, respectively. Each one is relevant and applicable to particular circumstances.

1.1.1   The accounting perspective

1.1.1.1   *The brand as an intangible asset*

IFRS Framework defines an asset as "a resource controlled by the entity as a result of past events and from which future economic benefits are expected to flow to the entity." International Accounting Standard 38 *Intangible assets* (issued 2004, amended 2008, para. 8) defines *intangible asset* as an "identifiable non-monetary asset without physical substance" and establishes that an asset is identifiable if it either arises from contractual or other legal rights or is separable (able to be sold individually or among other related assets).

IAS 38 (para. 21) indicates that "an intangible asset shall be recognized if and only if, (a) it is probable that the expected future economic benefits that are attributable to the asset will flow to the entity; and (b) the cost of the asset can be measured reliably."

Later we will evaluate some specific questions relating internally generated intangible assets, but we will now outline some examples of recognizable intangible assets acquired separately by the entity:

- *Marketing-related assets:* Trademarks, trade names, internet domain names, trade dress, etc.

- *Contractual assets:* Licensing agreements, contracts for advertising, construction, management, service or supply, lease agreements, franchise agreements.

- *Technology-based assets:* Patented technology, software, databases, trade secrets.

- *Customer-related assets:* Customer lists, customer relations and contracts, production orders.

- *Art-related assets:* Plays, operas, ballets, books, magazines, newspapers, musical works, films.

Clearly, this catalog omits several concepts popularly referred to as assets. Corporate reputation, human resources, and employee motivation do not constitute *recognizable* intangible assets because they are not identifiable (they may not be bought or sold), nor are they controlled by the company itself (its reputation is a consequence of its actions; employees have the right to end their contracts at any time). Later on we will evaluate whether these concepts can be considered non-recognizable assets, or intangible resources; or if they should be excluded from both classifications.

1.1.1.2 Non-recognizable intangible assets: Internally generated brands

Internally generated brands fall into the category of non-recognizable intangible assets. IAS 38 (para. 63) states: "Internally generated brands, mastheads, publishing titles, customer lists and items similar in substance shall not be recognised as intangible assets." These expenses are not distinguishable from the cost of developing the business activity as a whole. Although they do not meet the three requirements established in IAS 38 for tax and accounting-related recognition, they are still *controlled* by the firm, and do represent *a source of future economic benefits*. They therefore qualify as assets, despite their non-recognizability for tax and accounting purposes.

If the brand were acquired in the context of a business combination, the accounting conclusion could be different.

IAS 38 (para. 33) indicates that in accordance with IFRS3, "... The probability recognition criterion in paragraph 21 (a) is always considered to be satisfied for intangible assets acquired in business combinations. If an asset acquired in a business combination is separable or arises from contractual or other legal rights, sufficient information exists to measure reliably the fair value of the asset. Thus, the reliable measurement criterion in paragraph 21 (b) is always considered to be satisfied for intangible assets acquired in business combinations." Paragraph 34 also states that "an acquirer recognizes at the acquisition date, separately from goodwill, an intangible asset of the acquiree, irrespective of whether the asset had been recognized by the acquiree before the business combination."

Finally, the International Financial Reporting Standard 3 *Business Combinations* (IFRS 3, issued 2008, para. 13) comments regarding the recognition of intangible as distinct from goodwill, "... For example, the acquirer recognises the acquired identifiable intangible assets, such as a brand name, a patent or a customer relationship, that the acquiree did not recognize as assets in its financial statements because it developed them internally and charged the related costs to expense."

Thus, resources that are controllable by the company and that constitute a source of future economic benefits, such as internally generated brands, are considered assets though they are non-recognizable for accounting purposes (with the potential abovementioned exception when acquired in a business combination). From a pure "economic" perspective, these two features, together with the aforementioned non-monetary and non-substantial qualities, are the only ones truly relevant for the definition of intangible assets.

1.1.1.3 Trademark, brand and branded business

In various contexts and circumstances, *brand* is used to refer to three different concepts (Haigh and Knowles, 2004):

1. **A name, a logo and other associated visual elements:** This is the most specific definition, as it focuses on legally protectable verbal and visual elements that may be used to differentiate the products and services of one company from those of another. The principal legal elements at work in this definition are trade names, logos and trade symbols. According to Haigh and Knowles (2004) trademarks are valuable when they carry "associated

goodwill." Valuations based on this definition are referred to as "trademark valuations."

2. **A broader scope of elements including name, logo, other verbal and visual elements, and associated intellectual property rights:** Under this definition, the concept of *brand* is stretched to include a broader scope of intellectual property rights, such as domain names, product design rights, trade dress, packaging, copyrights on associated logotypes, descriptors, sounds, colours, smells, etc.[1] For example, under this definition, Guinness' valuation would not only have to look at its name and logo, but also consider its formula. This more holistic vision reflects the notion that a brand is an experience that transcends logo and related visual elements. This definition is generally applied in marketing-oriented brand valuations. But it may also apply to valuations for accounting purposes, as IAS 38 (para. 37) allows for the aggregation of acquired intangible assets when they have similar useful lives or their fair values cannot be reliably measured on an individual basis. In this case, the acquirer could combine the trademark and related intangible assets into a single group ("brand").

3. **A holistic company or organizational brand.** The term *brand* is frequently used to refer to the *business unit* that operates under that brand. For example, when Unilever speaks of having 1600 brands, and is hoping to reduce that

---

[1]Cf. FAS 141 para. 16 defines *brand* as a group of complementary intangible assets.

number to 400, what it means that it has 1600 individual branded businesses in its corporate business portfolio, and it needs to value and discard 1200 non-basic "brands." Both verbal and visual elements are taken into account in this definition, as well as associated intellectual property rights, along with the company's culture, personnel and programs, which provide the basis for the company's differentiation and value creation. Considered jointly, they represent a rather specific proposition of value, and lay the groundwork for building close relationships with consumers, providers and personnel. In this book, we will refer to this concept as "branded business."

English has two different terms for referring to the first two definitions: *trademark* (name, logo and other associated visual and verbal elements) and *brand* (formulas, know-how and other intellectual property assets). But in English, *brand* and *trademark* are often used synonymously. Certain authors, such as Smith (1997), distinguish between the two concepts, characterizing *brand* as a marketing concept referring to a set of assets including, but not limited to, *trademarks* (p. 42). For Smith, the term *brand* may also refer to formulas or recipes, trade dress, etc.

1.1.2 The economic perspective

1.1.2.1 Economic vs. accounting criteria

According to Burgman, G. Roos, Ballow and Thomas (2005), the debate regarding intangible assets in the realm of accounting has been fundamentally based on the definition of *intangible asset* for tax and accounting purposes. Burgman and his co-authors posit that the accounting classification of tangible and intangible assets presents a conflict regarding their recognition; while internally generated brands may not be considered intangible assets in the balance sheet, they do constitute intangible assets from an economic standpoint.

1.1.3   The management perspective

1.1.3.1   Brand and corporate reputation

The concepts of brand and reputation are often used interchangeably, particularly when referring to corporate brands like Sony or Vodafone. There are various viewpoints on the distinction between these two concepts. Before examining them, we shall first review the definition of *reputation*:

- According to the Oxford English Dictionary, *reputation* refers to "what is generally said or believed about a person's or thing's character."

- Reputation guru Charles Fombrun (1996) defines Corporate Reputation as "the overall estimation in which a company is held by its constituents, representing the 'net' affective reaction of customers, investors, employees, and the general public to the company's name" (p. 37).

There are at least six schools of thought with regard to the relationship between the concepts of brand and corporate reputation:

1. **Brand = Identity; Reputation = Perception:** For Terry Hannington (2006), *brand* refers to the visual reaction to a symbol, and therefore the visual identity, while *reputa-*

tion denotes "the attitudes and feelings to the specific qualities of the organisation" (p. 35). Hannington argues that the brand's advertising and visual style are just the tip of the iceberg; everything else is reputation.

2. **"Stock and flow variables":** *Brand* is the experience of the consumer, management actions (flow variable). *Reputation* is perception, the result of experience (stock variable). In other words, brand experience and company management are what ultimately generate reputation. But while the brand may be managed and controlled, reputation is awarded; it is the end result of brand management.

3. **"Contingent approach depending on the breadth of the definition of *brand*":** The correlation between the concepts of reputation and brand will ultimately be a function of how we define the latter. The broader the definition of *brand*, the more it will overlap with that of *reputation* (see Figure 1.1). Thus, the narrowest definition of *brand* will be synonymous with *visual identity*, while a broader definition will more closely resemble that of *corporate reputation*. This broader definition highlights the need for consistent communication with all relevant audiences, represented by various stakeholders. Brand then becomes a tool not only for increasing consumers' preference

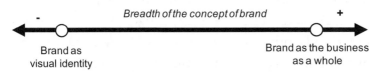

Figure 1.1 Corporate brand as reputation.

for the company's products and services, but for shaping corporate audiences' willingness to do business with the company as well (Haigh and Knowles, 2004). For example, the brand is able to favorably affect the perception of its personnel, providers, shareholders, regulators and fiscal authorities. In this context, certain academics and executives may use the terms *reputation* and *brand* synonymously. If there are problems with the brand or company reputation, this may have repercussions for some or all of the stakeholders.

4. **"Accounting Approach"**: Because it is not controllable, corporate reputation may not be considered an asset (cf. Section 1.1.1.1). However, brand is controllable, and therefore is an asset, even though it cannot be recognized as such without mediating a transaction.

5. **"Different Audiences"**: This school of thought distinguishes brand from reputation by comparing their respective audiences. There are two principal well-defined positions within this school. One suggests that while the brand's audience is limited to its current and potential consumers, the reputation's audience includes all stakeholders. The other holds that brand image can be measured among consumers while corporate reputation can be measured only by executives and other corporations.

6. **Brand and Corporate Reputation are "Synonyms"**: During an ESIC conference in 2006, Ángel Alloza, Director of Brand and Corporate Reputation at BBVA, used the concept of brand architecture to distinguish between the two concepts. For Alloza, in a company with a monolithic or

quasi-monolithic brand architecture, where the corporate brand coincides with the commercial brand (as happens with Samsung or BBVA itself), the concept of corporate reputation overlaps with that of corporate brand. However, in a company like SABMiller, where the product brands are not endorsed and do not coincide with the corporate brand, the final consumer hardly perceives the corporate name at all, making it unlikely for consumers' perceptions of the product brands to be tied to those of the corporation.

Chapter 8 will take a closer look at the essential difference between these two concepts and reproduce selected corporate brand and reputation valuation models that have appeared in prominent academic journals.

1.1.3.2 *Brand and visual identity*

Brand and visual identity are often confused, particularly in the field of brand management. Once again, we will start by reviewing the definition of *visual identity* and later examine it in relation to the concept of brand. There are numerous definitions for this term, spanning a wide range of both narrow and broad interpretations.

- *Narrow Definition of Visual Identity:* The sum of the individual elements that characterize a brand (name, logo, graphic symbols, slogan, characters, packaging, etc.).

- *Broad Definition of Visual Identity:* Any distinctive or manifested element inwardly or outwardly expressed by a company.

From a management standpoint, the trouble with defining *brand* as visual identity is that it compels the brand management department to act as the "logo police" or "photographic or visual style police." In marketing, brand is often defined as an idea, experience or relationship with the target market. In this sense, it is quite different from the concept of identity, which is simply the expression of this idea. According to this definition, the responsibility to create, develop and protect the brand lies in the company as a unit, and not solely in the marketing department.

1.1.4 Brand, intangible assets and intellectual capital – Everyday vocabulary and conflated terms

In informal settings, intangible assets are often said to theoretically include the satisfaction and motivation of a company's employees, its corporate reputation, customer loyalty, etc. A brief review of the accounting definition of *intangible asset* (cf. Section 1.1.1.1) will help us better understand which of these elements fall into the accounting framework of intangible assets.

1.1.4.1 Brand equity and intangible assets

Scholarly literature on the matter shows no consensus on the meaning of *brand equity*, nor on how a company could go about measuring the value of a brand. Winters (1991) writes: "There has been a lot of interest lately in measures of brand equity. However, if you ask 10 people to define brand equity, you are likely to get 10 (maybe 11) different answers as to what it means" (p. 70). As Winters demonstrates, brand equity is often considered an intangible asset. We will now turn to review various definitions of *brand equity* in order to determine whether it does or does not constitute an intangible asset:

- According to Aaker (1991: 15), *brand equity* is the "set of assets and liabilities linked to a brand, its name and symbol, that adds or detracts from the value provided by a product or service to a firm and/or to the firm's customers" – the concept of brand associations. For Aaker, brand equity includes not only the brand's incremental price premium, but also its loyalty, perceived quality, as well as a series of associations.

- Leuthesser (1988) defines *brand equity* as: "the set of associations and behaviour on the part of a brand's customers, channel members and parent corporation that permits the brand to earn greater volume or greater margins than it could without the brand name" (as cited in Wood, 1999, "Brand equity" section, para. 14).

- Simon and Sullivan define brand equity "in terms of incremental discounted future cash flows that would result from a branded product revenue, in comparison with the revenue that would occur if the same product did not have the brand name" (as cited in Motameni and Shahrokhi, 1998, "Different perspectives of brand equity" section, para. 1).

The first two definitions characterize *brand equity* as a "perceived" or "behavioral" value; the third interprets it as the brand's financial value or economic value. In fact, these two perspectives have always co-existed in the literature (see Figure 1.2). Wood (1999), Feldwick (1996) and Motameni and

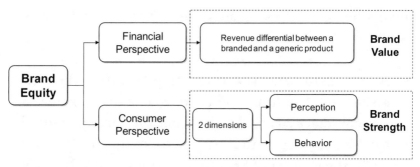

Figure 1.2 Different perspectives on the meaning of *brand equity*.
Source: Developed by author, based on Aaker (1991), Yoo and Donthu (2001)

Shahrokhi (1998) occasionally use the terms *brand value* and *brand equity* interchangeably. However, the most popular use of the term *brand equity* refers to the set of attributes related to consumer perception, and not to the brand's economic value (Aaker, 1991; Aaker and Keller, 1990; Keller, 1991; Martin and Brown, 1991; Srivastava and Shocker, 1991; Leuthesser, 1988 as cited in Wood, 1999). This is the definition we shall adopt in this book.

As we define it here, and similarly to the concept of reputation, *brand equity* may not be considered an intangible asset as it is not controllable (cf. Section 1.1.1.1).

1.1.4.2   Brand, intangible assets and intellectual capital

Human capital, *intellectual capital*, and other related terms are highly prevalent in scholarly literature, but appear so often with such diverse meanings, they have generated a mounting lexical confusion in the discipline. For example, some authors use *intellectual capital* to describe the difference between a company's market capitalization and its book value. Others interpret the term more narrowly, using it to denote intangible assets or particular skills. Thus, before analyzing the relationship between intangible assets and intellectual capital, we will need to examine the four principal conceptualizations of *intellectual capital*:

1. Intellectual capital as knowledge.

2. Intellectual capital as knowledge and the product of this knowledge.

3. Intellectual capital as intangible assets not recognized on the balance sheet.

4. Intellectual capital as the total set of recognized or non-recognized resources and intangible assets.

These sets of definitions often coincide in the *components* of intellectual capital, emphasizing either its source (the "dynamic concept" seen in definitions 1 and 2) or defining it as a differential variable (the "static-differential concept" seen in definitions 3 and 4).

The vast majority, however, agree that these components are:

- human capital

- structural capital.

Occasionally, a third component, relational capital, is detected and included as a sub-element of structural capital.

A well-known model of intellectual capital is that of Skandia, the Swedish insurance firm. For Skandia (Andriessen and Tiessen, 2000), intellectual capital is the sum of:

1. Human capital (the brains, skills, creativity, persistence, and dedication of the people who work for the company). J. Roos, G. Roos, Dragonetti and Edvinsson (2001) refer to it as "thinking capital."

2. Structural capital (encapsulating everything that remains in the company when the employees go home for the day). J. Roos et al. (2001) refer to it as "non-thinking capital." Structural capital may be divided into various sub-categories:

    2.1. Customer capital (which is not tangible, but still contributes significantly to the company)

    2.2. Organizational capital (the structure of the company, management knowledge, information systems, etc.) This category may then be split into:

        2.2.1. Innovation capital, which includes intangible assets (see Figure 1.3).

        2.2.2. Process capital.

We must take into account that each concept of intellectual capital will connect differently to the concept of brand (see Figure 1.4):

1. When intellectual capital is reduced to knowledge (Konrad Group, Andriessen), it excludes brand.

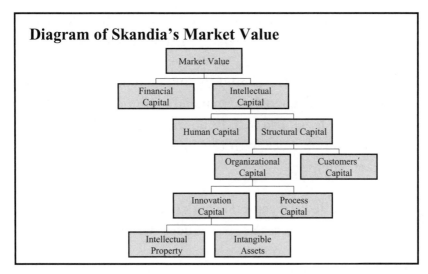

Figure 1.3   Intellectual capital model for Skandia.
Source: J. Roos et al. (2001) – Reproduced by permission of Skandia Insurance Company Ltd.

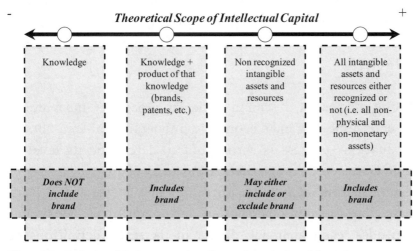

Figure 1.4   Relationship between intellectual capital and brand.
Source: Developed by author

2. When intellectual capital is understood as knowledge and the product of that knowledge, it includes brand.

3. When intellectual capital is understood as intangible assets not recognized in financial statements, it includes internally developed brands, but not acquired brands. This definition coincides with the concept of internally generated goodwill.

4. When intellectual capital is understood as all non-physical or non-monetary assets, it includes brand.

1.2 Brand value

1.2.1 What is brand value?

When we speak of brand value, we refer to a financial (monetary) economic value, and not to a subjective evaluation or opinion that a client or customer may have about a brand (we use *brand equity* to denote this last concept – cf. Section 1.1.4.1).

While the goal of the brand valuation process is indisputably to determine a brand's economic (monetary) value, a "brand evaluation" process is carried out to determine its level of brand equity. Although the vast majority of approaches to the determination of brand equity (or "brand *evaluation*") are based on consumer perception and quantifiable behavioral attitudes, each approach differs in its scale, definitions of indices utilized, and bases of comparison. They should therefore be considered as relative measures and indices. Some of the more well-known "brand *evaluation*" models are:

- Brand Asset Valuator (Young & Rubicam)

- Equitrend (Total Research)

- BranDynamics™ (Millward Brown)

- The Brand Equity Ten (David Aaker).

These models boost our understanding of brand strengths and weaknesses in competitive environments, and enhance our insight into the development of consumer perception. In general, although they serve as good tools for brand evaluation per se, they are not useful for estimating a brand's economic value. Still, they can be constructive resources for valuers and useful in understanding a brand's potential in the relevant market.

1.2.2 How do brands create value?

In economic terms, brands create value by affecting both supply and demand curves. On the *demand side*, they allow a product to be sold at a higher price, given a determined sales volume. Strong brands can also increase their sales volume and decrease their customer defection rate. In a complex and saturated market, brands play a fundamental role in consumer choice by introducing functional and emotional attributes. Therefore, they allow the firm to reach a more stable demand level. This brings obvious economic benefits, given that the cost of acquiring new customers is 10 or 20 times greater than that of retaining current customers. Strong brands are also capable of transferring values associated with the brand to new categories of products or services.

On the supply side, brands may reduce operating costs by increasing distributors' loyalty, improving personnel recruiting and retention costs, capital financial costs, and finally, by increasing economies of scale through greater volumes.

1.3 The growing importance of the economic value of brand

Intangible assets and brands are the objects of increasing attention in five rather different fields (see Figure 1.5).

1.3.1 Business evidence

Numerous initiatives, forums and institutions promoted by large business corporations demonstrate the increasing concern for the valuation and reporting of intangibles in the business world. The following are some such initiatives:

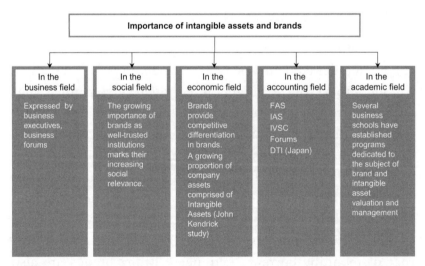

Figure 1.5 Evidence of the growing importance of intangible assets and brands.
Source: Developed by author

- The *Reputation Institute*, founded in 1997 by Charles Fombrun with the financial support of Shell, Pricewater-houseCoopers, WeberShandwick and MS&L, is committed to cultivating knowledge on corporate reputation and its management, measurement and valuation.

- The *Global Reporting Initiative* (GRI) is an independent institution comprised of multiple representatives from business, environmental, human resources, trade union and research agencies, and institutes from around the world. Its main objective is to develop and promote a global framework for reporting sustainability, to be used on a voluntary basis by companies concerned with the social, environmental and economic impact of their activities, products and services. Established in 1997, the GRI is an independent organization and now serves as an official UNEP (United Nations Environmental Program) center of collaboration. It also carries out projects in collaboration with Global Compact, supported by the Secretary General of the UN.

- The *Institute for the Analysis of Intangible Assets* in Spain was formed on the request of various companies, business schools and international consultants, among them Telefónica, Santander Group, BBVA, Unión Fenosa, Deloitte, PwC, KPMG, Ernst & Young and Brand Finance. Its main objective is to develop standards for the valuation, measurement and certification of intangible assets through laborious research endeavors.

- The *Corporate Reputation Forum*, boasting the support of various major Spanish companies.

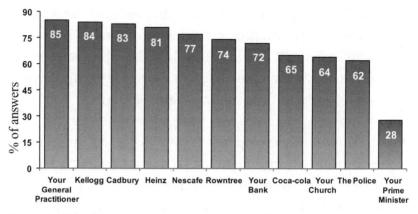

Figure 1.6 Which institution is the most trusted?
Source: The Henley Centre, Planning for Social Change (1998) cited in
Brand Finance (2002)

1.3.2 Social evidence

From a socio-economic point of view, a brand is an economic
contract based on trust. The level of trust in brands has grown
so dramatically in recent decades, it has actually managed to
dislodge the trust citizens put in other public institutions. In
a study by the Henley Centre in 1998 in England, the majority of those surveyed said they trusted brands more than other
institutions such as the Church or the police (see Figure 1.6).

1.3.3 Economic evidence

Numerous studies have manifested the growing importance
of intangibles over time. One of the most well-known is that
carried out by economist John Kendrick in 1994, which dem-
onstrated the increasing relevance assigned to intangible
assets, particularly the brand within a company's financial
structure.

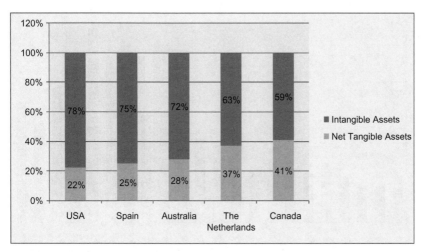

Figure 1.7 Market value breakdown for selected indices.
Source: Haigh and Chng (2005). Study on the S&P500, IBEX 35, S&P ASX200, AEX and TSX 223 – Reproduced by permission of Brand Finance PLC

According to a study by Brand Finance, intangible assets represent between 60 % and 75 % of capitalization value in the major stock indices (see Figure 1.7).

For some authors, the substantial growth of this proportion seen in the last twenty years is principally evidenced by the growing disparity between book value and market value in different indices. For example, in the S&P 500 index, the market-to-book ratio went from 1.3 in the 1980s to 4.6 by June 2004 (see Figure 1.8). For some commentators, the increasing proportion of intangible assets to market cap explains the growth of the market-to-book ratio. They reason that investors recognize that these companies' productive resources are increasingly represented by assets that do not appear on the balance sheet – patents, distribution rights, brands.

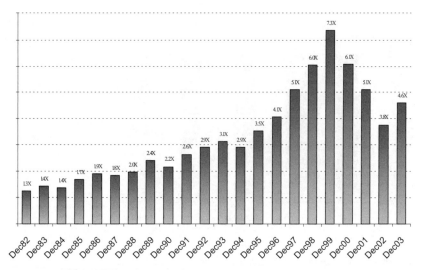

Figure 1.8 S&P 500 book-to-market ratio, 1982 to 2003.
Source: Haigh and Knowles (2004), © 2004 *Marketing Management*, 13: 3,
24–28. Reproduced by permission of the American Marketing Association

The substantial transfer of value from the tangible to the intangible realm has brought with it a growing level of investment in intangible assets. According to economist Leonard Nakamura of the Philadelphia Federal Reserve, in 2004, total investment in intangibles in the US was at 9 % of the Gross Domestic Product, and is rapidly approaching the percentage of investment in tangible capital (see Figure 1.9).

1.3.4 Normative and institutional evidence

Accounting standards: Recognition of acquired intangible assets as distinct from goodwill

The importance of understanding the value of the intangible assets that now represent the vast majority of business value has been buttressed by recent changes in accounting standards for business mergers and acquisitions. Until recently, no

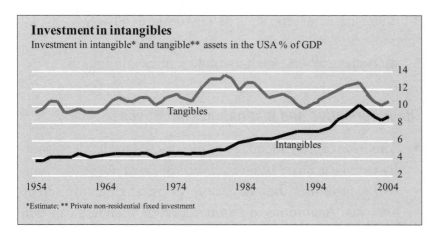

Figure 1.9 Rise in investments in intangible assets in the US as percentage of GDP.
Source: L. Nakamura, Federal Reserve Bank of Philadelphia (2005), cited in Hofmann, J. (2005) – Reproduced by permission of Jan Hoffmann

national standard required acquired intangible assets to be recognized apart from goodwill. FAS 141 in the US and the International Financial Reporting Standard 3 (IFRS 3) on *Business Combinations* require that goodwill (the difference between book value and the price actually paid in the transaction) that arises from an acquisition and represents the value of the set of intangible assets in a business, be specifically allocated to such assets. As a result, the number of defined intangibles is expected to grow. Goodwill will be allocated to five broad categories of assets:

- technology-based assets, such as patents

- contract-based assets, such as licensing agreements

- artistic assets, such as theatrical works and movies

- client-based assets, such as customer databases

- marketing assets, such as trade names and brands.

Other normative and institutional initiatives

- The new capital adequacy requirements for lenders established in the *Basel II Revised International Capital Framework* promote the valuation of intangibles in credit
  analysis. According to Hofmann (2005), lenders can take
  two approaches under *Basel II:* either opt for the IRB
  (Internal Rating-Based) Approach or for the Standard
  Approach. A lender taking the IRB Approach needs to
  include not only balance sheet information but also "qualitative information" on the assets when evaluating. In
  principle, this regulation will also allow intellectual property to be recognized as collateral. If, on the contrary, the
  bank takes the Standard Approach under the new capital
  regulation, it must resort to ratings elaborated by external
  agencies.

- In order to avoid duplication and confusion, the International Valuation Standards Committee (IVSC), based in
  London, is backing an initiative to standardize methods
  of intangible asset valuation. In 2006, a group of experts
  was established to work on the "standardization of the
  approach to take in the determination of the fair value of
  intangible assets for the purpose of reporting under IFRS"
  (IVSC, 2007: 7). The discussion paper released in July 2007
  ("Determination of fair value of intangible assets for IFRS
  reporting purposes") is the result of the work of the group
  of experts. The final objective is to develop a Guidance

Note on the Determination of Fair Value of Intangible Assets for IFRS Reporting Purposes.

- In March 2000, the ICAEW (Institute of Chartered Accountants in England & Wales) published the study *New Measures for the New Economy*, which analyzed the necessity and difficulty associated with the development of new measurements for intangible assets.

- In 2003, The United Nations Economic Commission for Europe (UNECE) published a report entitled *Intellectual Assets: Valuation and Capitalization*.

- Various initiatives in the public sector, most often carried out in conjunction with the private sector, have been launched in numerous countries in order to promote the voluntary disclosure of "intangible capital" (Hofmann, 2005). The following represent the most relevant among these initiatives:

  - Since the end of the 80s, the Government of Denmark, through the Danish Ministry of Commerce, Industry and Development, and the Danish Agency for Commerce and Industry, with the collaboration of universities, consultants, auditors and the Danish Patent Office, has carried out a series of studies on the measurement of intangible assets.

  - In 1999 the Netherlands Ministry of Economics published *Intangible Assets, a Balance between Accounts and Knowledge*, which compiled models proposed by four auditors (KPMG, Ernst & Young,

PricewaterhouseCoopers and Walgemoed) for the reporting of intangible assets.

- Sweden, along with Denmark and the Netherlands, has been rather active in working towards a standardization of intangible asset reporting.

- In Japan, the Ministry of Economy, Trade and Industry has sponsored a committee focused exclusively on the establishment of a rigorous definition and methodology for brand valuation, based on publicly accessible data released in balance sheets. The goal was to develop an "objective" brand valuation methodology (Beccacece, Borgonovo and Reggiani, 2006). In June 2002, this committee, known as the Hirose Committee, produced a brand valuation methodology. In January 2004, the Ministry published a *Guide for the Reporting of Intellectual Property Information* with the objective of promoting greater understanding among companies and capital markets through the voluntary disclosure of information regarding patents and technology.

- In the United Kingdom, the Department of Trade and Industry is conducting a "best practices" analysis known as the MARIA project, on the reporting of intangible assets in OFR (Operative Financial Review).

- Since 1994, the European Commission has endorsed research projects and conferences in hopes of better understanding the relevance of intangibles as factors of competitiveness. Among the research projects are MERITUM (Measuring Intangibles to Understand and

Improve Information Management) and the MAGIC (Measuring and Accounting Intellectual Capital). The former focuses on the measurement and reporting of intangibles, and features the participation of Denmark, Finland, France, Norway, Spain and Sweden. The latter hopes to develop a low-cost practical solution for the measurement, valuation (both quantitative and qualitative) and reporting of intellectual capital.

- In the United States, multiple initiatives in the institutional and normative realm have been carried out. Three worth mentioning are: the creation of a Research Committee for the reporting of values of intangible assets within the Financial Accounting Standards Board (FASB); the Brookings Project, a study of the sources of intangible value, funded by the Brookings Institute in Washington. This project arose as the continuation of a conference on intangible assets sponsored by the SEC, and is focused primarily on promoting the discussion of various ways of measuring, monitoring and reporting intangible sources of wealth, both on the private business level and on the national level. Other major goals include evaluating various projects dedicated to the measurement of intangibles, examining decision processes at work in intangible investments, and looking at how public policy (regulations, information requirements and fiscal standards) may affect this process. Finally, the United Nations Economic Commission for Europe (UNECE) and the United Nations Statistics Division (UNSD) have supported various groups and conferences with the objective of studying the valuation and capitalization of intangible assets.

1.3.5 Academic evidence

Within the past 10 years, numerous programs and specialized courses on or concerning intangible assets have sprung up in European, Asian and American universities:

- The Wharton School at the University of Pennsylvania in the United States offers a course in accounting at the undergraduate level that devotes an entire class module to intellectual capital valuation. This business school has also recently launched an academic program called "Marketing Metrics: Linking Marketing to Financial Consequences."

- The Vincent C. Ross Institute of Accounting Research at New York University, United States, launched the Intangibles Research Project in 1996, directed by Baruch Lev.

- The Kellogg School of Management at Northwestern University, United States, offers a course on "Intellectual Capital Management."

- Nanyang Polytechnic in Singapore offers a course in Brand Management.

- The Spanish business school EOI and the José Pons Foundation have recently developed a master's program in "Industrial and Intellectual Property and New Technologies." EOI also offers a module on the "Presentation of Intellectual Capital in Accounting States" in its Knowledge Management Executive Master's Program.

- HEC School of Business, in France, is currently promoting various research projects and conferences on intangibles.

- The Technological University of Dresden, Germany, has published two studies directed by Thomas Guenther on "Management, Control and Brand Valuation."

- Chalmers University of Technology, Sweden, has founded a "Center for Intellectual Property Studies" (CIP).

These initiatives are just a few examples of the developments currently underway in the academic world, and serve to illustrate the growing interest in the management and valuation of intangibles.

1.4 Conclusions

In this chapter, we have reviewed the basic concepts that will lay the groundwork for our understanding of the approaches and models presented in Chapters 4 and 5. We may summarize this introductory chapter by asserting the following points:

- There are various ways of defining brand. In this work, we shall subscribe to both the accounting and economic definition of *brand as an intangible asset* (recognizable or not), thereby discarding the various marketing and management-oriented definitions.

- Recent decades have seen vast proliferation, excessive usage, and adverse conflation of terms like *brand equity* and *intellectual capital*. We need to understand the relationship between these terms and the definitions we accept for *brand* and *brand value*.

As conceptual and methodological divergences show the rapid evolution of this modern phenomenon, the growing importance of brands is evidenced by the initiatives and developments underway in the institutional, normative, social, economic and academic realms.

2

The Origin and Evolution of Valuation Methods

I N THIS CHAPTER, WE WILL REVIEW THE ORIGIN AND evolution of valuation methods and examine their current status by looking at their application and discussing the key players in the brand valuation industry today (providers, corporations/users, investors and investment analysts). We will also consider the various factors that have hindered the development of valuation models.

2.1 The origin and evolution of valuation methods

2.1.1 Origins: The series of acquisitions in the 1980s

The series of brand acquisitions in the late 1980s revealed the hidden value of companies with strong brands, and generated growing interest in brand valuation. When the British company GrandMet acquired Pillsbury in 1988, it paid an estimated 88 % of the price as goodwill (Haigh, 1999). Since then, other acquisitions have shown that brands can create value and justify high market-to-book multiples (see Figure 2.1). For

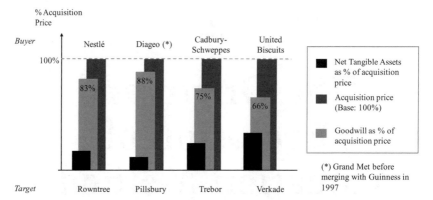

Figure 2.1   Goodwill as percentage of the acquisition price in M&A transactions in the 1980s.
Source: Adapted from D. Haigh (1999)

example, in 1998, Volkswagen acquired Rolls-Royce Motor Cars' assets for £430 million. The acquisition included all physical assets of Rolls-Royce and Bentley auto production, but the brand was left out of the agreement. Through a separate transaction, priced at £40 million, BMW acquired the rights to use the Rolls-Royce plc name and logo (Haigh and Knowles, 2004b).

The overall trend was that acquisition prices for companies with strong brands were consistently higher than the value of their net tangible assets. This discrepancy between market value and book value is known as *goodwill*, and may include various types of intangible assets, among which the brand is a major factor. In short, these transactions have manifested brands' tremendous capacity to create value. But they have also raised the issue of how corporate purchasers can possibly set an objective value for companies based on intangible assets that do not appear on their balance sheets. How can we measure brand value?

2.1.2   The first brand valuation: Rank Hovis McDougall

In 1988, the management firm Rank Hovis McDougall carried out a valuation of RHM brands in order to oppose a hostile takeover bid by Good Fielder Wattie (GFW). GFW's offer followed a series of transactions during the 1980s in which corporate raiders and asset strippers were acquiring undervalued companies with strong brands at very economic prices. In 1986, for example, Hanson Trust paid £2.3 billion for Imperial Group and later sold the food portfolio alone for £2.1 billion, retaining the tobacco business, a major cash generator, altogether resulting in a net price of £200 million (McAuley, 2003). This situation elucidated the fact that analysts were severely undervaluing the principal assets of businesses with strong brands. To avoid this "valuation breach," RHM decided to carry out its own brand valuation process. In its defense document, RHM called attention to the power of several of its brands, asserting that the offer was inferior to the company's true value:

RHM owns a number of strong brands, many of which are market leaders, which are valuable in their own right, but which the stock market tends consistently to undervalue. These valuable assets are not included in the balance sheet, but they have helped RHM build profits in the past and provide a sound base for future growth (as cited in Haigh, 1999: 6).

With its brand value information, RHM was able to convince investors that the offer was very low. The investors re-evaluated the business, RHM's market value increased, and GFW withdrew its offer. The majority of academics in the field locate the birth of the brand valuation industry in this event.

After rejecting GFW's hostile takeover bid, RHM recorded the value of its externally acquired and internally generated brands in its 1988 annual report at £678 million, while its intangible assets were valued at less than £400 million.

2.1.3   The accounting conflict generated by brand capitalization

The fact that RHM had included both internally generated and externally acquired brands in its balance sheet might seem like evidence of a consistent approach to some. But in the accounting profession, it led to major controversy. Valuations for externally acquired brands may not exceed a set maximum figure, given by the price paid in the transaction; in other words, the brand should not be worth more than the price that the acquirer paid for the business. In the case of internally generated brands, however, there is no such "ceiling." This is why RHM's action generated not only intense debate among accounting professionals, marketing directors and board members, but also a greater awareness of the brand valuation issue.

According to Haigh (1999), originally, the difference between the book value of tangible assets and the price paid was known as *goodwill* and included an indeterminate blend of intangibles, among them, brands. But as the debate about brands grew deeper, and methodologies developed for quantifying brand value, goodwill began to be broken down into different categories. Ultimately, this highlighted the need for a method of accounting for brands and other intangible assets that recognized their true value. The developments that arose from the accounting debate then led to:

- the recognition of brand value and the possibility of measuring it;

- the improvement of valuation methods and accounting for intangibles;

- the proliferation of all kinds of brand valuation providers; and

- in short, the development and consolidation of brand valuation.

2.1.4 Rapid development and applications

In 1992, Tomkins plc purchased RHM at a price higher than the original Goodman Fielder Wattie offer. After the acquisition, Tomkins wrote off all RHM's intangible assets (McAuley, 2003). The brand valuation had met its objective. But in 2000, Tomkins sold RHM to Doughty Hanson, a private equity fund, for £1.1 billion. Doughty Hanson needed financing to pay off the bank loan of £650 million it had requested to acquire RHM. The problem was that the assets on the company's balance sheet – which were to be offered as security – were valued at £300 million. Therefore, it decided to structure a loan in which all brands were transferred to separate intellectual property companies, licensing them back to RHM's operating divisions. With the backing of these intangible assets, it issued a bond which securitized five of the company's oldest brands – those with the most stable cash flows. By issuing and placing bonds at a value of £650 million, they were able to pay off the bank and reduce annual financing costs.

Transactions such as these helped generate understanding of the true value of brands and build awareness of the valuation tool. Today, because accounting standards require separate recognition of brand value and intangible assets in mergers and acquisitions, valuation tools have acquired greater relevance.

2.1.5   Who values brands today?

Prior to 1995, there were only nine proprietary[2] brand valuation models. Of these, at least five were developed by commercial providers. Of those five, four were elaborated by two providers. Over the course of the next 13 years, at least 28 additional brand valuation models were developed,[3] not including other corporate brand valuation models developed in the same period. This indicates that of the models identified and described in Chapter 5, over 75 % were developed within the past 13 years (see Figure 2.2). As we will see in later chapters, the majority of these were commercial models developed in the United States, Germany and the United Kingdom. Within the past decade, many new and diverse providers have entered the field of brand valuation,

---

[2] As we only consider proprietary models, we leave out of the analysis some suppliers, such as Houlihan Advisors and AUS Consultants, the intangible valuation firm based in New Jersey, as they seem to use general methodologies rather than proprietary methods. Other providers that apply proprietary methodologies developed by third parties are also excluded from the analysis. For example, absoluteBRAND applies the proprietary methodology developed by Intangible Business.

[3] This figure does not include models for which we do not have enough information (cf. Chapter 5, Section 5.32). It refers to models, and not to commercial providers, as various commercial providers may share a single model. Where a commercial provider has developed more than one model, all models have been counted.

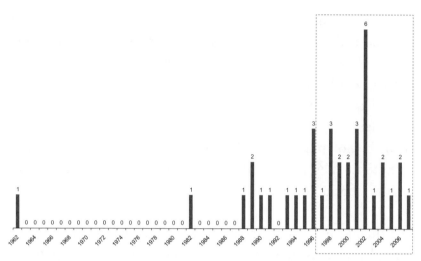

Figure 2.2 Number of valuation methods developed annually from 1962.
Source: Developed by author

broadening the spectrum of practising specialists. Today, brand valuation services are provided by:

- auditors and accountants

- consultants specializing in intangible and brand valuation

- consultants specializing in company valuation

- advertising groups, branding consultancies, media centers

- market research specialists

- intellectual property specialists and lawyers

- independent academics and business schools

- brokers and traders specializing in intellectual property.

In total, 39 distinct proprietary brand valuation models for commercial brands, developed by 31 providers, scholars and standardization bodies, have been identified. Chapter 5 presents a detailed description of different valuation models for commercial brands[4] developed or applied by 31 commercial providers and academics, and lists 34 additional providers who do not publish detailed information on their models. Chapter 8 describes corporate brand valuation models in greater depth.

But this development has not been without problems. While it might seem as though today, anyone would be able to value a brand, it actually requires a very specific skill set not necessarily shared by experts in many related specialty fields. In order to perform a successful valuation, one needs profound knowledge of corporate finance and valuation, as well as expertise in statistical and research tools so as to understand brand performance from the consumer perspective.

2.1.6 How do corporations use this tool?

Despite increasing recognition of intangible assets' major role in value creation, their management and control are currently at a very early stage of development. In 2003, Accenture carried out a survey among 120 top executives worldwide to investigate state-of-the-art intangible asset management techniques (Accenture, 2003). 96 % of those interviewed affirmed that intangible assets were important to their companies'

---

[4]We distinguish "valuation models for commercial brands" from "valuation models for corporate brands," such that the former refers to valuing product or service brands, in B2C or B2B, while the latter refers to the valuation of corporate brands.

success, but only 5 % had implemented an effective method for measuring these assets and comparing their performance. The cost of this negligence can be very high. According to economist Leonard Nakamura (2001), capital markets' undervaluing of intangible assets is largely due to the lack of information disclosed by companies.

According to a recent study by Deutsche Bank Research (Hofmann, 2005), various factors have led to widespread company silence on intangible assets:

- *Limitations imposed by accounting regulations* that do not allow intangible assets to be capitalized, except in cases of mergers and acquisitions.

- *Corporations' reluctance to disclose competitive advantages by publishing information on their intangible assets.* Companies do not want to share information on organizational processes, methods of production or models of consumer retention, with their competitors.

- *The lack of generally accepted vocabulary in the field of intangible asset valuation and evaluation.* Even were companies willing to publish more information on intangibles, in many cases, there is no common language in the communications between companies and capital markets, nor among capital market players.

2.1.7 How do investment analysts use this information?

In a recent survey by Howrey (2002) of 100 fund managers, private equity investors, venture capitalists and bank analysts, 89 % of those surveyed considered the company's intellectual property to be a major factor in their investment decision. However, only one third affirmed that they "always" or "usually" formally analyzed and evaluated the value of the company's intellectual property upon weighing a potential investment. This third was mostly comprised of communications and technology company analysts.

According to the Deutsche Bank Research study (Hofmann, 2005), various factors have prevented capital market analysts from adopting brand and intangible valuation methods:

- *Analysts, fund managers, venture capitalists and private equity investors sense a lack of tools for properly valuing intellectual property.* In the Howrey study, over half of those surveyed were convinced that intellectual property could not be measured, and over two thirds said that since the market lacked reliable tools for effectively valuing intellectual property, they resort to subjective valuations. Baruch Lev, Doron Nissim and Jacob Thomas provide quantitative evidence of the faulty valuation of intangible assets determined by capital markets (as cited by Hofmann, 2005: 4).

- *The diversity of the methods employed by companies for the reporting of intangible "resources" and assets.* Although monetary valuations are not always necessary, and the kind of valuation will depend on its particular objectives, a model that only reports purely statistical measures has very limited applications. For example, in the absence of a standard measure for comparison, how could one judge whether a certain number of hours of training is or is not enough?

- *The lack of familiarity with valuation models.* Although there are various existent models for valuing intangibles, many analysts, lenders and corporations are simply not familiar with them.

- *The lack of credibility in valuation models.* Due to insufficient experience with intangible asset valuation, as well as analysts' scanty training in these matters, capital markets are scarcely trusting of the results of these valuations. Intangibles will have a major influence on analysts' valuations only when there is standardized knowledge available on their valuation. Without generally established proven methods, the level of confidence in the results yielded by valuations in capital markets will remain minimal, and ultimately hinder the development of liquid markets that might work to advance their valuation.

- *The impossibility of comparing intangible assets.* The fact that transparent and liquid markets for intangible assets exist only in isolated cases severely complicates comparability.

- *The very concept of "intellectual property" varies among analysts and other capital market participants.* Figure 2.3 shows the various elements that intellectual property may be said to include, according to market players.

2.1.8 How do other players use this information?

Aside from providers, analysts and corporations, there are various other players involved in the field of brand valuation:

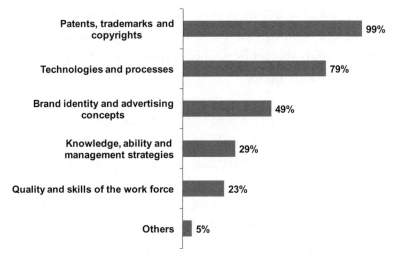

Figure 2.3 Elements of intellectual property, according to capital market players.
Source: Howrey (2002) – Reproduced by permission of Howrey LLP

- *Lenders* who accept intangible assets from borrowers as credit guarantees.

- *Judges* who resolve disputes involving intangible assets.

- *Witness experts* who provide professional opinions in disputes or conflicts involving intangibles.

- *Fiscal authorities* that collect and control the taxes corresponding to intangible asset transactions (sales, purchases, internal or external licenses).

In many cases, and with the exception of fiscal authorities and specialized experts, there is a profound lack of knowledge regarding the usage, scope and limitations of valuation tools among analysts and other capital market players. Clearly, this hinders their correct application and subsequent development, particularly in the fields of law and credit.

2.2 Conclusions

Since its birth 20 years ago, the brand valuation industry has undergone dramatic changes. At least 39 proprietary brand valuation models have been elaborated by 31 providers, scholars and standardization bodies, and at least 63 providers and authors of valuation models for commercial brands have been identified. Despite the spectacular growth on the supply side of the industry, numerous studies have manifested the lack of understanding and the apprehensive or incorrect application of these tools on the part of their different "users": corporations, analysts, judges, experts and lenders.

3

Brand Valuation
Method and Process

A s we saw in Chapter 2, there is still a certain degree of generalized ignorance or skepticism surrounding valuation tools, at least among investors and corporate financial managers. In this chapter, we will discuss the possible uses of brand valuation, and examine the questions that should be answered before launching a brand valuation project.

3.1 Brand valuation process

Nearly 20 years after the debate generated by the RHM incident, there are still many brand valuation detractors. Patrick Barwise, Professor of management and marketing at London Business School, holds that brand value cannot be separated from business value and is reluctant to accept what he calls "theoretical brand valuations" (those that take place when a business is not being bought nor sold), preferring what he calls "brand evaluations" that use metrics as management tools (as cited in McAuley, 2003). The problem is that over the last 20 years, brand valuation has often been misunderstood, and as a result, many industry players are skeptical about the use of valuation models. In this section, we will assess the current state of the debate on brand valuation, primarily from the user's standpoint, and examine the questions that ought to be answered before launching a project of this nature.

3.1.1 What is brand valuation?

Asset valuations are expert opinions on the asset's monetary value based on data analysis and assumptions rooted in a particular moment in time; this is so in the valuation of any kind of asset, work of art, wine or brand. Therefore, brand valuation may be defined as the process through which a qualified expert forms an opinion on the value of a brand, based on a set of premises or hypotheses, and taking into account the objectives, and audiences for which his or her expert opinion has been solicited.

3.1.2 The current debate: Why bother with brand valuation?

As we saw in Chapters 1 and 2, most top executives recognize that intangible assets, and brands in particular, play an important role in long-term financial success. This understanding has led to a growing interest in the appropriate tools for measuring their value, evidenced partly by the great number of articles and brand value tables recently published by business and marketing magazines such as *Business Week, Forbes* and the *Financial Times*. Figure 3.1 shows the vast increase in the number or brand value league tables seen in the last seven years.

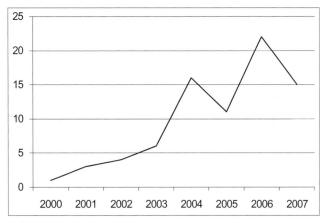

Figure 3.1 Evolution of the number of brand league tables published since 2000.
Source: Developed by author

But amidst the proliferation of new brand league tables, we face deeper questions: Is brand valuation necessary? In which circumstances? To satisfy which objectives?

As David Haigh and Jonathan Knowles suggested in a brilliant article entitled "Don't Waste Your Time with Brand Valuation" in 2004:

Most companies do not need an answer to the question, *What is the value of my brand?* except for the specific purpose of accounting for goodwill after an acquisition. Rather, they need an answer to the question, *How – and for how much – can my brand contribute to the total success of my business?* It is this insight into the sources of customer value and the economic cost of delivering that value that will enable them to run more successful businesses (Haigh and Knowles, 2004b: 1).

These authors are part of a growing school of thought; one which holds that brand value on its own grants no more than a chance to toot your own horn at a corporate cocktail party (Ehrbar and Bergesen, 2002; Haigh and Knowles, 2004b).

This is why clarifying the objective of a brand valuation is essential before embarking on these types of projects. We must answer the question: *What is the purpose of the valuation?* And we must distinguish between technical valuations (for accounting and transactional purposes) and brand management valuations.

The determination of the objective of the brand valuation exercise is closely related to the second key step in the process, given by answering the question: *What exactly are we valuing?* We must determine if we want to value the trademark or the entire branded business. The fuzzy definition of "brand" can often cause confusion here.

Once we have answered the previous two questions, we will be able to choose the methodology best suited to our objectives. This leads to a very important conclusion: that the selection of the brand valuation methodology will be contingent on the project's objectives.

In the following sections, we will discuss the three key steps of a brand valuation exercise.

3.1.3 The purpose of brand valuation[5]

In the past 10 years, brand valuation techniques have become generally accepted tools with a wide range of applications. There are three major groups of applications:

[5]Based on Haigh and Knowles (2004b).

- valuations for brand management purposes

- valuations for accounting purposes

- valuations for transactional purposes.

Valuations for accounting or transactional purposes are done for balance sheet reporting, tax planning, litigation support, securitization, mergers and acquisitions, and investor relations. Thus, they focus on a value at a given point in time.

Valuations for brand management purposes are necessary for brand architecture, brand portfolio management, marketing strategy, marketing budget allocation and management scorecards. They are based on dynamic business models and on the role that the brand plays in the model's key variables.

3.1.3.1 Brand management

On certain occasions, brand valuation can be used as a management tool, and implemented to compare the levels of success of various brand strategies and the relative performance of different marketing teams. In this context, valuations have been used to defend marketing budgets, or to make decisions on brand extensions and architecture, as well as to measure the return on brand investment. But Ambler and Roberts (2006) point out several challenges to this usage (as cited in Salinas and Ambler, 2008). In general, when brand valuation is implemented for management purposes, the model will consider segmented values and sensitivity analysis, as the objective is to understand the impact that different brand investment levels will have on the business performance.

3.1.3.2 Accounting purposes

New accounting standards require that all identifiable intangible assets of acquired businesses be recorded at their "fair value." This breaks with the older practice of recording the purchase price in excess of the net acquired assets as a single figure under goodwill. Current regulations require that the value of acquired brands be included in the balance sheet. A recent example of this is South African Breweries' acquisition of Miller Brewing Co. The Miller brand represents $4500 million of the $6500 million of intangible assets that appear in SABMiller's 2003 balance sheet.

3.1.3.3 Internal or external transaction purposes

There are two types of transactions that may require a brand valuation: internal and external (see Figure 3.2).

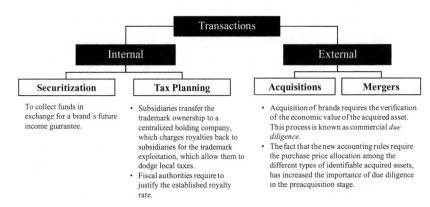

Figure 3.2 Transactional purposes: internal and external transactions. Source: Based on Haigh and Knowles (2004b)

Internal transactions

The two most common types of *internal* transactions involving brands and trademarks are:

- Trademark-backed securitization and

- Tax planning.

In trademark securitization, funds are collected in exchange for collateral based on future revenues generated by licensing the trademark, i.e. trademark licensing royalties (Eisbruck, 2007). According to Hillery (2004), trademark-backed securitizations have not been as frequent as music or film; however, some high-profile examples of trademark-backed securitizations have recently been observed. According to this author, in 2003, Guess Inc. securitized royalty streams from 14 trademark license agreements for US$ 75 million.

Brand valuation may also be used for *tax purposes*. Usually, subsidiaries transfer brand and other intellectual property assets to a centralized holding company, which charges operating companies royalties for the use of these assets, such that a portion of the operating companies' profits may evade local taxes. Of course, fiscal authorities require the justification of the brand value, to determine if it has been transferred to another fiscal jurisdiction by a fair value and to ensure that no fiscal obligations have been dodged.

External transactions

External transactions tend to take the form of *acquisitions* of companies with brands. In these cases, commercial due diligence is required in order to verify the economic value of the acquired asset, and to substantiate negotiations of the terms of the transaction.

3.1.4 Defining the scope of valuation and the concept of brand

In Chapter 1, Section 1.1.1.3, we reviewed three alternative definitions of *brand*. Each definition has distinct implications as to what other intangibles need to be considered in the valuation. For example, a "trademark valuation" (definition 1) would require the valuation of other associated intellectual property separately (like a formula for example). In a "brand valuation," (definition 2), there would be no need to value those other intangible assets separately. For example, in the valuation of a beer brand, the trademark and the formula would be valued jointly. Sometimes the *brand* is confused with the *business unit* that operates under the brand (definition 3). "Branded business valuations" (definition 3) are really no more than business or company valuations, commonly used in strategic and financial decision-making.

Most CEOs are primarily interested in the impact that different brand strategies can have on the value of the branded business. On other occasions, such as in the case of a company that decides to transfer brands for fiscal reasons, brands are valued independently.

3.1.5 Choosing an appropriate methodology

The valuation model to employ will depend on the answers to the two questions we have posed in this chapter regarding the purpose of the valuation and the scope of the concept of brand. Salinas and Ambler (2008) classify the applications or purposes of brand valuation in two general categories: technical purposes and "other brand management purposes."

Brand valuations with technical applications are generally undertaken for business combinations, impairment tests, tax planning, securitization, etc. They are therefore focused on a value at a given point in time. They commonly refer to the valuation of the *trademark* or *brand*. *Brand valuations for management purposes* are used for restructuring brand portfolios, performance evaluation and budget allocation. These valuations are typically based on dynamic models of the *branded business* and aim to measure *the role that the brand plays in the model's key variables*.

Previous research has shown the correlation between the type of application and the methodology of choice. Salinas and Ambler (2008) analyze the methods employed by a sample of commercial providers previously classified as "providers positioned in technical practices" and "providers positioned in management practices." They conclude that most of the providers oriented towards technical applications applied the "royalty relief" methodology, while those providers more geared towards management applications favored methodologies that focused on measuring the role the brand plays in generating demand ("Demand driver analysis," cf. Section 4.3.3).

Salinas and Ambler's findings (2008)[6] are consistent with the opinions of other scholars who have noted the royalty relief

[6]Their results and research are based on previous research by Salinas, G. (2008) "Valoración económica de marcas: ¿existe un método óptimo para valorar marcas?" in *La comunicación empresarial y la gestión de los intangibles en España y Latinoamérica*, Pearson Educación, Madrid.

methodology as the methodology of choice for valuations with accounting and reporting purposes (Mard, Hitchner, Hyden and Zyla 2002; Woodward 2003; Anson 2005). The "Big 4" accountancy firms tend to view royalty relief as the most reliable method, from a technical perspective (cf. Harms, 2008).[7]

3.2 Conclusions

Before embarking on any brand valuation project, we must define the purposes of the valuation as well as the scope of the definition of the asset to be valued. Different objectives and applications will lead to different definitions of "brand," and will determine the appropriate methodology to use. Methods valid for internal management purposes will not necessarily satisfy accounting requirements or tax regulations.

"Royalty relief" is the methodology most commonly used for technical valuations, while "brand management-oriented valuations" are typically based on dynamic models of the *branded business* and aim to measure the *role that the brand plays in the model's key variables.*

---

[7]http://www.ey.com/GLOBAL/content.nsf/UK/CF_-_Services_-_SFS_-_ Library_-_Methodology_-_Valuing_IP; http://www.ey.com/global/content. nsf/WebPrint/8b8e23cdd699f2b680256cc5004dafbb?OpenDocument& Click=; http://www.deloitte.com/dtt/newsletter/0,2307,sid%253D3631%2 526cid%253D58029,00.html.

4

General Approaches to Brand Valuation

It is important to carefully distinguish between approaches, providers and models of brand valuation. *Approach* refers to the three general ways in which any kind of asset can be valued; *model* refers to the specific relationships between the variables that determine brand value. Valuation models have most often been designed by commercial providers and scholars, and tend to vary substantially in their use of different variables and their expression of the relationships between them.

At least 39 different proprietary valuation models for commercial brands[8] have been proposed by different providers and scholars. These models fall under three basic general valuation approaches (International Valuation Guidance Note 4 by the International Valuation Standards Committee, 2003; Cravens and Guilding, 1999; Seetharaman, Nadzir and Gunalan, 2001):

---

[8]The reader should recall that we have defined *commercial brand* as a product or service brand, as opposed to *corporate brand*.

4.1 cost approach

4.2 market approach

4.3 income approach.

We shall now examine different methods and models used within each approach and consider their respective advantages and disadvantages. The methods presented in this chapter are general ones, while those discussed in Chapter 5 will be proprietary methods proposed by specific providers or scholars.

4.1 Cost approach

With this approach, the brand is valued by considering the cost of developing it (brand acquisition, creation or maintenance) during any and all phases of its development (testing, product concept R&D, product improvements, promotions).

Options
(a) *Historical cost of creation*
This method measures the sum spent on brand development at the time it was developed. This model may serve as a reference, but it is not sound from a conceptual point of view, as the cost of creating a brand can have little to do with its present value.

(b) *Replacement cost*
Replacement cost is the monetary value of the expenditure and investment necessary to replace the brand with another brand with the same characteristics, i.e. with an equivalent utility to the owner (Smith, 1997). This does not include the inadequacies and obsolescence present in the subject intangible asset (Reilly and Schweihs, 1999: 122). While this criterion

is more logical than that of historical cost (as it is based on equivalent utility rather than incurred expenses), it is not useful on its own, as it does not consider profits generated by the brand.

(c) *Reproduction/recreation/replication cost*
This approach determines the potential costs of developing the brand to reach its current status. This includes the same inadequacies and obsolescence as the subject intangible assets (Reilly and Schweihs, 1999: 122).

(d) *Capitalization of brand-attributable expenses*
The development cost attributable to the brand is the proportion of expenses incurred historically to develop it. Often, brand value is estimated as the value of the business attributable to the brand, based on the accumulated advertising expenses over total marketing expenses incurred. Table 4.1 shows a specific example of this methodology.

With this method, if the business is valued at €100 million, the brand value would represent 75% of this figure; that is, €75 million.

This represents a mixed criterion, whereby the percentage of residual costs attributable to the brand is used as an indicator of the proportion of business value attributable to it. The formula is problematic because it assumes that the returns, and thus the business value, will be divided proportionally between the "brand investment" and the investment made in other selling and distribution activities.

Table 4.1 Example of residual development cost

Brand: A	2001	2002	2003	2004	Total	%
In €000						
Annual inflation rate	3.00%	3.00%	3.00%	3.00%		
Personnel expenses	1542	1034	1009	1513		
Selling and distribution expenses	694	743	563	593		
Sales commissions	1284	1106	802	853		
Total selling and distribution expenses	3520	2883	2375	2959		
Inflation-Adjusted Annual distribution expenses	3625	2970	2446	3048		
Constant accumulated selling and distribution expenses	*3625*	*6703*	*9350*	*12679*	*12679*	*25%*
Advertising expenses	*12024*	*7524*	*7069*	*8023*		
Inflation-Adjusted Annual investment	*12385*	*7749*	*7282*	*8264*		
Constant accumulated investment	*12385*	*20506*	*28403*	*37519*	*37519*	*75%*
Total selling, distribution and promotion expenses					*50197*	

Characteristics of the cost approach

- It is not a good indicator of value.

- It does not capture the value added by brand management, i.e. the brand's competitive position, brand strength or risk relative to relevant competitors.

- If the brand has been in the market for a long time, it can be difficult to identify all incurred costs.

- In determining the historical cost of creation, it can be difficult to pinpoint the intangible asset's initial moment of development (Boos, 2003).

Applicability of the cost approach

The cost method, in any of its variants, is not appropriate for brand valuation. It is more commonly applied in cases of easily replaceable assets, such as software or customer databases.

4.2 Market approach

The market approach considers recent transactions (sales, acquisitions, licenses, etc.) that have involved similar brands, and for which data regarding the transaction price is available.

Options

(a) *Sales transactions comparison*

Brand value is calculated with reference to open market values where there is data on prices at which similar brands have been transferred.

(b) *Royalty savings*[9]

This technique is based on the assumption that a company that does not possess the ownership rights to a brand will need to license it from a third party. Ownership, therefore, "relieves" the company from paying the royalty rate to a third party for the use of its brand. This method entails estimating likely future sales, applying an appropriate royalty rate to them, and later discounting the future after-tax royalties to

[9] This method is described in detail in Section 4.3.2.

arrive at the present value. This amount then represents the brand value.

This method is often described as "mixed" or "income" because even when it involves the comparison of licensing contracts for similar brands in similar sectors to obtain a referent range for royalty rates, these royalty rates are applied to projected sales in order to arrive at future income attributable to brand, taking into account market transactions and sales revenues.

Characteristics

The market approach (sales transaction comparison) has limited application in the field of brand valuation, since there is no active market for brands.

Applicability

- The market approach is ideal for valuing assets that are not unique. In the case of brands, this approach may be applied – though not as a primary method – to calculate fair value or value in use when the transaction involves a similar brand in the same industry.

- This approach is also applicable when:

  - there is a sufficient number of comparable transactions, for example, in the case of airport landing rights and commodity quotas (milk production quotas or energy emissions);

  - the transaction is conducted among independent parties ("arm's length" transactions);

  - the transaction is effected on a relevant date.

4.3 Income approach

This approach requires the identification of future income, profits or cash flow attributable to the brand over its expected remaining useful life, and discounting or capitalizing them to present value. In order to arrive at a capital value, the estimated future cash flows or earnings attributable to the brand are discounted back to present value ("Discounted Cash Flows" – "DCF" approach) or multiplied by a capitalization factor (direct capitalization).

Some authors are more restrictive than others in the way they interpret the income approach. For example, Cravens and Guilding (1999) classify the methods based on P/E multiples such as Financial World or Interbrand as "Formulary Approaches," while Smith (1997) classifies the techniques that "utilize price/earnings multiples or brand strength multipliers to convert an income to a value indication," as "other Income-Related Valuation Approaches" (p. 155). Within this work, we will take the latter approach.

Options
There are various ways of determining income attributable to the brand; we shall now examine the most prevalent methods.

1. *Price premium*

    1.a. Conjoint analysis

    1.b. Hedonic analysis

2. *Royalty savings*

    2.a. Brand strength and market comparables method

    2.b. Excess margin

    2.c. The Knoppe formula

    2.d. Cluster or group analysis

    2.e. Other: Kleineidam, Kuebart and Contractor benchmarks

3. *Demand drivers/brand strength analysis*

4. *Comparison of gross margin*

5. *Comparison of operating profit*

6. *Comparison with theoretical profits of a generic product*

7. *Cash flow or income differential with a benchmark company ("subtraction approach")*

8. *Incremental cash flow ("value of the company with and without the brand")*

9. *Free cash flow less required return on tangible assets*

10. *Excess earnings*

11. *Firm value less value of net tangible assets*

12. *Real options.*

4.3.1 Price premium

This method estimates the brand's incremental profits by comparing its price with that of an equivalent generic or unbranded product (Seetharaman et al., 2001).

Price premium-oriented methods operate under the assumption that certain characteristics, such as perceived quality or awareness, allow a goods manufacturer to charge a price premium for its brand (Aaker, 1991; Zimmermann et al., 2001). In other words, it assumes that the brand generates an additional benefit for consumers, for which they are willing to pay a little extra. According to Aaker (1991), price premiums can be measured through direct observation or consumer research.

Brand value is established by comparing the price of a branded product with that of an otherwise identical unbranded product. Total brand value is estimated as the present value of the stream of the after-tax profits attributable to the brand. To obtain annual profits attributable to the brand, unit price differentials are multiplied by the unit sales volume.

Advantages

- In theory, this approach is desirable because price premium represents a universally understood methodology.

Disadvantages

- In practice, this approach is problematic, and will be difficult to apply in companies that:

- depend on independent distribution channels that may not be willing to participate in the experiment;

- sell bundled goods and services that are hard to compare with the competitors' offer.

- A premium price position based solely on brand is hard to maintain for an extended period of time; therefore, we cannot consider the entire price premium as a profit generated by the brand (Smith, 1997: 88).

- When a branded product does not involve a price premium, the profit is generated in the dimensions of cost and units sold. By focusing only on price, the method ignores costs and other factors, such as economies of scale of high-volume brand production (Tollington, 1999).

Perhaps it is due to these disadvantages that no company has reported the price premium method in its accounting policies (Tollington, 1999). However, various providers offer methodologies based on determining the price differential or utility between the brand being valued and other benchmark brands or products. Such methodologies may consider various elements:

- The difference in forecasted sales for the branded product and a generic product, for a given period of time, assuming that both companies will sell the same volume of products or services.

- The difference in unit price between a branded and unbranded product, multiplied by forecasted sales volume.

- The average price premium differential of the past three years between the branded product and a generic product in the same category, multiplied by forecasted sales volume.

- Relative brand utility compared to other benchmark brands (and not generic products), multiplied by forecasted sales volume.

- Variation in brand sales per unit when the brand varies as a characteristic of the product, multiplied by forecasted volume and unit price.

4.3.1.a Conjoint analysis

Conjoint analysis may be thought of as a deductive price premium-oriented approach to brand valuation (Zimmermann et al., 2001).

This statistical technique is used to determine the importance that consumers assign to different product characteristics and the impact of these individual features on consumers' general preferences for the product. Through choice experiments, researchers ask consumers to choose between different combinations of attributes. Specifically, consumers are asked how much of a certain attribute they'd be willing to do without in order to obtain a little more of another attribute. This question may then be repeated for different pairs of attributes. Analyzing how these kinds of choices are made sheds light on the utility of each attribute, and offers an indication of consumer willingness to pay for specific product characteristics, the brand among them; the brand's value is thus determined. According to Keller (2008), Ogilvy & Mather has used a simplified version of conjoint analysis, reflecting just two variables (brand and price) to determine brand value.

Advantages

Quantitative statistical methods can reduce the degree of subjectivity to which brand valuations are generally prone.

Disadvantages

- *Restrictive assumptions:* Conjoint analysis demands that there be no influences between the brand, the other product characteristics and the price; a prerequisite that is hardly realistic, given that the halo effect lends the brand substantial influence over the perception of other characteristics (Zimmermann et al., 2001).

- *Subjectivity moved to a different level:* Conjoint analysis introduces certain elements of construction and application that make it largely unreliable for the estimation of fair value of all intangible assets; under certain conditions, it may yield an individual measure of brand equity, but not an aggregate measure at the level of the market or certain segments thereof (Kamakura and Russell, 1993, as cited in Jourdan, 2001).

4.3.1.b Hedonic analysis

According to Boos (2003), hedonic price models have recently been introduced as potential valuation approaches within the context of setting transfer prices for intangible assets. Under a hedonic price model, price or value is considered a function of the asset's characteristics. To value the brand, brand is treated simply as another product characteristic. Provided a set of n characteristics x_i, the function of price y would be given by the following expression:

$$y = \beta_0 + \beta_1 * x_1 + \beta_2 * x_2 + \ldots + \beta_n * x_n + \varepsilon$$

where:

y = the price of the asset

β_0 = a constant that represents price not explained by the individual characteristics present in the equation

β_i = the coefficient of the individual characteristics

x_i = the individual asset characteristics relevant to the transaction

ε = a random error term

Hedonic price analysis quantifies the effect of every characteristic on the price of the asset. Therefore, it allows for the identification and "separation" of the value of each individual product characteristic, including brand, if it is to be considered among them. If the brand were characteristic x_1, and its coefficient β_1 were positive, the brand attribute would be desirable, and would therefore have a positive market value (Boos, 2003).

As the hedonic function can predict price changes that would occur if certain product characteristics were altered, the final product price may be calculated with and without brand (Zimmermann et al., 2001). The differential is the unit revenue generated by the brand. By multiplying the unit revenue directly attributable to the brand by the total quantity sold, we arrive at the amount of revenue that would not have been obtained without the brand. To establish the net income attributable to the brand, we must deduct the specific brand expenses, i.e. those that would not have been incurred in the absence of the brand.

Advantages

Quantitative statistical methods can reduce the degree of subjectivity to which brand valuations are generally prone.

Disadvantages

The hedonic method is a very complex one in both theory and practice, and effectively places the subjective judgment inherent in any valuation process on another level; it is in the selection of a product's variable characteristics and associated costs that we see a vast potential for bias (Boos, 2003). Therefore, this method should not replace traditional analyses, but rather complement them. In Chapter 5, we shall consider several other disadvantages of this model, particularly Sanders' hedonic price model (see Section 5.26).

4.3.2   Royalty savings

The royalty savings method, also known as "royalty relief" or "relief from royalty," is based on the royalty rate that a company would have had to pay to use the brand if it did not own it and instead had to license it from a third party. Thus, in this approach, brand value is determined as the present value of the royalty stream after taxes.

The royalty savings methodology based on brand strength is as follows:

1. Estimate the *branded net sales* for the planning horizon (generally three to five years).

2. Determine a *reasonable royalty rate* that two unrelated parties would have set for the transfer of comparable brands in an "arm's length" transaction.

3. Multiply the estimated royalty rate by the projected sales of the brand over its economic life. The result represents annual royalty savings.

4. Apply a fiscal charge in each period to estimate the after-tax royalty savings for each.

5. Estimate the brand's *perpetual growth rate*, economic useful life and *discount rate*.

6. *Discount* the royalty stream after taxes at present value.

Table 4.2 shows an example of a trademark valuation using the royalty savings method.

In brand valuation exercises, much time and effort is spent on determining an appropriate royalty rate. Comparable licensing agreements are often used to determine a range of royalty rates "for the sector." To access these agreements,

Table 4.2 Royalty savings method – Valuation of trademark

Variables					
Royalty rate				4%	
Discount rate				16%	
Tax				40%	
Annual growth rate				10%	
Useful economic life				Indefinite	
After-Tax Royalty Rate growth rate post 2007				5%	

Year	2003	2004	2005	2006	2007
Net Sales	58,800	64,680	71,148	78,263	86,089
Pretax Royalty Stream	2,352	2,587	2,846	3,131	3,444
Tax Payable	941	1.035	1.138	1.252	1.377
After-Tax Royalty	1,411	1,552	1,708	1,878	2,066
Discount factor	0.928	0.800	0.690	0.595	0.513
Present Value After-Tax Royalty Stream	*1,310*	*1,242*	*1,178*	*1,117*	*1,059*
Sum of Present Value of After-Tax Royalty Stream	5.908				
2008 After-Tax Royalty	2,169				
Terminal Value 2008	19,722				
Present Value of Residual	10,113				
Trademark Value (as of December 31, 2002)	**16.021**				

Source: Adapted from Mard et al. (2002: 103[10]). Reproduced by permission of John Wiley & Sons Inc.

appraisers use databases that contain historical data on international royalty rates for the relevant product and industry. During this stage, it is important to bear in mind that the *royalty rate* is a function of:[11]

[10] The example presented by Mard et al. (2002) has been slightly modified excluding the calculation of the Tax Amortization Benefit and assuming a 10% annual growth during the explicit forecast period.
[11] Some of these factors have been previously quoted in different works such as: Smith and Parr (2000), Boos (2003), Cohen (2005), etc.

- the brand strength, generally used to establish the royalty rate via interpolation or another mathematical relationship;

- the duration and termination provisions of the agreement;

- the license's exclusivity;

- the parties' negotiating power;

- the product's life cycle;

- the local market conditions, particularly the margins earned in the local market

- the level of operating margin or licensee's sales. There are two general guidelines in determining the royalty rate: "the 25% rule" and "the 5% rule" (Smith and Parr, 2000). The 25% rule suggests that the royalty rate ought to be 25% of operating profit. The 5% rule places it at 5% of sales. Both rules arose within the pharmaceutical industry. Smith and Parr (2005) cite various sources that indicate that the 25% rule was developed decades ago by Robert Goldsheider, who carried out an empirical study on commercial licenses in the late 1950s. In the study, licensees tended to generate profits at figures around 20% of sales, on which they paid royalties at 5%. Therefore, the royalty rate effectively represented 25% of the licensee's profits. Although Goldsheider wrote about this rule for the first time in 1971, he noted that it had been used by valuation experts prior to that date (Smith and Parr, 2005: 411).

Advantages

- It calculates brand value by reference to documented third-party transactions.[12] That is, it is based on observable, contrastable and objective market parameters (comparable royalty rates).

- The value yielded by the application of this method is industry-specific.

- It is also theoretically appealing, as it removes the intrinsic difficulty of estimating the differential profitability attributable to the brand. According to Pablo Fernández (2001), "for a company whose main activity is the management of a name (a brand) that it transfers to other companies (franchises) in exchange for the payment of royalties, this difficulty disappears because brand management is the company's sole activity" (p. 670, own translation). In this case, brand value would be given by the market value of the company that manages the brand but is wholly uninvolved in the production of goods sold under that brand name.

- It has been accepted by many fiscal authorities as a suitable model.

Disadvantages

- The major disadvantage of this approach is that very few brands are actually comparable.

[12]Cf. http://www.brandfinance.com/docs/royalty_relief.asp.

- The royalty rate generally includes more than just the brand. The problem lies in determining what part of the royalty derives exclusively from the brand, and what part from the set of obligations outlined in the contract. Some find that this method does not adequately isolate brand value, because royalty rates tend to cover not only payment for the exploitation of the brand, but also other rights transferred from the licensor to the licensee (Barwise, Higson, Likierman and Marsh, 1989). For example, the licensor generally commits to providing a set of raw materials, know-how and services to ensure that the licensee maintains the required quality standard.

- Similarly, Smith and Parr (2005), Lasinski (2002) and Pavri (1999) note that the royalties estimated through this method may represent only a portion of the profit attributable to the brand. They make three objections to this approach:

  - *The royalty savings methods provides a "floor" or a "minimum value" for the brand that does not consider the "upside value" of having total control of the brand.* Licensing contracts only transfer a portion of the ownership rights (and the licensor reserves the right to exploit intellectual property himself). Therefore, the payment for these limited rights (royalties) is not a reliable measure of the "total" economic profit derived from ownership. Smith and Parr (2005) cite a legal decision made recently by the 2nd Circuit Court of Appeals of the United States with regard to a verdict on Nestlé

Holdings, Inc., in which the expert witnesses for both the taxpayer and the IRS used the "royalty relief" methodology to value the trademarks. The Court was not convinced that the resulting values were appropriate, remarking that "the relief-from-royalty method necessarily undervalues trademarks" (p. 194). The Court found that royalty models are appropriate for estimating the profit derived from the unjust use of the brand on the part of the infringer, but that it is ultimately not appropriate in the case of a sale, since it "fails to capture the value of all rights of ownership, such as the power to determine when and where a mark may be used, or moving a mark into or out of product lines" (Smith and Parr, 2005: 194). The Court decided that "ownership of a mark is more valuable than a license because ownership carries with it the power and incentive both to put the mark to its most valued use and to increase its value" (Smith and Parr, 2005: 194). Clearly, a license does not entail the same kind of incentive. Although it criticized the method, the Court did not suggest an alternative approach.

- Smith and Parr (2000) also object to this methodology, resorting to the "bundle of rights" theory originally applied to real property. According to this theory, certain rights may be transferred, while others are retained by the owner. Therefore, only by adding the rights retained by the owner/licensor and the rights of the licensee would we have a complete representation of the ownership rights

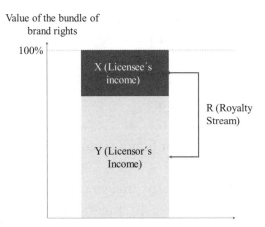

Figure 4.1 "Bundle of Brand Rights" Theory.
Source: Adapted from Smith and Parr (2000). Reproduced by permission of John Wiley & Sons Inc.

and the value of the brand. In Figure 4.1, the value of all the rights in the brand would be obtained by discounting the X and Y income streams. R is a portion of X income and its present value would represent the value of the license contract for the owner. According to Smith and Parr (2005), if we had to value the owner's rights to the brand, we would have to discount the R and Y income streams. And if we were to value the licensee's rights to the brand, we would need to discount X income stream less R royalty expenses.

- Referring to royalty rates as a "surrogate for the income attributable to the brand," Smith (1997: 100) affirms that while understanding that the reasonable return on the brand is fundamental to determining its value, many professionals take the industry's royalty rates as an indicator of this return, assuming that such rates were fixed in light of the values of the underlying assets and rates of return, and that they are somewhat stable in time.

In practice, there are at least five methodological options for estimating the royalty rate:

4.3.2.a Method based on brand strength and market comparables

In this methodology, royalty rates are estimated by surveying the range of royalty rates in the industry. Common data sources tend to be subscription databases such as *Royalty-Stat®* or publications such as *Licensing Economic Review* or *The Licensing Letter*. To determine a specific royalty rate for a particular brand within this range, one must review and understand the key clauses of every pertinent license contract (exclusivity/non-exclusivity, duration, rights of the parties, etc.) as well as the relative strength of the brand in relation to its relevant competitors. Brand strength is measured based on a list of qualities or attributes of the brand compared with those of its competitors. The royalty rate, then, will be a function of the range of comparable royalties as well as brand strength. Smith and Parr (2000: 369) critique this method, arguing that if the selected attributes are not those that generate the range of industry rates, the results will not be representative of the asset's value. The authors question whether the royalty rates at the bottom of the bracket really correspond to brands with low margins, low awareness, and low growth, or merely to disadvantageous contracts.

4.3.2.b Operating margin differential

This method analyzes the annual differences in operating margin and uses them as implicit royalty rates. In many ways, it resembles the method presented in Section 4.3.5, the sole difference being that it assimilates the margin differential with the theoretical value of the royalty rate. In general, the operating margin of the company being studied is compared with that of companies that do not have brands (generic manufacturers or private labels) or companies with similar but inferior brands (less known brands with poor distribution or less time in the market).

Once the excess income (as surrogate for the royalty rate) has been calculated based on any of these criteria, it is allocated to the brand.

4.3.2.c   The Knoppe formula

The Knoppe formula takes its name from Helmut Knoppe, who introduced it in 1967 (Boos, 2003). It is the German version of the rule of 25% of profits or 5% of sales as well as other norms proposed in the United States (Boos, 2003). The formula is as follows:

$$\text{royalty rate in \%} = \frac{\text{profit of licensed product} * 100}{\text{sales of licensed product} * 3} \quad (4.1)$$

Although the formula is a center of controversy among brand valuation experts, it is generally employed for auditing purposes (Boos, 2003). The formula is based on the German administrative principle by which a business manager should only pay the royalty rate up until the point at which it leaves him with an operating profit appropriate for the exploitation of the licensed product. For Knoppe, the optimum sum corresponds to a royalty rate with a maximum 25% to 33.33% of the licensor's profits before taxes.

The formula is no more than a rule of thumb, and represents a general guideline more than a basis of sound calculation. According to Boos (2003), its application beyond a simple control check is not recommended, particularly for fiscal purposes.

4.3.2.d Cluster or group analysis

Cluster analysis is a multivariate analytical technique used to organize variables or individuals of a population into homogeneous groups or clusters. The objective is to maximize the degree of intra-cluster homogeneity among variables and minimize it among inter-cluster variables.

Cluster analyses for the determination of the royalty rate encompass four stages (Boos, 2003):

1. *Data collection and determination of clustering variables.* For brands, this implies collecting data on licensing contracts and then selecting the variables that will be used to group the contracts. These clustering variables can either be different contractual characteristics (terms of contract, exclusivity, duration, etc.) or measures of profitability (sales to assets, operating margin, average inventory, etc.).

2. *Selection of a clustering method and data standardization.* For brand valuation purposes, the agglomerative hierarchical method is preferred.

3. *Establishment of the optimal number of groups or clusters.* Three models may be used to achieve this step: the dendogram (tree structure), the agglomeration table, or the

cluster distance vs. number criterion. The objective is to find an appropriate cluster that contains data on the brand to be valued, as well as on its comparables.

4. *Determination of the royalty rate.* In the last step, the cluster with data on the brand and its comparables is used, based on median royalty data or profit levels on the cluster companies.

Advantages

Boos (2003) points out two general scenarios that favor the application of this method:

- *Data availability.* This method may be used to value intangible assets in circumstances in which there is a great number of potential comparables and factors of comparability.

- *Low-profit intangibles.* This method is useful in the search for comparables to low-profit intangible assets.

Disadvantages

Boos (2003) indicates three main drawbacks of this methodology:

- *Too much discretion.* Although quantitative statistical methods are generally thought to reduce the level of subjectivity of brand valuation, they really only shift it into the realm of methodological decision-making. There is a lot of discretion in each of the four stages that in turn affords ample room for manipulation.

- *Access to necessary data may be severely limited.*

- *Not applicable to high-profit intangibles.* Cluster analysis is difficult to apply in the case of unique high-profit intangibles, as the necessary data would not be available.

4.3.2.e Other: Kleineidam, Kuebart and Contractor benchmarks

These models are centered on analyses of the negotiation process between independent licensors and licensees (Boos, 2003).

4.3.3 Demand drivers/brand strength analysis

This model focuses on the effects that brand strength and/or demand drivers have on supply and demand in order to determine the brand's "influence" on consumer decision-making/value creation as well as the proportion of the business "related to brand." Several companies employ different versions of this approach by analyzing demand drivers and/or brand strength attributes. Although the demand driver analysis approach is statistical at times, the methodology involved in determining the drivers and their relative relevance may be completely arbitrary. This method is also known as "reasons-to-buy." The approach commonly involves the use of quantitative and qualitative market research or the Delphi method.

Various specific algorithms are used to estimate the brand's contribution to income or profits generation. The following are among the numerous options for calculating the brand's contribution:

- *Absolute techniques*

  - This approach is based on the proportion of brand-related factors relative to the total number of factors considered during the buying process, without weighting them by importance. This process entails deciding which factors are brand-related and adding their relative frequencies. Distinguishing brand-related factors from non-brand-related factors is generally a subjective process and lends itself to general confusion depending on the structure and composition of the survey, as well as the analyst's judgment. We therefore find this model to be arbitrary, lacking a stable system of logic, and, as shown in Table 4.3, not always capable of rendering appropriate results.

- *Relative techniques:* There are two ways of applying this approach: one that considers the brand as a factor that

Table 4.3 "Reasons-to-buy" analysis

Reasons for choosing brand	% (frequency)	The lower limit assumes attributes related to:	The upper limit assumes attributes related to:
1. Brand quality and status	25%	Brand	Brand
2. Track record and historical performance	5%	Business	Business
3. Brand image	15%	Brand	Brand
4. Models and design	40%	Business	Brand
5. Other reasons	10%	Business	Business
Sum of frequencies associated with "brand"		**40%**	**80%**

Source: Developed by author based on experience with projects within Europe

influences all the product or service relevant attributes; and one that considers the brand as an independent attribute.

- The first "relative technique" ranks each demand driver's *importance* and determines the *relative perception/brand contribution* for each driver. Subsequently it weights the brand's contribution to each factor by its relative importance. This approach assumes that the brand has an effect on the perception of every key attribute in the purchase decision. Figure 4.2 shows an example of an estimation of the "brand's role in generating customer demand" carried out under this approach.

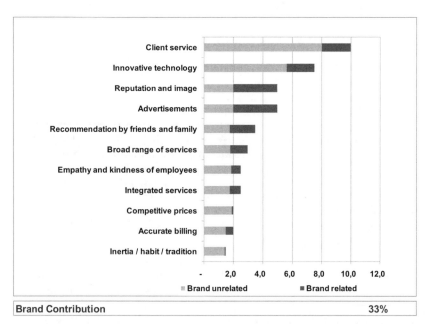

Figure 4.2 Analysis of the brand's contribution, treating brand as an independent attribute that influences the perception of the other attributes. Source: Based on Marketing Leadership Council (2003: 8) and Binar (2005)

- The second "relative technique" determines the importance of each demand driver, brand among them. The brand is considered an independent attribute that does not influence the perception of other attributes (see Figure 4.3). Brand contribution is given by the "weight" of the brand importance compared with that of the other attributes. Brand contribution can be estimated through different statistical techniques, among them, regression analysis.

Both approaches under this analysis yield an "index" or "percentage" that may later be applied to sales, earnings, cash

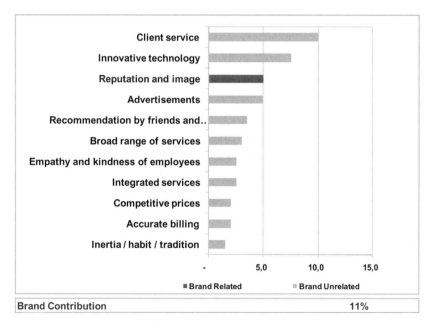

Figure 4.3 Analysis of the brand's contribution, treating brand as an independent variable that does not influence the perception of other attributes. Source: Adapted from Haigh (2000). Reproduced by permission of Brand Finance PLC

flow Economic Value Added, or EVA[13], in order to estimate the brand-related proportion of each of these variables.

Advantages

- From a marketing perspective, this method is useful for determining the key demand drivers that add value for the company. However, the determination of these demand drivers does not require a brand valuation procedure, and may instead be accomplished simply through thorough market research analysis.

- With this method, calculating the proportion of profits attributable to the brand does not always depend on obtaining data on benchmark transactions or firms.

Disadvantages

- Companies that employ this method often do not reveal their calculation algorithms ("black box"[14] methodologies) and/or apply them on a case-by-case basis, depending on the information available; therefore, the results obtained through this approach are not easily comparable.

- The index yielded by demand driver analysis is often applied to different bases (EVA, free cash flow, sales, etc.).

[13]EVA is a registered trademark of Stern Stewart & Co. and EVA Dimensions, and BRANDECONOMICS is a registered trademark of Stern Stewart & Co.
[14]A "black box method" is one in which at least one essential component is opaque and undocumented.

- Caution must be exercised when applying the statistical regression techniques used to determine brand contribution when the brand is considered a product attribute. Although this technique may seem very appealing at first, likening the brand to a product attribute may lead to several conceptual problems:

  - Statistical measures of the effects of the interaction between the brand and other attributes can be very complex (Rangaswamy, Burke and Oliva, 1993, as cited in Jourdan, 2001).

  - As the consumer associates the brand with specific characteristics, the manipulation of these variables within experimental research may sometimes lead to unrealistic results, jeopardizing the external validity of the analysis (Green and Srinivasan, 1978, as cited in Jourdan, 2001).

  - Because the results of these analyses often point to an individual value, in my opinion, this type of analysis is valid for strategic or management-related objectives, but never for estimating the fair value of intangible assets for accounting purposes.

  - This type of analysis also presents problems in its implementation. In my experience, these analyses leave a lot of room for subjectivity in various core elements, among them:

    - The formulation of the questions relative to the additional "brand" attribute.

- The selection of independent variables.

- The type of regression analysis to perform; this measure may be effected through a Logit regression (Swait, Erdem, Louviere and Dubelaar, 1993 and Kamakura and Russell, 1993, as cited in Jourdan, 2001) or through conjoint analysis (Park and Srinivasan, 1994, Srinivasan, 1979 as cited in Jourdan, 2001).

- The selection of a particular multi-attribute model for measuring utility is, generally speaking, arbitrary, and often entails systematic errors.

- Any unit contribution index calculated in this fashion does not value the impact of the brand alone; due to its constitution, it also inevitably encompasses a measuring error deriving from the use of a particular multi-attribute model – additive linear or others – as well as the arbitrary nature of the selection of criteria for product evaluation (Mazis, Ahtola and Klippel, 1975, as cited in Jourdan, 2001).

- The validity of conjoint analysis methodology depends highly on the selection of attributes and their determining characteristics within the consumer's selection process (Green and Srinivasan, 1978, as cited in Jourdan, 2001).

- Other typical problems with statistical analysis that may affect the reliability of their results include the size of the sample, measuring errors, sampling, etc.

4.3.4 Comparison of gross margin with that of relevant competitors

Smith (1997) introduces this technique, also known as the "Economies of Scale method," for companies that have strong brands but cannot charge a price premium. A company may enjoy economies of scale in its production or procurement that may be attributed to the brand. To capture the value of economies of scale attributable to the brand, the gross business margin of the firm unable to charge a price premium is compared with the average gross margin yielded by a set of comparable competitors. The difference is then multiplied by the net sales corresponding to the brand. Thus, earnings attributable to brand m due to economies of scale in production are expressed mathematically by the following equation (Smith, 1997):

$$ESE_m = (GM_m - GM_c) * S_m \qquad (4.2)$$

where:

ESE_m = the economies of scale earnings attributable to brand m

GM_m = the gross margin corresponding to the business associated with brand m, defined as:

$$GM_m = \left(\frac{GP_m}{S_m} \right)$$

GM_c = the average gross margin yielded by the set of comparable competitors, defined as:

$$GM_c = \frac{\sum\limits_{i=1}^{n} GP_i}{\sum\limits_{i=1}^{n} S_i}$$

S_m = the net sales of the business associated with brand m

S_i = the net sales of the business of competitor i of the set of n comparable competitors

GP_i = the gross profit corresponding to competitor i of the set of n comparable competitors, defined as:

$$GP_i = S_i - CGS_i$$

CGS_i = the cost of goods sold under the brand of competitor i of the set of n comparable competitors

GP_m = the gross profit corresponding to the products sold under brand m, defined as:

$$GP_m = S_m - CGS_m$$

CGS_m = the cost of goods sold under brand m

This technique assumes that the difference between gross margins is due to the fact that brand m is reaping the profits of the economies of scale in production because of its dominant market position. In other words, it assumes that the business associated with brand m would earn ESE_m less (during the period under study) if the gross margin were the same as the average of its competitors.

The brand value is calculated as the present value of the after-tax gross profit attributable to the brand.

Advantages

Because it considers cost advantages, this approach is useful in valuing brands that do not enjoy price advantages.

Disadvantages

Because it does not consider other non-brand-related variables that might influence the gross margin, this approach is likely to under- or overvalue the brand.

4.3.5 Comparison of operating profit with that of relevant competitors

Operating profit comparisons are more complex than gross margin comparisons, and consider a wider spectrum of brand advantages. A truly strong brand can also increase profitability through lower promotion expenses and administrative and general expenses; these concepts are not included in the cost of goods sold (Smith, 1997). One way of taking these factors into account is to compare the branded business' levels of operating profit (EBIT) with those yielded by a set of benchmark companies.

Brand value is then calculated as the present value of after-tax operating profit attributable to the brand.

This approach is expressed mathematically as:

$$EBIT_m = \left[\left(\frac{EBIT}{S} \right)_m - \left(\frac{\sum_{i=1}^{n} \left(\frac{EBIT}{S} \right)_i}{n} \right) \right] * S_m \qquad (4.3)$$

where:

$EBIT_m$ = the operating profit attributable to the brand

$\left(\dfrac{EBIT}{S}\right)_m$ = the ratio of operating profit to branded business

 sales

$\dfrac{\sum\limits_{i=1}^{n}\left(\dfrac{EBIT}{S}\right)_i}{n}$ = the average operating profit/sales ratio yielded

by the set of comparable competitors

S_m = branded sales revenue

Advantages

This approach considers a wider spectrum of brand advantages than the techniques of "economies of scale" and price premium.

Disadvantages

As there may be other non-brand-related variables that influence operating profits, this approach is likely to over- or undervalue the brand.

4.3.6 Comparison with theoretical profits of a generic product

This method estimates brand value as the operating profits differential between the branded company and the unbranded company multiplied by a multiple. There are three models based on this technique that stand out in the literature: those developed by Financial World, Interbrand and Global Brand Equity (by Motameni and Shahrokhi). They are based on an analysis of the brand's operating profits and those estimated for an equivalent generic product. The profits attributable to the brand are determined in one of two ways:

1. By deducting the estimated EBIT for an "equivalent generic product" from the EBIT of the branded business. The calculation of profits for an equivalent generic product assumes a 5% return on capital employed (RCE) and a ratio of capital employed to sales equivalent to the median ratio in the sector.

2. By deducting the EBIT for an "equivalent generic product" and the remuneration of the resources from the EBIT of the branded business.

Estimation of the EBIT of an equivalent generic product:

$$EBIT_{eq} = Med\left(\frac{CE}{S}\right)_s * S_m * RCE(5\%)$$

where:

$EBIT_{eq}$ = the EBIT of an equivalent generic product

$Med (CE/S)_s$ = the median ratio of capital employed to sales in the sector

VS_m = the sales of the branded products

$Med(CE/S)_s * S_m$ = the capital investment required to produce VS_m sales volume

RCE = the return on capital employed for a generic product arbitrarily set at 5%

Advantages

Conceptually, comparing profits of the branded company with those of the unbranded company is sound.

Disadvantages

- The disadvantages of this method lie in its application, given that obtaining reliable data and estimations for the unbranded company can be difficult.

- The quantification of the EBIT differential involves a highly subjective procedure (Fernández, 2001).

4.3.7 Cash flow or income differences with a benchmark company ("subtraction approach")

This technique, presented by Smith and Parr (2005: 258), assumes that differences between the net cash flows of the subject company (the firm owning the brand being valued) and that of the set of comparable companies that have no trademark is fully attributable to the brand factor.

Advantages

One could argue that the primary advantage of this method is its simplicity; however, this simplicity is jeopardized by the fact that cash flow differentials cannot reasonably be attributed exclusively to the brand.

Disadvantages

- This approach does not consider other variables that may contribute to cash flow differentials.

- According to Smith and Parr (2005: 259), in everyday practice, it is difficult to find an unbranded comparable company (i.e., one that has the same mix of monetary, tangible and intangible assets). Even generic products can have significant associated intangible assets (for example, a long-term contract with a private-label distributor).

- In practice, the unbranded comparable company might have higher returns or cash flows than those of the branded company. Would this indicate that the brand being studied has no value? The earnings of the branded company may be lower for many reasons unrelated to the brand's contribution.

4.3.8 Present value of incremental cash flow (the company's value "with" and "without" brand)

More than a method to determine the income attributable to the brand, this is a valuation technique in itself. The value of the business *with* and *without* brand may be calculated through the DCF approach, wherein the differential indicates brand value. The income attributable to the brand is estimated by considering the brand effect on different value drivers. The brand effect might be reflected in an increased growth rate, increased advertising expenses or lower risk (Smith, 1997).

Advantages

This method is conceptually sound.

Disadvantages

According to Smith (1997), the key to the correct application of this kind of model lies in appropriately reflecting the brand effect on different business value levers. This task is not a simple one.

4.3.9 Free cash flow (FCF) less required return on other non-brand-related assets

Smith (1997) and Houlihan Advisors determine the free cash flow (FCF) attributable to brands and/or intangible assets as free cash flow less remuneration of other tangible and/or intangible non-brand-related assets. An example of an application of this methodology is shown in Table 5.23.

Advantages

None

Disadvantages

This approach is conceptually flawed. Here, free cash flow attributable to the brand is similar to EVA, but, as noted by Pablo Fernández (2001), cash flow attributable to an unbranded company is substituted by the assets employed by the branded company multiplied by their required return. For this reason, this method has been heavily criticized by various authors (Roos, 2005; Fernández, 2001).

4.3.10 Excess earnings

This technique estimates the excess earnings on all intangible resources, by subtracting the normal returns on physical or financial assets from the firm's total return rate. It is therefore not useful for determining the value of a particular intangible asset. Preliminary work is required in order to estimate the portion of excess earnings attributable to the intangible asset being valued. This allocation is done on the basis of the analyst's experience. It is difficult to consider this process an objective one, as each analyst will arrive at a different conclusion.

There are multiple variations in the application of this technique:

- U.S. Revenue Ruling 68-609

- Baruch Lev's intangibles scoreboard

- Analysis of required return on investment.

Let us take a closer look at these various options.

4.3.10.a U.S. Revenue Ruling 68-609
In U.S. Revenue Ruling 68-609 (RR 68-609), also known as "The Formula Approach," intangible assets are valued by determining the earnings in excess of a fair rate of return on net tangible assets. Below are the specific steps that need to be followed when applying this approach (Pratt, 2002: 178):

1. Normalize historical pre-tax earnings and recalculate taxes based on normalized pre-tax earnings.

2. Determine the value of the company's net tangible assets.

3. Determine a reasonable rate of return (at the date of the valuation) on the estimated value of the company's net tangible assets. The average annual rate of return on tangible assets should be the normal return in the industry at the time of valuation. When such information is unavailable, a figure of 8% or 10% may be used, depending on business risk.

4. Multiply the reasonable rate of return (step 3) by the value of the company's net tangible assets (step 2). The result is the "reasonable margin" on such assets.

5. Subtract the reasonable rate of return (step 4) from the normalized net earnings (step 1). The difference is the company's excess earnings.

6. Determine an appropriate capitalization rate (at the date of the valuation) for the company's excess earnings, which are assumed to be attributable to goodwill and other intangible assets. This rate may fall either at 15% or 20%, depending on business risk.

7. Capitalize excess earnings (by dividing their value by the appropriate capitalization rate).

Figure 4.4 visually represents this process:

We now turn to an example of the application of this method presented by Pratt (2002), shown in Figure 4.5 below. It involves KLM, a fully equity-financed company in the garden and landscape design sector. The excess earnings method is applied on the basis of the following assumptions:

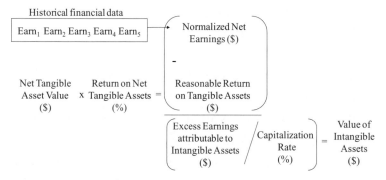

Figure 4.4 Revenue Ruling 68-609.
Source: Developed by author based on Shannon Pratt (2002)

Tangible asset value	$20 000
Net cash flow	$50 000
Required return on tangible assets 0.08 × $200 000	$16 000
Return attributable to intangible assets	$34 000
Value of intangible assets (capitalized excess earnings) 34 000 ÷ 0.20	$170 000

Figure 4.5 Valuation in conformity with Revenue Ruling 68-609.
Source: Pratt (2002: 180). Reproduced by permission of John Wiley & Sons Inc.

1. An expert from the American Society of Appraisers in Machinery and Equipment Appraisal with experience in gardening valued KLM's tangible assets at $200 000.

2. The reasonable rate of return on the company's tangible assets was set at 8%.

3. The appropriate capitalization rate for the company's excess earning was 20%.

4. KLM's normalized net cash flow after the owner's reasonable compensation was $50 000 per year.

5. Cash flow growth is estimated at 3%, equivalent to the annual rate of inflation.

4.3.10.b Baruch Lev's Intangible Scoreboard

Professor Baruch Lev of New York University based his Knowledge Capital Scoreboard and Intangibles Scoreboard on the excess earnings method. But rather than setting the reasonable rate of return for tangible assets at 8% or 10%, he sets the after-tax fair rate of return at 7% on physical assets and 4.5% on financial assets (Hofmann, 2005). The intangible assets driven margin is the margin in excess of the 7% assigned to the tangible assets, and the 4.5% assigned to the financial assets.

4.3.10.c Analysis of required return on investment

This technique, also known as the *analysis of required return on investment* or *residual return*, and presented by Smith (1997), does not assign a fixed return to the tangible assets. It goes a little further than the methods previously presented, by allocating the intellectual property driven earnings among various intellectual property assets. For Smith (1997), total business income derives from the exploitation of the assets that comprise it, such that return attributable to the brand may be isolated based on the expected returns for the other assets. The allocation of earnings among different asset categories is determined by the assets' relative values and risks. Smith (1997) notes that although it is tempting to cut corners and allocate the total business income to assets simply on the basis of their relative value, this shortcut would not adequately recognize their relative risks. For that reason, this analysis introduces market risk rates. To estimate them, Woodward (2003) suggests assuming that the owner must rent the assets in order to generate earnings. Table 4.4 shows an example taken from Smith (1997):

Table 4.4   Allocating income among assets

Category of asset	Value of assets (in $000)	Required return	Earnings (in $000)
Net working capital	135 000	5.0%	6 750
Tangible assets	187 500	9.0%	16 875
Intangible assets	52 500	13.0%	6 825
Intellectual property	80 000	18.81%	15 050
Total	455 000	10%	45 500
Patents	20 000	17%	3 380
Proprietary technology	22 500	22%	4 858
Trademarks	37 500	18%	6 806
Intellectual property	80 000	18.81%	15 050

Source: Adapted from Smith (1997). Reproduced by permission of John Wiley & Sons Inc.

The income attributable to the assets is $45.5 million, the same as the estimated net cash flow. On the top part of the table, earnings attributable to intellectual property are calculated at $15.05 million. But to be able to calculate the required rate of return and earnings attributable to intellectual property, the appraiser must know the business value, its earnings and the values and return required for all the other assets. Once the intellectual property earnings are estimated, earnings attributable exclusively to brand (in this case $6.8 million) are isolated, "using judgement," (p. 150) keeping the general return on intellectual property at a constant 18.81% and intellectual property value at $80 million.

Advantages of excess earnings

- Although this methodology is conceptually sound, assigning a return rate to each intangible asset is somewhat subjective.

Disadvantages of excess earnings

- In the case of companies with valuable brands, numerous obsolete physical assets, and cash surplus, the brand will be undervalued because of the high rate of return assigned to the idle assets.

- The determination of each intangible asset's required return is very subjective.

- Wherever the return rate on tangible assets is considered to be fixed (Baruch Lev's Intangibles Scoreboard, RR 68-609), the return rate on intellectual property assets is determined in an arbitrary fashion.

4.3.11   Company valuation less value of net tangible assets

More than a method to determine the income attributable to the brand, this is a valuation technique in itself. According to the AASB (2001), in this methodology, brand value is established by first determining the entity or operation's fair value (using a generally accepted valuation model such as the present value of expected cash flow) and subtracting the fair value of the net tangible assets employed by the entity. The resulting value is then the value attributable to the brand.

Advantages

According to Lonergan (1998) this approach can be useful to set a maximum upper limit of the brand's value (p. 269 as cited by AASB, 2001).

Disadvantages

According to the AASB (2001), this approach assumes that aside from the brand, there are no other intangible assets (identified or not identified) used in the company or operation, or that these other intangible assets have no value.

4.3.12 Real options

In the absence of comparable transactions, real option models may be useful for quantifying a brand's royalty rate (Torres, 2006).

An option is essentially the right to choose. Financial options are contracts that convey the right but not the obligation to buy or sell an asset at a previously fixed price over an agreed period of time or at a given date. The theory of real options applies financial option valuation tools to non-financial assets; assets are treated as a set of options that, if exercised, generate more options and cash flow.

According to Pablo Fernández (2001), a brand may be considered an asset that provides its owner with a set of real options:

- of geographical growth

- of growth by broadening distribution coverage

- of growth by using new formats

- of growth by extending the brand into new categories

- to abandon, etc.

However, in practice, real options methods are rarely used to value brands. Lamb (2002) highlights the fact that most investment banks and consultants do not use real options to value trademarks.

Put simply, a real option valuation includes a basic value plus the value of the option or volatility. The following variables must be determined in order to value an option:

- Risk-free interest rate (r_f)

- Implicit volatility of the underlying asset (σ^2)

- Current strike price (E)

- The current market value of the underlying asset (S)

- Time to expiration (t)

The crucial assumption is that the brand owner has the option to terminate or renew the brand license when a contract expires. The value of the underlying asset would be the value of the cash flow deriving from the licensing contract and the cost of developing the brand is the strike price. This method may be useful for determining the potential value of brand extensions, but the assumptions inherent in this approach make its application very difficult.

Advantages

- Because this method considers the value associated with the uncertainty of cash flows, flexibility, and future opportunities for growth, it provides excellent tools for management decision-making (extension, expansion, etc.).

Disadvantages

- Though the theory of real options may constitute a reliable method of estimating share values, it is less effective when applied to intangible assets, due to their unique nature. The reliability of this approach is diminished, as the value of the variables involved in the valuation (r_f, σ^2, E, S, t) must either be approximated roughly or set arbitrarily.

- While this approach provides ideas for decision-makers, it does not provide results acceptable for fiscal authorities.

There are two alternative methods of applying the real options approach.

4.3.12.1 Binomial method (time as a discrete variable)

The binomial valuation model is used to determine the value of real options. It describes price movements within a period of time, such that the asset may have two possible prices (in Figure 4.6, the success and failure values).

Woodward (2003) discusses this methodology in detail, outlining the following steps:

1. Make a tree diagram that includes all relevant possible decisions.

2. Use a utility function (or expected value) and probability of occurrence on each node. The probability of occurrence reflects the specific risk.

3. Choose the branch with the highest value on any decision node.

4. At the end of the tree, estimate the value discounting the outputs at WACC.

Figure 4.6 shows an example of a tree diagram used in real options analysis:

Advantages

- This model is more intuitive and flexible than the Black-Scholes model, and is based on the simplification that the underlying asset can only move between two possible price levels within a short period of time.

- Given that the binomial model allows for the estimation of the option's value at any point of its life, the advantage

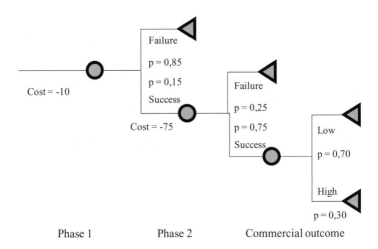

| Phase 1 | Phase 2 | Commercial outcome |

The probability weighted present value is is $64

Figure 4.6 Tree diagram used in real options analysis.
Source: Woodward (2003). Reproduced by permission of Pricewaterhouse-Coopers

this model has over the Black-Scholes model is that it may be used to calculate the value of American options, which can be exercised at any time.

Disadvantages

This method requires laborious calculations. For example, the risk associated with the asset fluctuates with time, and the discount factor must be adjusted in function of the varying risk, which further complicates the process.

4.3.12.2 Black-Scholes model (continuum)

The Black-Scholes equation is used to calculate the value of a call option, as shown in equation (4.4):

$$c = s\varphi(d_1) - xe^{-rt}\varphi(d_2) \qquad (4.4)$$

$$d_1 = \frac{\ln(s/x) + (r + \sigma^2/2)t}{\sigma\sqrt{t}} \qquad (4.5)$$

$$d_2 = d_1 - \sigma\sqrt{t} \qquad (4.6)$$

where:

S = the price of the underlying asset

X = the strike price

r = the risk-free rate

t = the time to expiration

σ = the implicit volatility of the underlying asset and

φ = the standard normal probability density function

Advantages

- Speed is often considered an advantage of this technique, but it applies more to shares, because estimating the parameters for real options can be very time-consuming.

Disadvantages

- It is difficult to determine all the parameters needed to apply this equation.

- While the equation assumes a single exercise date (European options), this is not always the case in real situations.

5

Brand Valuation Methods and Providers

THIS CHAPTER PRESENTS REVIEWS OF VARIOUS VALUATION procedures used by brand valuation service providers from all over the world, and models developed by prominent academics in the field. Each model is described in terms of its methodology, as well as its advantages and disadvantages, where appropriate. This chapter is designed to serve as a source of reference for analysts interested in the various applications of each methodology described in Chapter 4.

The description of each model starts with a summary table that indicates the ownership of the mode, the approximate year in which it was developed, the author, the country of origin, and the approach and methodology used. Later, an in-depth description of the main variables and modules or stages of the model is presented. Finally, the main advantages and disadvantages of each proprietary methodology are discussed.

All of the models discussed in this chapter are applicable for the valuation of both product and service brands. Chapter 8 will discuss various methods of corporate brand valuation. Chapter 6 offers a comparative look at the various models based on relevant criteria.

5.1 AbsoluteBrand

Table 5.1 AbsoluteBrand model

Model name or ownership	Uses the model developed by Intangible Business, with whom it has a joint venture[15]
Year of development	2003
Author	Whitwell, Stuart
Country	USA
Approach	Mixed (income/market)
Principal methodology	Royalty savings

Source: Developed by author

AbsoluteBrand's website[16] shows the general stages of the company's brand valuation process without alluding specifically to the ways in which it differs from other brand valuation methods. These stages include:

• identifying the brand

• segmenting the business

• creating market maps

[15] As of 27 July 2008, on AbsoluteBrand's website, one could read that Intangible Business is their European partner: http://www.absolutebrand.com/RESEARCH/brand_trademark.asp.
[16] http://www.absolutebrand.com/services/VALUE/default.htm.

- checking financial forecasts against value levers

- determining value drivers

- determining royalty rates

- calculating segmented "branded business" and "brand" value

The main assumptions behind this approach are:

- forecasted annual revenues

- royalty rates

- marketing, promotional, research, development and other costs

- segmentation

- value drivers

- taxes

- discount rates

- growth rates beyond the forecast period

After examining the relevant milestones in the brand's history, this model applies the royalty savings method for the brand in its key markets and segments. To do this, it analyzes the brand's value drivers and compares brand strength in these criteria with that of its competitors. Later, and based on a database containing information on transactions effected in the market among independent parties (arm's length), the model determines the applicable royalty rate within a range of comparable license contracts. It also considers comparable sales and historical/replacement cost approaches as a sense check.

AbsoluteBrand model critique

This model is subject to criticisms applicable to all royalty savings-based models.

5.2   AUS Consultants

Table 5.2   AUS Consultants model

Model name or ownership	It seems that the company does not have a proprietary model and thus applies different models in different circumstances
Year of development	1983[17]
Authors	Not applicable (the models presented by G. Smith and R. Parr are not proprietary).
Country	USA
Approach	Income (mainly)
Principal methodology	Free cash flow less the return required on other non-brand-related assets and value of the company "with" and "without" the trademark, among others

Source: Developed by author

---

[17] The Year of development of the practice and the first brand valuation models is assumed to be the Year of development of AUS Consultants within the group. Cf. http://www.ipmall.info/news_activities/news/smith_050101.asp.

Gordon V. Smith (1997), president of AUS Consultants, rec-
ommends methods "that have basis in financial principles"
(p. 158). As many of these methods are not exclusive to AUS
Consultants, we will list them below and later provide an
example of the application of one of them.

The methods recommended by Smith (1997) and presumably
applied by AUS Consultants include:

(a) trademark valuation based on estimation of reproduction
cost by trending historical costs or deriving the cost to
reproduce the trademark;

(b) trademark valuation based on market transactions
comparison;

(c) residual trademark valuation;

(d) trademark valuation based on price premium;

(e) trademark valuation based on gross margin advantage;

(f) trademark valuation based on operating margin advantage;

(g) trademark valuation based on royalty savings;

(h) trademark valuation based on free cash flow less the
required return on other non-brand-related assets;

(i) trademark valuation based on the difference in value of
the business "with" and "without" the trademark;

(j) trademark valuation by allocation of income, based on the
investment rate-of-return analysis.

Table 5.3 Trademark valuation based on free cash flows less the required return on other non-brand-related assets ("DCF-based technique")

	1995	1996	1997	1998	1999	2000
Sales, less returns and allowances	373 500	388 440	403 978	420 137	436 942	454 420
Less – Cost of Goods sold	205 001	213 201	221 729	230 598	239 822	249 415
Gross Margin	168 499	175 239	182 249	189 539	197 120	205 005
Less – Selling, general and administrative expenses	74 700	77 688	80 796	84 027	87 388	90 884
Net operating income	93 799	97 551	101 453	105 512	109 732	114 121
Other income or (expense)	-32 000	-32 640	-33 293	-33 959	-34 638	-35 331
Net Income before income taxes	61 799	64 911	68 160	71 553	75 094	78 790
Less – State and federal income taxes	24 720	25 965	27 264	28 621	30 038	31 516
Net income before extraordinary items	37 080	38 947	40 896	42 932	45 056	47 274
Extraordinary items of income or (expense)	-5 000					
Net income	32 080	38 947	40 896	42 932	45 056	47 274
Calculate net cash flow						
Add: extraordinary items to normalize	5 000					
Add: Depreciation expense	12 000	12 240	12 485	12 734	12 989	13 249
Subtract: Additions to working capital	2 000	1 800	1 836	1 873	1 910	1 948
Subtract: Capital expenditures	3 000	4 500	4 590	4 682	4 775	4 871
	44 080	44 887	46 955	49 111	51 360	53 704
Assets Employed						
Net Working Capital	90 000	91 800	93 636	95 509	97 419	99 367
Tangible Assets	225 000	229 500	234 090	238 772	243 547	248 418
Intangible Assets	75 000	76 500	78 030	79 591	81 182	82 806

Intellectual Property – Patents		10000	10200	10404	10612	10824	11041
Intellectual Property – Proprietary Technology		15000	15300	15606	15918	16236	16561
Less Returns Required on Assets Employed							
Net Working Capital	6.0%	5400	5508	5618	5731	5845	5962
Tangible Assets	9.0%	20250	20655	21068	21489	21919	22358
Intangible Assets	14.0%	10500	10710	10924	11143	11365	11593
Intellectual Property – Patents	14.5%	1450	1479	1509	1539	1569	1601
Intellectual Property – Proprietary Technology	20.3%	3045	3106	3168	3231	3296	3362
Allocable to Trademark		*3435*	*3429*	*4668*	*5978*	*7365*	*8829*
Present Value of FCF Allocable to Brand (@16%)			3184	3736	4125	4381	4527
Terminal Value							76516
Present Value of Terminal Value							39237
Total Present Value (@ WACC 16%; growth rate after 2000 = 4%)		**59190**					

Source: Smith (1997: 151–152)

Smith (1997) discusses the limitations of each of these techniques in their applications to trademark valuation. He refers to the methodologies based on the differential value of the business "with" and "without" the brand (j) and on free cash flow less the required return on other assets (i) as "DCF-based techniques" (p. 150) and emphasizes that these DCF-based methodologies "capture all of the elements of value" (p. 148).

Valuation based on the differential between free cash flow and the required return on other assets

Smith (1997) suggests that this methodology might surpass those not based on the DCF approach. To be able to apply this methodology, the appraiser must know the value of the business, the income that the business generates and the values and rates of return of some of its assets. Table 5.3 on p. 114/115 shows an example of a trademark valuation based on this methodology provided by Smith (1997) and corrected by the author.[18]

AUS Consultants model critique

From Smith's literature, we can infer that AUS Consultants uses different methods for different purposes. Chapter 4 discussed the advantages and disadvantages of each of these methods. Although Smith (1997) does not clearly state any preference for one valuation method over another, his description of the advantages of what he calls "DCF-based techniques" indicates that these might be his (and AUS Consultants')

---

[18] In the original example presented by Smith (1997), the trademark value is calculated at 53 157 rather than 59 190. The difference derives from the calculation of terminal value. While the author calculates terminal value as [$8829(1 + 0.04)/(0.16 − 0.04)]/(1 + 0,16)∧4.5, which yields a discounted terminal value of 39 237, Smith (1997) computes the discounted terminal value as [$8829/(0.16 − 0.04)]/(1 + 0,16)∧4.5, yielding a result of 37 728.

methodologies of choice. With respect to the determination of the royalty rate under the "royalty savings" method, while Smith (1997) criticizes score-based methods, as well as the 25% rule, the methods that he deems best for calculating royalty rate are somewhat circular or highly subjective.

5.3 BBDO

Table 5.4 BBDO model

Model name or ownership	Brand Equity Evaluation System (BEES); Brand Equity Evaluator®; and BEVA ("Brand Equity Valuation for Accounting") developed jointly with Ernst & Young
Year of development	2001; 2002; 2004
Authors	Zimmermann et al. (BEES and BEE); BBDO and Ernst & Young (BEVA)
Country	Germany
Approach	Income (BEES), Income (BEE); Income/Market (BEVA)
Principal Methodology	Income capitalization based on brand strength analysis (BEES); cash flow discount and demand/ brand strength analysis (BEE); royalty savings (BEVA)

Source: Developed by author

BBDO has developed two brand valuation models independently (Zimmermann et al., 2001 and 2002) and one model jointly with Ernst & Young (BBDO, 2004):

- BEES, Brand Equity Evaluation System®

- BEE, Brand Equity Evaluator®, a revision of the above model, and

- BEVA, Brand Equity Valuation for Accounting®.

Each of these three models is described below.[19]

Before embarking on the description of these models, I feel obliged to say that the research undertaken by BBDO between the years 2001 and 2002 and condensed in two thorough papers (cf. Zimmermann et al., 2001 and 2002), is one of the most complete and honest I have come across in the industry. Although I may not agree with all their conclusions and conceptual developments, their work demonstrates a great deal of academic rigor, dedication and professionalism.

5.3.1 Brand Equity Evaluation System (BEES)

This model first identifies eight brand equity determinants:[20]

- *Brand sales.*

- *Net operating margin* (averaged from the past three years).

- *Perspectives of brand development:* industry analysts' opinions used as an indicator of the brand's future potential.

- *International orientation:* the proportion of income deriving from foreign markets as an indicator of potential for international development.

- *Advertising investment:* pre-tax percentage of earnings invested in advertising.

---

[19] These models were developed in Germany. BBDO Spain cautions that although the models are included on BBDO's website in Germany, it is not to be understood that they are currently in use. Rather, they should be regarded as elements of BBDO's knowledge and historical background.
[20] This model uses "brand equity" and "brand value" interchangeably.

- *Brand strength in the sector:* measured relative to sector competitors by comparing sales with those of the leading manufacturer.

- *Brand image:* brand attractiveness among stakeholders.

- *Pre-tax earnings* within the past three years: an indicator of potential brand value.

In a second stage, the determinants that compose the brand environment – sales, net operating margin and development perspectives – are combined to form a brand quality factor. Later, this factor, together with the four remaining factors, constitutes the *adjustment factor* to be used as a multiple for pre-tax earnings. The brand's economic value is the product of the average pre-tax revenue (in the past three years) and the adjustment factor.

The model uses pre-tax earnings in order to avoid fiscal distortions. When it averages earnings, it considers older earnings less significant than recent earnings, and weights them accordingly.

Figure 5.1 shows a snapshot of the BEES® model.

BEES model critique

- Within the context of this model, *brand equity* is synonymous with *brand value*.

- Zimmermann et al. (2001) do not indicate how the eight brand equity determinants are combined in order to calculate the adjustment factor or income multiple.

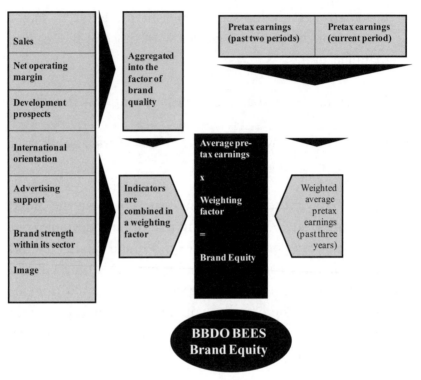

Figure 5.1 BEES® model.
Source: Zimmermann et al. (2001). Reproduced by permission of Schmindt Axel/BBDO Consulting GmbH

- While according to the authors, this model serves to value corporate brands exclusively, the majority of the determinants involved refer to product brands.

- The model is quite similar to Interbrand's first Annuity model (cf. Section 5.18.1), in which brand income is multiplied by a factor determined as a function of seven brand determinants. The models differ in three basic areas:

  - *Different multiple determinants:* The Interbrand model uses seven factors instead of eight. Among these, many coincide or are similar in content, although they are worded differently; international orientation (termed "international image" in the Interbrand model), advertising investment (more restricted but similar to Interbrand's "support" factor), development perspectives (similar to Interbrand's "market factor"), brand strength (analogous to Interbrand's "leadership factor").

- *Different methods of determining the multiple:* While Interbrand applies an "s-curve," BEES does not disclose the mechanism it uses to determine the "weighting factor."

- *Different methods of determining brand income:* The Interbrand Annuity model determines brand income by comparing the branded product's EBIT with that of a theoretical generic product; the BBDO BEES model simply uses the average pre-tax earnings as a basis. Both models weight recent income more heavily.

5.3.2   Brand Equity Evaluator®

This model is based on the BEES model and involves four stages:[21]

- **Stage 1:** Measurement of "brand equity" or brand value determinants (dominance of relevant market, international orientation, brand status and market quality)

- **Stage 2:** Calculation of the brand discount rate

---

[21] Based on the adaptation of the BEE® for the purpose of sale or acquisition (cf. Zimmermann et al., 2002: 21).

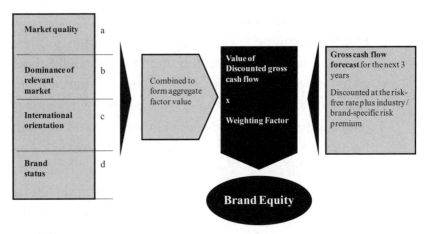

Figure 5.2 BEE® model.
Source: Zimmermann et al. (2002)

- **Stage 3:** Calculation of the present value of gross cash flow[22]

- **Stage 4:** Calculation of the brand's present value.

Figure 5.2 summarizes the main components of the BEE® model.

Stage 1: Brand equity determinants

The BEE model references four brand equity determinants:

(a) Market quality

This component refers to the environment in which the brand operates, and is measured by tracking the following indicators:

---

[22] Again, gross cash flow is used if the brand is being valued for sale or acquisition purposes. According to Zimmerman et al. (2002), the specific monetary basis used will vary with the valuation purpose.

- *Industry sales* (growth, trends, etc.): expressed as the average sales growth rate for the past three years, and serves as an indicator of the brand's sales potential.

- *Industry net operating margin:* expressed as the average return on sales for the past three years.

- *Degree to which sector is brand-led:* measured as the advertising investment in the sector, as percentage of total sales.

Once isolated, these three factors are fused into a single market quality indicator.

(b) Market dominance

This factor refers to the brand's relative strength in terms of sales, compared to those of competitors in the same sector. For Zimmermann et al. (2002), this ratio may be thought of as an indicator of the brand's capacity to control the relevant market. This valuation is based on the brand's sales share in relation to those of the leading company in the sector.

(c) International orientation

This factor is expressed as the ratio of the brand's international sales to its total sales and is interpreted as an indicator of the brand's potential for global development.

(d) Brand status

Brand status is expressed as brand attractiveness and brand strength as perceived by consumers. The BBDO Five-level Model© is used to determine brand status. This model does not distinguish between various industries in the calculation

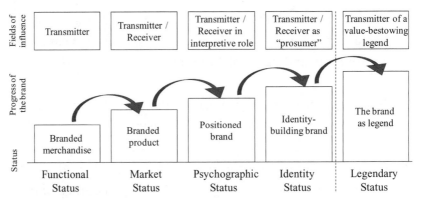

Figure 5.3 The BBDO Five-level Model®.
Source: Zimmermann et al. (2002)

of this value. Figure 5.3 shows a graphical depiction of the Five-level Model®.

These four factors – market quality, market domination, international orientation and brand status – are later combined as a weighting factor.

Stage 2: Calculation of the discount rate

The calculation of the discount rate is based on CAPM.[23] The BBDO commercial literature suggests that they use a pre-tax equity discount rate to discount the cash flows attributable to the brand (cf. Zimmermann et al., 2002: 22). The market risk premium is adjusted by a brand-specific risk premium.

BBDO distinguishes two scenarios for the calculation of the discount rate:

---

[23] Capital Asset Pricing Model: $r_e = r_f + (R_m - r_f)^* \beta_e$, where r_e is return required by the shareholder, r_f is the risk-free rate represented by the performance of the American government bond, R_m is the rate of performance of the market assets portfolio, and β_e is the stock's sensitivity to market movements.

- In corporate brand valuation, the company's beta is applied to the calculation of the brand's discount rate ($\beta_{brand} = \beta_{company}$), if the brand constitutes a significant proportion of the firm's assets.

- In product brand valuation, a separate beta must be calculated for the brand. However, BBDO recognizes that this is a difficult process and instead applies an average beta derived from benchmark companies in the same industry, especially from listed companies.

Stage 3: Calculation of the net present value of cash flow

To value the brand for a merger or acquisition purpose, BBDO uses the net present value technique and calculates the monetary base as the three-year forecast for gross cash flow (before interest, after taxes). This cash flow is discounted to obtain the present value at a CAPM-based discount rate (cf. Stage 2).

Stage 4: Calculation of brand value

Finally, the value yielded in Stage 1 is used as a weighting factor for the present value of discounted gross cash flow.

BEE model critique

- Like the previous model, the BEE model takes *brand equity* to mean *brand value*.

- While the authors indicate that the model may be adapted to appropriately value corporate or product brands, the majority of the brand value indicators make sense only in the context of the latter.

- Zimmermann et al. (2002) suggest that the choice and weighting of the components or brand equity determinants (market quality, market dominance, international orientation, brand status) are based on the purpose of the valuation and the type of brand being valued (corporate vs. product brand). But it is not clear if any other components are considered outside of these four. If so, the choice of brand equity determinants would be arbitrary.

- In determining brand strength or brand status, the BBDO Five-level Model© does not distinguish between industries.

- The model first calculates the present value of gross cash flow, which would be quite similar to the value of the company (or identical in the case of a corporate brand, since the model would use the company's beta in this case). A percentage calculated in function of the "brand equity determinants" is then applied to the present value of gross cash flow. However, no BBDO report makes reference to any empirical study that supports the validity of this relationship.

- In determining the discount rate, and using CAPM as the basis for its calculation, the model assumes an unlevered firm.

5.3.3 "Brand Equity Valuation for Accounting" (BEVA)

Developed jointly by BBDO Consulting and Ernst & Young AG Assurance and Advisory Services Company, this model was created to simultaneously satisfy both accounting and marketing requirements. The model fuses a *marketing-oriented perspective* and a *brand management* perspective furnished by BBDO Consulting (BBDO Five-level Model of Brand Management©) as well as a *quantitative and accounting perspective* provided by Ernst & Young AG Assurance and Advisory Services (royalty savings).

Marketing or behavioral module: brand strength

Brand strength is determined through BBDO's Five-level Model of Brand Management© based on consumer surveys. Taking into account market royalty rates and the relevance of the brand within the industry, brand strength is transformed into a *company-specific royalty rate*. Neither BBDO nor Ernst & Young explicitly describe the algorithm behind this transmutation, but as illustrated in Figure 5.4, and published in BBDO's commercial literature, the functional relationship between these variables takes on an "S-curve" shape.

Financial model: royalty savings

In this stage, *branded sales* are calculated on the basis of accounting information. A specific royalty rate is used to derive *brand income*. A brand risk-adjusted *discount rate* applicable to brand income is also calculated. Brand value is then yielded by applying a discount rate to brand income, and adding the discounted brand income. This value represents the amount saved by not having to pay royalty fees for using the brand.

Within the financial module, the "value of strategic options" may be added to brand value (for example, the value that would be added by extending the brand). The model must

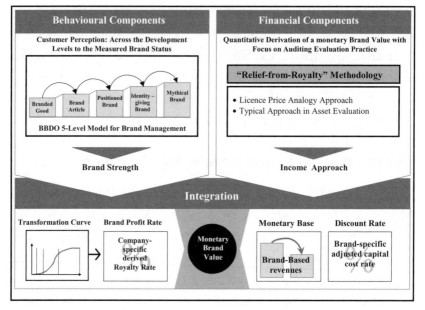

Figure 5.4 BBDO and Ernst & Young's BEVA model.
Source: BBDO (2004)

define the "life span" for the brand, which may either be finite or indefinite.

The model in all its modules is illustrated in Figure 5.4.

BEVA model critique

- Because it is based on BBDO's Five-level Model©, this method is subject to the same general criticism (cf. BEE model critique).

- Brand strength "is transformed" into a company-specific royalty rate via an "s-curve," as shown in Figure 5.4. BBDO does not give any theoretical or empirical arguments that justify this functional relationship between "strength index" and "royalty rate."

- Nor does BBDO disclose the algorithm for "adjusting" the brand income discount factor.

- As we will see in other models later on, the attempt to fuse marketing and accounting perspectives in a single model is a growing trend.

5.4   Brandient

Table 5.5   Brandient model

Model name or ownership	Brandient
Year of development	2004[24] (model based on demand driver analysis); 2006 (model based on royalty relief)
Author	Brandient
Country	Romania
Approach	Income
Principal methodology	Driver/brand strength analysis; Royalty savings

Source: Developed by author

The text on Brandient's website suggests that the firm applies what seems to be a model with "proprietary" modules or formulas based on demand driver analysis, as well as a general methodology based on royalty relief.

5.4.1   Brandient's model based on demand driver analysis

The Brandient brand valuation model (Obae and Barbu, 2004) involves four steps:

[24]Based on the first written evidence of the application of the Brandient "proprietary model." Cf. http://www.brandient.com/en/news_and_viewpoints/interviews_articles/capital_is_a_valuable_brand.html.

Step 1: Financial analysis

The objective of this step is to forecast the "branded revenues."

Step 2: Determination of the brand's role in the generation of income

The model uses market research to determine the proportion of income generated by the brand. In other words, it attempts to identify the drivers that influence demand and how closely they are related to the brand. Based on data from market and financial data, Brandient calculates the proportion of earnings attributable to the brand.

Step 3: Determination of Brand Stamina™

The risk associated with the future earnings stream is determined based on the Brand Stamina™ index, which measures the brand's strength and vitality. According to Obae and Barbu (2004), the components of the Brand Stamina™ index coincide with *brand equity* in the minds of consumers (i.e., perceived positive attributes and attitudes towards the brand, such as brand awareness, loyalty, personality, favorability), *brand mechanisms* (name, design), *brand support* (i.e., the brand management's strategic decisions on brand level of price, distribution channels, promotion, etc.), *brand positioning* (i.e., relative price in the market, market share and trends) and *legal protection*.

Step 4: Calculation of brand value

Obae and Barbu (2004) explain that in subsequent stages, "value is calculated by applying widely used financial techniques and considering all aforementioned dimensions" (para. 9)

5.4.2 Brandient's model based on royalty savings

The fact that Brandient used the royalty relief method to estimate the value of the "Top 50 most valuable Romanian brands" suggests that this might be a method that the brand consultancy applies regularly. According to Brandient (2006) the royalty relief method demonstrates the principle that "a brand can be measured in a way similar to a tangible asset, through the discounting of the cash flow *(Net Present Value)* generated by the brand compounded by its strength on the market" (p. 2). Although it does not describe the methodology in detail, Brandient outlines the key elements necessary for its application. This includes information concerning:

- historic branded sales;

- sector growth prospects;

- the risk-free rate given by sovereign bonds with long maturity;

- sector risk premium or "Category risk" taken from Ibbotson statistics;

- category royalty rates range;

- "brand equity" or brand strength based on market research.

Although Brandient does not explicitly explain the link between all of the abovementioned elements, the inputs listed suggest that the firm applies a scoring method based on "brand equity" or brand strength to derive the applicable royalty rate within the range of relevant comparable royalty rates in the sector.

Brandient model critique

Model based on demand driver analysis

- The model is highly reminiscent of the methodology used in FutureBrand's principal model (cf. Section 5.12), and Brand Finance's secondary model (cf. Section 5.6). The main difference is that competitive benchmarking analysis here is termed *Brand Stamina*™.

- The model does not clarify the basis upon which it applies the percentage derived from the analysis of the brand's role in the generation of income: EBIT, NOPAT, free cash flow, etc. Similarly it does not explicitly state how the Brand Stamina™ index is linked to the discount rate.

Model based on royalty savings

- While neither the relationships between the model's various elements, nor its process for determining the royalty rate is disclosed, the list of required inputs suggests that this process is based on a scoring system. Such a basis would make this model susceptible to the criticism directed at scoring-based royalty relief methodologies.

5.5 BrandEconomics

Table 5.6 BrandEconomics model

Model name or ownership	BrandEconomics
Year of development	2002
Authors	Stern Stewart & Co. and Young & Rubicam
Country	USA
Approach	Income
Principal methodology	Drivers/brand strength analysis

Source: Developed by author

Figure 5.5 General components of the BrandEconomics model.
Source: BrandEconomics (2003)

BrandEconomics® is the brand consulting division of Stern Stewart & Co.[25] Based on findings from various studies discussed in this section, BrandEconomics designed a brand valuation model founded on the assumption that there is a strong correlation between brand strength and business value. Instead of beginning with brand profits, this model uses a deductive approach to estimate the role of the brand in the creation of business value (Ehrbar and Bergesen, 2002: 4). Its brand valuation approach thus combines methodologies from Stern Stewart's Economic Value Added (EVA)® model with those of Young & Rubican's Brand Asset® Valuator (BAV) model – see Figure 5.5.

Phases in the application of this methodology

The methodology of this model encompasses five principal phases:[26]

---

[25] Another BrandEconomics LLC partner, Landor, is a brand consultancy firm that also offers BrandEconomics valuation services.
[26] These stages are not stated as such in the BrandEconomics literature. They reflect the author's interpretation of the complex descriptions of the model and are therefore subject to error.

1. Separation of the total market or entrerprise value of the companies that operate in a determined category (including the company being valued) in two areas: tangible capital and intangible value.

2. Determination of the degree to which differences in brand health explain differences in intangible values, i.e., the determination of the brand's role in the sector (brand health/financial performance correlation as shown in Figure 5.7).

3. Estimation of brand health for the brand being valued. This is a relative index established as a function of all the brands in a particular country rather than category.

4. Determination of an intangible value multiple (multiple of annual sales) for the company that operates the brand being valued, using the future EVA vs. BAV impact matrix.

5. Determination of the brand's intrinsic value as a function of the brand's role in the sector, the brand's intangible value multiple and its annual sales.

1. Separation of the company's total market or enterprise value

The valuation process begins by dividing the company's total market or enterprise value (market value of shares plus book value of debt) into tangible capital and intangible value which Ehrbar and Bergesen (2002: 4) define as follows:

- *Tangible capital* excludes goodwill and may be defined as the book value of property, plant and equipment, and net working capital.

- *Intangible value* is the total market value less the value of tangible capital. This definition of intangible value assumes that tangible assets will earn a return equivalent to the cost of capital. Any return in excess of the cost of capital represents a return on the intangible assets.

Based on the two previous definitions, the authors conclude that:

- any variation between market value and tangible capital book value will reflect the intangible assets' contribution to profits.

- with respect to the EVA valuation model, intangible value is equivalent "to the present value of current and expected EVA, which is mathematically equivalent to the present value of forecasted free cash flows" (p. 4).

Figure 5.6 provides a visual depiction of the abovementioned conclusions.

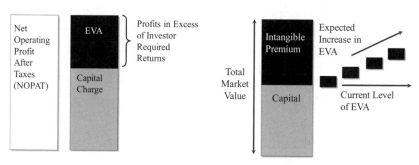

EVA = NOPAT less a charge for the use of capital

Figure 5.6   The role of EVA in the BrandEconomics model.
Source: BrandEconomics (2002). Reproduced by permission of Stern Stewart & Co.

2. Determination of the role of the brand

BrandEconomics models the role of the brand within the sector by using multivariate regression techniques in order to calculate the impact that brand health BAV measures have on the intangible values of public companies. This modeling not only allows for the determination of the brand's role within the sector, but also for the identification of the BAV's specific parameters and image attributes that define brand health in the sector.

In this way, the model yields a calculation of the relative impact value of changes in economic performance against changes in brand health. This indicator does not correspond to a particular brand, but rather to the sector as a whole.

Through this analysis, the brand's impact on financial performance is isolated from that of other intangible assets. Figure 5.7 shows a graphical depiction of the relationship between

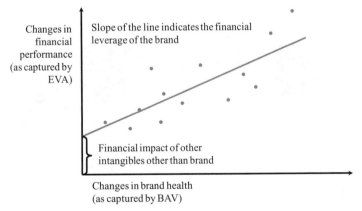

Figure 5.7 Relationship between brand health and financial performance based on BAV and EVA Databases.
Source: Developed by author based on BrandEconomics (2002: 9)

changes in brand health and changes in financial performance, where the slope of the regression line represents the degree of brand leverage (β_b) and the y-intercept represents the contribution of other intangibles.

3.   Determination of brand strength: Young & Rubicam's Brand Asset Valuator

Young & Rubicam defined brand health as a composite of four pillars, as shown in Figure 5.8:

- *Differentiation* measures how distinctive the brand is within the market.

- *Relevance* measures if the brand has meaning or relevance for those surveyed.

- *Esteem* measures if the brand has a good reputation and is considered among the best in its category.

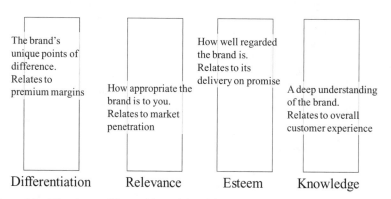

The brand's unique points of difference. Relates to premium margins

How appropriate the brand is to you. Relates to market penetration

How well regarded the brand is. Relates to its delivery on promise

A deep understanding of the brand. Relates to overall customer experience

| Differentiation | Relevance | Esteem | Knowledge |

Figure 5.8   The four pillars of brand health.
Source: BrandEconomics (2003). Reproduced by permission of Stern Stewart & Co.

- *Knowledge* measures the degree to which the public understands the brand's concept and what it represents.

These components are determined through surveys that ask consumers to evaluate various brand elements. The model groups the differentiation and relevance components that comprise *brand strength*, which in turn is a key indicator of the brand's future growth. The esteem and knowledge components make up *brand stature* and represent brand presence.

Fifty-two criteria are analyzed in order to determine the value of the components individually and jointly. However, it remains unclear how individual criteria are determined within the components and how these values are combined. Finally, the brands analyzed via Brand Asset Valuator are illustrated as points in the "Power Grid of Brand Health," a four-quadrant grid based on brand strength and brand stature (see Figure 5.9).

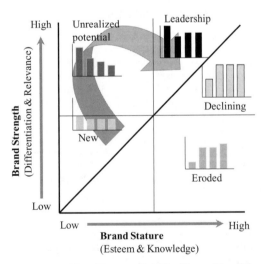

Figure 5.9 The "Power Grid" of brand health.
Source: BrandEconomics (2003: 8). Reproduced by permission of Stern Stewart & Co.

4. Determination of intangible value multiple (a multiple of annual sales, IV/AS) for the company that operates the brand being valued, using future EVA vs. BAV impact matrix

For Young & Rubicam, the exhaustive analysis of BAV data shows that brands undergo progression along four consumer dimensions. According to this agency, these dimensions are linked to the brand's capacity to generate increasing income and higher margins, which in turn creates value.

The *Brand Strength Power Grid* manifests a brand's position in the brand universe on the dimensions of brand strength (a future indicator of brand health) and brand stature (a lagging indicator of brand health). This grid constitutes a useful visual tool for understanding brand progress: how brands develop, achieve leadership, lose their positions, and sometimes regain them.

The logic behind the grid is as follows: the relationship begins with *differentiation*; something attracts consumers and incites them to find out more about the product. Later they decide whether or not this step is worthwhile (i.e., whether the product has *relevance*) for them. A brand's reputation – depending on factors of quality, popularity and how success-fully it delivers on promise – constitutes *esteem*. Finally, *knowledge* comes in; in other words, the product comes to be well-understood after a sufficiently long period of use. Brand-Economics carried out a study of 400 monobrands (companies in which 80% or more of income derives from a single brand) in order to determine the relationship between brand

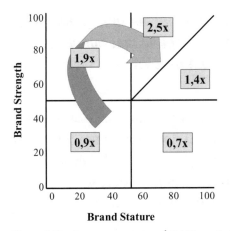

The intangible value of a company, i.e., market value less tangible capital (standardized as a multiple of annual sales) increases as brand strength increases.

The intangible value multiple declines sharply in the lower right section of the leadership quadrant as brand strength begins to erode (most often as a result of a loss of differentiation).

Figure 5.10 Impact matrix of BAV vs. intangible value.
Source: BrandEconomics (2002, 2003). Based on an analysis of 400 "monobrands". Reproduced by permission of Stern Stewart & Co.

strength (BAV) and intangible values. The results are expressed in terms of multiples – see Figure 5.10.

5. *Determination of the brand's intrinsic value*

In this stage, the intangible value multiple given by brand health is linked to the brand contribution calculated in earlier stages.

The principal product of the model is a brand multiple that may be applied to any brand in the sector to estimate its "intrinsic value" (Ehrbar and Bergesen, 2002). Here, "intrinsic" indicates the value that the brand would reach were it operated by a competent and efficient manager. This concept is very important to BrandEconomics; the real value of a business unit or the market value of a company depends heavily on aspects of strategy and execution, and may vary or not completely reflect brands' intrinsic value.

The brand value equation that fuses all these elements is shown below (5.1):[27]

Calculation of Brand Value within the BrandEconomics model

$$
\begin{aligned}
V_b &= M_{BV} \times AS \\
M_{BV} &= \beta_b \times IV/AS \\
IV/AS &= f(S_b, ST_b) \\
S_b &= f(D_b, R_b) \\
&= f(E_b, C_b)
\end{aligned}
\tag{5.1}
$$

6 BAV measurements of Brand Health and Brand Personality

where:

V_b = Brand value

M_{BV} = Brand value multiple

AS = Annual sales

IV = Intangible value

[27] This equation, like equations (5.2) and (5.3) and Figure 5.11, were developed based on several commercial pamphlets and articles published by BrandEconomics. They demonstrate the author's collective interpretation of the contents of these publications, and are therefore not explicitly described by BrandEconomics.

β_b = Brand leverage in the sector (β_b = $\Delta EVA/\Delta BAV$) or the brand's contribution to business value

S_b = Brand strength

ST_b = Brand stature

D_b = Differentiation

R_b = Relevance

E_b = Esteem

C_b = Knowledge

Expressed as a function of its individual components, the brand value equation appears as follows:

$$V_b = \beta_b * \left(\frac{IV}{AS}\right)_b * AS_b \qquad (5.2)$$

$$V_b = \left(\frac{\Delta EVA}{\Delta BAV}\right)_s * \left(\frac{IV}{AS}\right)_b * AS_b \qquad (5.3)$$

where:

BAV = Brand health

The model in its entirety is illustrated in the graphic in Figure 5.11 below:

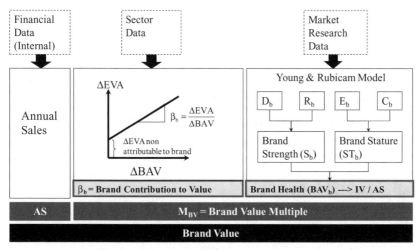

Figure 5.11 BrandEconomics® brand valuation model.
Source: Developed by author

BrandEconomics model critique

- The intangible value multiple grid is based on findings from a BrandEconomics study of 400 monobrands between 1993 and 2000 in the US. These results are not necessarily applicable in other scenarios.

- The role of the brand is determined for the sector, assuming that the brand has an intrinsic value and that such a value could be obtained by an efficient manager. This aspect of the model has no economic justification when, actually, β_b is no more than an "average value" and cannot properly determine an "intrinsic" value defined as the highest potential value obtainable through effective management strategy.

- The model considers that the present and future value of *EVA* is equivalent to *intangible value* or the difference between total market value and the accounting value of tangible assets. In Chapter 7 we will see that the conflation of *EVA* and *intangible value* is a very common error in the practice of brand valuation, and that the accounting/market capitalization differential cannot accurately be attributed to intangible value, especially in the presence of market imperfections.

5.6 Brand Finance

Table 5.7 Brand Finance model

Model name or ownership	Brand Finance
Year of development	1996
Author	D. Haigh
Country	United Kingdom
Approach	Mixed (income/market) for the primary methodology; Income for the secondary methodology
Principal methodologies	Royalty savings (primary); driver/brand strength analysis (secondary)

Source: Developed by author

Brand Finance applies different methodologies to suit different types of objectives. "Discounted cash flow" methods are recommended for intangible assets when future cash flow attributable to these assets may be "reliably measured." Among the principal methods for calculating cash flow attributable to a specific intangible asset under the "cash flow discount" method, Brand Finance utilizes:

- price premium

- excess margin

- economic substitution (value of the company "with" and "without" the brand)

- earnings split

- royalty relief

The earnings split and royalty relief methods are the most commonly used by Brand Finance, and are selected on the basis of the valuation's principal objective:

- For more technical valuations, the royalty savings approach is recommended.

- For valuations with brand strategy objectives, the brand value added (BVA®) or earnings split method is recommended.

5.6.1 Royalty savings

This methodology (see Figure 5.12 below) determines brand value with respect to the royalty rate that would be payable for the use of the brand if it had to be licensed from a third party. The royalty rate is applied to forecasted sales to determine a stream of income attributable to the brand. The stream of brand income is later discounted at present value. The advantage of this approach is that there are abundant examples of royalty rates used by companies that license brands to one another. The royalty savings method consists of four phases:

Phase I: Sales forecast

In this phase, net sales for the branded business are forecasted. The value of the branded business is often calculated as a benchmark value.

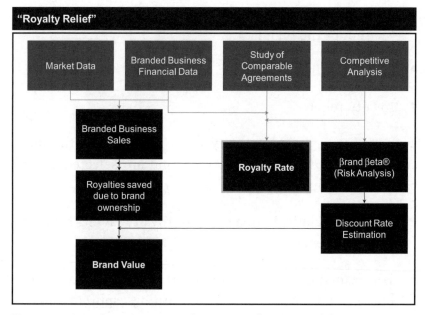

Figure 5.12   Royalty savings Brand Finance valuation model.
Source: Developed by author based on Brand Finance (2000)

Phase II: Calculation of brand risk

Brand Finance has developed a proprietary method for estimating brand-specific risk. The βrand βeta® reflects a brand's strength relative to the competition. The logic behind this model is that brand strength may influence business risk, either increasing or decreasing it. To estimate brand risk, or the βrand βeta®, Brand Finance carries out a benchmarking study of the performance and strength of the brands being studied in relation to their competitors. This process, also known as competitive benchmarking, is used not only to determine the brand risk but also to estimate the future income attributable to the brand, as we will see in Phase III. The βrand βeta® is later referenced in the calculation of an appropriate discount rate.

Phase III: Calculation of the specific royalty rate

This phase encompasses a three-step process:

1. *Establishing a range of royalty rates:* The range of royalty rates is set by reviewing license agreements for other brands in comparable sectors and researching royalty rates set among third parties in independent transactions.

2. *Determining the appropriate royalty rate within the range established for the brand being valued:* Once the royalty rate range is established, the specific royalty rate applicable to the brand being studied is established based on the brand strength index yielded in Phase II.

3. *Analyzing the economic sustainability of the determined royalty rate:* It is important to ensure that the established royalty rate is sustainable and affordable for the licensee; in other words, it must be a rate to which the licensee would have consented with a third party acting as licensor. This analysis involves calculating the royalty rate's potential impact on the licensee's operating profits.

Phase IV: Brand value calculation

The brand value is estimated as the present value of the stream of future royalties.

5.6.2 Earnings split

The "earnings split" valuation model (see Figure 5.13 below) adopts an approach "of economic use" (Haigh, 2001). It begins

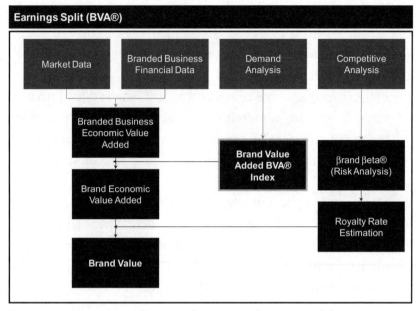

Figure 5.13   "Earnings Split" Brand Finance valuation model.
Source: Adapted from Brand Finance (2000). Reproduced by permission of
Stern Stewart & Co.

by reviewing the appropriate segmentation, analyzing research and all existing information. This might include interviews with senior executives in order to determine the key trends and issues for the sector and the brand under study. The "earnings split" approach generally combines elements of the financial business/marketing and planning process models already in place in the firms. It consists of five phases:

Phase I: Segmentation

This is a key step in ensuring the success of a brand valuation exercise. The process begins by defining or reviewing the standard criteria of segmentation and determining an appropriate and relevant definition for segmentation. It would be unsuitable to choose a segmentation based on grouping customer or product groups that shroud underlying relevant differences. Similarly, it would not be sound to propose a detailed segmentation from which the appropriate economic information could not be extracted.

Phase II: Financial forecasts

This phase generally involves financial forecasts for a period of three to five years. The Brand Finance "earnings split" method uses EVA as the basis for calculation.

Phase III: Analysis of demand drivers (BVA® or brand value added)

Market analysis, business analysis, and assessment of demand drivers are the basis for the "sense-check" of the financial forecasts. Close evaluation of these key elements and the relationships between them will lead to more reliable projections and a deeper understanding of how different aspects of the brand experience affect brand value. Demand driver analysis produces an index called BVA® that enables the EVA-based calculation of earnings attributable to brand.

Phase IV: Assessing brand risk

The fourth step calls for the determination of an appropriate rate for discounting income attributable to the brand. The discount rate is based on the CAPM (Capital Asset Pricing Model), and its required inputs: the risk-free rate in the relevant geographical market, market risk premium (the excess return of equity over the risk-free rate) and market beta (that reflects equity volatility). This sector-specific discount rate is adjusted by the relative strength of different brands within a given market (βrand βeta®). The analysis also considers appropriate competitors for each segment. Once the cost of equity is determined, the cost of debt is used to calculate the weighted average cost of capital.

Phase V: Brand value calculation

Brand value is calculated as the present value of business earnings attributable to the brand in each segment.

Brand Finance model critique

BVA® model
The BVA® model was originally developed as an index that applied to EVA. It is not suitable for the calculation of fair value. Instead, it is useful for understanding the demand drivers in a particular sector in order to ultimately enhance decision-making and strategic analysis. Additionally, although Brand Finance does not speak of EVA as "intangible earnings," the BVA® index could be applied to different "income or profit bases" because there is no existing theoretical or empirical argument that justifies the relationship between BVA® and EVA. Therefore, the numeric results yielded by this approach are generally dispensed with and greater emphasis is put on demand driver analysis itself.

Royalty model
This model is subject to criticism applicable to all models based on royalty savings. It is also susceptible to Smith and Parr's (2005) critique of the determination of royalty rates through scoring systems: "a royalty rate analysis technique

(...) based on the use of scoring or rating criteria (...) to quantify the qualitative difference between the trademark being studied and trademarks that have been licensed, and for which the royalty rate is known. This technique gives an aura of academic precision to an otherwise subjective process" (p. 258).

5.7 BrandMetrics

Table 5.8 BrandMetrics model

Model name or ownership	BrandMetrics
Year of development	1998[28]
Author	R. Sinclair and J. de Viliers
Country	South Africa
Approach	Income
Principal methodology	Driver/brand strength analysis

Source: Developed by author

According to Keller (2008), BrandMetrics is a "no-frills" methodology "based on the premise that the accounting definition of asset applies to brands" (p. 416). That is, BrandMetrics correctly conceives brands as resources under the control of an entity and that will likely generate future income for the entity.

The BrandMetrics methodology encompasses four key stages:

1. Financial analysis for the determination of the economic profit.

---

[28] The BrandMetrics website states that the model was developed and tested between 1993 and 1998 and has been marketed through BrandMetrics Ltd, since its establishment in 1999.

2. Expert workshops for the determination of brand premium profits.

3. Category and Brand Strength Analysis (BKS) for the determination of brand expected life.

4. Brand value calculation.

Figure 5.14 summarizes the main components of the Brand-Metrics Model.

Phase I: Financial analysis for the determination of the economic profit

This model requires data on the after-tax net operating profit (NOPAT), capital employed, cost of capital and financial fore-

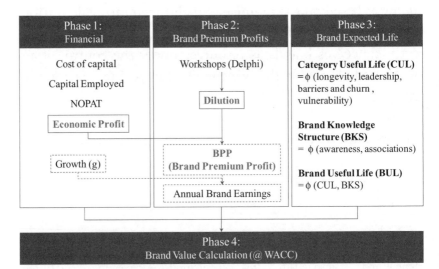

Figure 5.14 Four components of the BrandMetrics brand valuation model.
Source: Developed by author based on BrandMetrics (n.d.) and Keller (2008)

casts to estimate the Economic Profit, defined here as "the amount of after-tax operating profit a company earns that exceeds the cost of the capital the company has employed in operating the business" (Keller, 2008: 416).

Phase II: Expert workshops for the determination of brand premium profits (BPP)

In order to calculate the brand premium profits, the model estimates the percentage of profits attributable exclusively to the brand (known as "dilution" in the context of the Brand-Metrics model). A special procedure based on a variation of the famous Delphi forecasting technique is used to estimate the "dilution percentage." This procedure is called "Resource Recognition Procedure" (RRP) and, according to Keller (2008), is an iterative process based on the gathering of internal experts from different functional areas. The process can be conceptually divided into four stages:

1. *Elaborate a catalog of resources that generate economic profit:* Typically, under the leadership of a trained facilitator, the experts list and rank the resources that drive economic profit. After four or more rounds, the experts reach a consensus on five to eight items.

2. *Determine the relevance of each resource in terms of economic profit generation:* Once they have reached a consensus, each expert allocates 100% among the five or eight resources they had agreed on. Then, the scores are averaged to yield a final result.

3. *Determine the degree of influence of brand equity on each resource:* Experts allocate a score from 0 to 10 that reflects

the impact of brand equity on each key resource that generates economic profit.

4. *Determine the percentage of economic profit attributable to the brand (dilution):* According to Keller (2008), "the weighted scores are summed to produce a percentage that, when applied to the economic profit, produces the (...) portion attributable to the brand." Figure 5.15 shows a selection of dilution percentages proposed by BrandMetrics for various industries.

After the portion of profit attributable to the brand is isolated by applying the dilution percentages to economic profits, brand premium profits are forecasted into the future using an

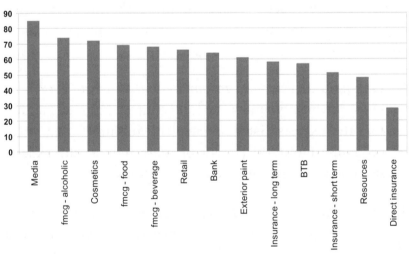

"Dilution calculates the influence of the brand on core premium profit generators – the resource set. This percentage is the portion of profit that could be lost if the brand name were sold, changed or damaged. It is, most crucially, the impact of Brand Equity on company profits. These are mean percentages from the BrandMetrics database."

Figure 5.15 Dilution percentages by sector.
Source: BrandMetrics (n.d.). Reproduced by permission of Brand Metrics (Pty) Ltd.

appropriate growth rate, thus obtaining a projection of annual brand profits.

Phase III: Determination of the brand expected life

The number of years to include in the model is a function of the relative strength of the brand. BrandMetrics uses two types of analysis in order to determine the brand useful life:

- *Category Expected Life analysis:* BrandMetrics has developed a process that calculates the economic useful life for the category in which the brand operates based on the idea that the capacity of a brand to drive economic profit is determined by its category or sector. This process sets a time limit for the valuation and determines the shape of the DCF slope (cf. Figure 5.16). According to Keller (2008), "Brand Metrics evaluates profits according to four variables: longevity (category maturity); leadership (market share stability or volatility); barriers and churn (competitive activity); and vulnerability (external forces)" (p. 417). Each variable receives a score from 1 to 5 and the sum of the scores is interpolated to produce a number of years in a rank that allocates 40 years for the notional dominant brand and 10 years for the notional marginal brand.

- *Brand knowledge structure (BKS) analysis:* This module is based on Kevin Lane Keller's concept of Brand Knowledge (awareness and associations). On the basis of data extracted from the surveys, a "brand knowledge structure" index is calculated as a function of awareness and associations. This index, calculated relative to competitors in the category, reduced to a single score out of 100%, is interpolated on the scale of years 10–40, determining a specific number of years of expected useful life for the brand under study.

Phase IV: Calculation of brand value

All collected data is then added to the model to yield brand value. Annual brand premium profits are discounted at present value using the weighted average cost of capital. Once the base case has been calculated, the model allows a sensitivity analysis to be carried out, flexing certain variables to understand their impact on brand value.

Figure 5.16 shows an example of the curve that BrandMetrics employs in the calculation of brand value. The shape of the curve represents forecasted profits attributable to a hypothetical brand. In the example, the time that the brand has been established in the market is seven years, and its economic useful life is 18 years.

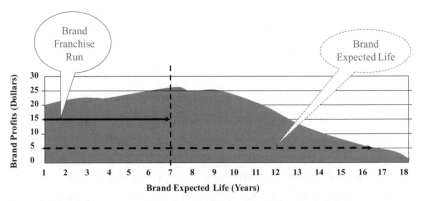

Figure 5.16 BrandMetrics brand valuation calculation: brand profit "curve." Source: BrandMetrics (n.d.). Reproduced by permission of Brand Metrics (Pty) Ltd.

BrandMetrics model critique

- This model is based on the premise that the accounting definition of asset applies to brands. This concept needs to be highlighted, not only because I believe it to be the right one in the context of valuation, but also because I have heard a lot of different and incorrect definitions in the industry. As we saw in Chapter 1 (cf. Section 1.1), there are different perspectives to define brand. But from the valuation point of view, the relevant definition equates brand with an intangible asset.

- The dilution percentage – applicable to NOPAT to determine profits attributable to brand – constitutes the central element in this model and is determined subjectively via expert workshops.

- It explicitly models the remaining useful life of the brand, not just five years plus a perpetuity, which can constitute an advantage in certain circumstamces.

- It is not explicitly suggested that the particular criteria used for the Category Expected Life Analysis and BKS Analysis will vary depending on relevant circumstances.

- A priori, the scale from 10 to 40 years applied for the estimation of the category expected life seems to be arbitrary and applicable to any sector.

- Comparative loyalty is treated in certain articles as a determinant of the brand's remaining useful life. Here, there is no mention of brand strategy analysis as an essential factor that may affect the remaining useful life.

5.8 Brand Rating

Table 5.9 Brand Rating model

Model name or ownership	Brand Rating
Year	2000
Authors	Alexander Biesalski (Dr Wieselhuber & Partner; Icon Added Value)
Country	Germany
Approach	Income
Principal methodology	"Modified Price Premium." Actually this can be considered as a hybrid methodology that considers price premium and the brand investment necessary to achieve it.

Source: Developed by author

Icon Added Value, together with the Dr Wieselhuber & Partner consultancy, developed a brand valuation method known as the "Brand Rating" in 2000. Upon the development of the model, they founded a company with the same name.

The "Brand Rating" brand valuation method is comprised of five modules and a final step that integrates them.[29]

---

[29] In reality, the Brand Rating method also comprises a brand evaluation module that encompasses a thorough behavioral analysis that is based on the concept of the brand value chain. That is, how the marketing activities impact on perceptions, attitudes and behaviors and, in turn, behaviors impact on price and volume premiums. The behavioral dimensions indicate how brand preference can be improved and the marketing mix can be applied more effectively. But as this is part of their brand evaluation module, and not an integral part of the specific brand valuation modules, a thorough description of this methodology is beyond the scope of this book.

Module I: "Icon iceberg model"

Brand strength is understood as the product of "visible" and "hidden" factors, and is graphically represented by the image of an iceberg (see Figure 5.17 below). *Brand iconography* refers to the holistic perception of the brand. It encompasses the elements of a brand that are "visible" to consumers, such as packaging design, communications, advertising, etc. *Brand credit* refers to the long-term effects of brand consumer attitudes and behaviors that constitute the hidden part of the iceberg. In other words, it is the emotional tie of target group and brand and includes the brand's appeal and the consumers' trust therein (brand loyalty). The iceberg analysis results in a qualitative brand strength index.

The brand strength index reflects the sum of brand iconography and brand credit. The degree to which each dimension

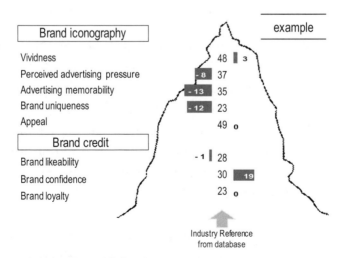

Figure 5.17 Icon value-added iceberg.
Source: Brand Rating (2008)

contributes to the value will depend on the brand's age, given that it takes time to develop many of these factors, particularly loyalty and trust. The brand strength is then calculated using industry reference values from a Brand Rating proprietary database.

For Brand Rating, the brand strength is related to price premium or added value (Module II):

- A differentiated brand profile (brand iconography) has a positive impact on the price premium.

- Increased brand credit strengthens customer retention, keeping and increasing current market share.

The results of the iceberg analysis are validated through the calculation of discounted price differentials.

Module II: Calculation of the brand added value

The price differential Δp is calculated by comparison with the cheapest competitor in the same category. To circumvent distortions, Brand Rating uses the average value of the price differentials within the past three years. According to Brand Rating, "the central task in determining the price bonus is to identify a suitable benchmark product or group of products, compared to which the price differential can be measured (Biesalski and Sokolowski, 2008: 6)."

The *achieved price differential* arrived at by price analysis in the target market is then validated against the perceptions of the target group or *perceived price differential*. The price differential Δp is then multiplied by the number of units sold. The brand-specific investments and expenses and corporate taxes are then deducted to arrive at the "brand added value."

Module III: Calculation of the brand future score

Through an analysis of the "Brand Shift Potential," Brand Rating determines an index that represents the brand potential in terms of its capacity to access new distribution, expand into new segments and geographical regions, etc. The Brand Future Score allows one to forecast the brand added value into future periods.

Module IV: Brand added value forecast

In this module, the brand expected life is determined and the brand value added is forecasted throughout the brand expected useful life. The brand value added forecast is based on the brand future score determined in Module III.

Module V: Calculation of brand-specific discount rate

The brand added value calculated in Module IV is discounted using an interest rate that accounts for the industry-specific risk premium, as well as the brand-specific risk.

Brand Rating starts with the WACC of the company that is later adjusted to reflect the brand-specific risk. To estimate the brand-specific risk, several factors are taken into account (Brand Rating, 2008):

- general market environment

- legal and political context

- threat from competitors and substitutes

- attractiveness of brand

- brand's role in purchase process, etc.

Module VI: Calculation of the brand's monetary value; synthesis of modules I–V

To calculate the brand's monetary value, the forecasted brand earnings calculated in Module IV are discounted using the brand-specific discount rate calculated in Module V. Figure 5.18 summarizes the main components of the Brand Rating model.

Brand Rating model critique

As a general comment, it is fair to point out that this methodology is not a "pure" price premium methodology but rather a modified price premium-based methodology that

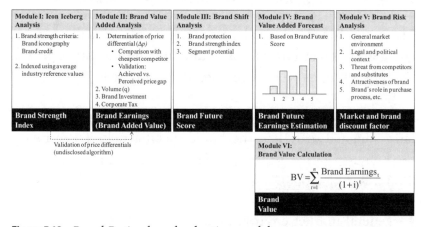

Figure 5.18 Brand Rating brand valuation model.
Source: Based on Brand Rating (2008) and Brand Rating's website and Zimmermann et al. (2001)

takes into account brand investment in the calculation of the brand earnings.

Advantages

- In general, methods oriented towards price premium have an intuitive logic; they are easy to use and understand in practical terms.

Disadvantages

The Brand Rating website states that brand value "originates and evolves in the *heads and hearts* of the target group. Brand value is therefore independent from current cost structures and corporate revenue."[30] This is clearly an arguable statement.

Zimmermann et al. (2001) note various methodological problems with this model:

- *Interdependence between brand iconography and brand credit.* Because Brand Rating assumes interdependence between brand iconography and brand credit, these components should not be combined in the determination of brand value.

- *Offsetting brand strength differentials between brand iconography and brand credit.* Can differences in brand iconography and credit strength offset one another? If so, definitively determining the brand iconography and brand credit indicators' impact on total brand value would prove unfeasible.

---

[30] http://www.brand-rating.de/cms/index.php?page=philosophy.

- *The common price premium method downfalls.* This approach is also subject to the general criticism of price premium methods (choice of benchmark brand, absence of price advantage, etc.).

5.9 Consor

Table 5.10 Consor model

Model name or ownership	*VALMATRIX®, ValCALC®, BVE$_Q$™ (Brand Value Equation) e IVE$_Q$^{SM}*
Year of development	1989 (Valmatrix®);[31] 1991 (VALCAL®);[32] n/a for the rest of the models
Author	W. Anson
Country	USA
Approach	Valmatrix® (Mixed – income/market); VALCALC® (Income); BVE$_Q$™ (Income)
Principal methodology	Royalty savings; Excess Earnings; "Core value plus the incremental brand based asset values"; market cap less the value of tangible assets

Source: Developed by author

This international consulting agency, previously known as Trademark & Licensing Associates, has developed several valuation models for brands and other intellectual property assets:

- Royalty relief methodology based on *Valmatrix®* analysis, which compares brand value drivers.

---

[31] Approximate date. According to Business Wire (1998), "Valmatrix® was developed in the late 1980s ..." (para. 6).
[32] Approximate date. Consor's website states, "The ValCALC Methodology, developed by CONSOR in the early 1990s (...)." Cf. http://www.consor.com/sec_page7165.html?page_idno=34695&parent_idno=34694.

- *ValCALC®*, based on "Excess Earnings" methodology.

- BVE_Q™ (Brand Value Equation), based on the concept that brand value is composed of a "core value" plus an "incremental value" generated by the incremental efficiencies that the brand produces for the other elements of the business. These incremental efficiencies are called IVE_Q™.

- *Residual Approach*, which calculates brand value as the difference between market cap and the Net Book Value of Tangible Assets.

5.9.1 Royalty savings model based on Valmatrix® analysis

Consor's royalty savings model values brands on the basis of the hypothetical royalty rates a brand owner would pay were he or she to license the brand from a third party. The royalty rates are set on the basis of typical royalty rates charged by competitors who own similar brands operating in the same sector.

Brand value is calculated as the present value of the royalty savings stream. To arrive at this value, Consor applies its Valmatrix® proprietary model, which serves as "the basis for an objective comparison of a trademark or brand's strengths relative to its competition" (Anson and Martin, 2004: 9). Through this model, relative brand strength is evaluated and measured against 20 dimensions or attributes that represent key brand value drivers.[33]

---

[33] According to Anson (2005) the analysis is based on the "the 20 factors associated with trademarks and marketing assets" (p. 44). This phrase would suggest that the dimensions to evaluate brand strength are the same independently of the sector in which a brand operates.

These drivers include legal protection, consumer awareness, profit margins, marketing activities, brand life cycle, breadth of distribution, etc. (Zimmermann et al., 2001; Anson, 2005). The brand is evaluated on a scale of 0 to 5 for each of the 20 dimensions (cf. Anson, 2005: 42).

In the comparative process, the company uses a database with over 20 years' worth of information on more than 10 000 sales and licensing agreements.[34] The result of the brand strength evaluation is used to determine a specific royalty rate within a range of comparable royalty rates. Later, as shown in equation (5.4), royalty rates are combined with the brand's remaining useful life, annual income growth rate, annual sales and discount rates to estimate brand value.

The resulting equation expresses brand value as a function of the abovementioned variables:

$$
BV = \phi \left(\begin{array}{ccc} \text{Average royalty rate} & & \text{Average annual} & \text{Current annual sales} \\ \text{as \% of wholesale,} & \begin{array}{c} \text{Remaining} \\ \text{useful life} \end{array} & \text{brand revenues,} & \text{discounted at a normal} \\ \text{product prices} & & \text{growth rate (\%)} & \text{rate over useful life} \end{array} \right)
$$

$$(5.4)$$

Source: Adapted from Zimmermann et al. (2001)

Figure 5.19 summarizes the three steps of the *VALMATRIX®* methodology.

---

[34] Cf. http://www.inta.org/annual/2004/pdfs/exhibitors.pdf.

Step 1: Brand Strength Estimation (VALMATRIX® Analysis)	Step 2: Determination of a specific royalty rate	Step 3: Calculation of brand value
Based on 20 dimensions: • Profit margins (0-5) • Industry/product maturity (0-5) • Brand transferability • International legal protection (0-5) • Sales growth (0-5) • Awareness and recognition (0-5) • Breadth of distribution, etc.	• Range of royalty rates for the sector (database with information on 10 000 brand sale and licensing transactions) • Brand strength (the greater the strength, the higher the royalty rate)	Applying financial techniques to reflect: • The brand's remaining useful life • The annual growth in brand revenues • Current annual brand revenues • Discount rates

Figure 5.19   Consor valuation model.
Source: Developed by author based on Anson (2005), Zimmermann et al. (2001) and Consor's website

Consor royalty savings model based on Valmatrix® analysis critique

This model is subject to the criticism applicable to all royalty savings-based models, as well as Smith and Parr's (2005) critique of the determination of royalty rates via scoring systems. Additionally, the dimensions or value indicators used here appear to be the same across all industries, despite potential significant differences in brand strength determinants and normal royalty rates among various sectors.

5.9.2   ValCALC® model (excess earnings)

A variation of the excess earnings method, the ValCALC® model aims to establish a rate of return or profit attributable to the brand. It basically allocates a market rate of return to all tangible assets in a company, taking the balance as the return attributable to brand.

Consor ValCALC® model critique

This model groups all intangible assets together, making it more appropriate for entities with a single key intangible asset (Anson, 2005: 39). See Section 4.3.10 for a more in-depth description of the advantages and disadvantages of the "excess earnings" methodology.

5.9.3 BVE$_Q$™ model (core brand value plus the value of incremental efficiencies)

This technique is based on the concept that a brand is a bundle of intellectual property rights (Anson, 2005: 40). Here, brand value is calculated as a "core brand value" (CBV) plus the values for the associated intellectual property rights. Anson (2005) applies this technique not only to the valuation of product brands, but to corporate or umbrella brands as well. For this author, an "umbrella brand" consists of a "core name and trademark plus the supporting elements" (p. 57). Based on this concept, he developed a methodology known as "Brand Value Equation" that considers that a corporate umbrella brand can be valued as the sum of its "core brand value" (CBV) plus the "incremental brand efficiencies that it generates for its products and sub-brands" (IVE), such as distribution, purchasing or advertising efficiencies. For example, in the case of General Motors, Anson (2005) highlights that the corporate brand GM generates savings and incremental revenues for Pontiac, Buick, Camaro or Cadillac, through higher efficiency in purchasing advertising, and lower distribution expenses.

The resulting brand value equation (BVE$_Q$®) expresses the Umbrella Brand Value (UBV) as:

$$UBV = CBV + (IVE_1 + IVE_2 + ... + IVE_n) = CBV + IBV$$

where,

UBV = the total value of the umbrella brand

CBV = the core brand value

IVE_i = the incremental brand efficiencies

IBV = the total incremental brand efficiency

In turn,

$$CBV = f(S, RR, t, r)$$

where,

S = the amount of sales for the relevant period

RR = the applicable royalty rate

t = the brand remaining useful life

r = the applicable discount rate

and

$$IBV = f(S, IBV_{rs}, t, r)$$

where,

S = the amount of sales for the relevant period

IBV_{rs} = the incremental efficiency rates on sales

t = the brand remaining useful life

r = the applicable discount rate

Consor BVE₀™ model critique

This model is conceptually appealing, as it separates the core brand value from the "halo" effect the corporate brand has on sub-brands. If the estimations yielded by this equation are sound, this can be an interesting indicator for making some brand architecture decisions.

The problem with this model is that the estimation of the incremental efficiencies is far from being objective.

5.9.4   Residual approach (market cap less the value of tangible assets)

According to Anson (2005), if corporate identity is quasi-monolithic, brand could be valued using a residual approach. He applies this methodology to the Coca-Cola brand (i.e., a brand that according to him is quasi-monolithic). To value Coca-Cola, the appraiser should take its market cap and deduct the value of its tangible assets. The remaining value, according to Anson, can be attributed to the intangible assets and "goodwill" since Coca-Cola "has one key intangible asset," the Coca-Cola brand.[35]

---

[35] Anson calculates this example as of 1 September 2004. The value of the Coca-Cola corporate brand under this methodology is $109 billion, i.e., the market cap at that date ($138 billion), less the value of tangible assets ($29 billion).

Consor residual approach critique

The differential market cap-tangible asset value can incorporate market inefficiencies and does not necessarily represent the value of all the intangible assets in the company. Even if it represented the value of all the intangible assets, to attribute all that value exclusively and systematically to brand is an error, especially in the Coca-Cola case. Firstly, because Coca-Cola is not as monolithic as Anson argues (reviewing its brand architecture the reader will realize how many sub-brands not related to the corporate name Coca-Cola has in its portfolio: Minute-Maid, Aquarius, etc.). Finally, the distribution contracts in the case of Coca-Cola play a fundamental role in its value. Assuming that this differential can be exclusively attributed to the brand is an extreme simplification.

5.10 Damodaran's valuation model

Table 5.11 Damodaran model

Model name or ownership	A. Damodaran
Year of development	1994[36]
Author	A. Damodaran
Country	USA
Approach	Income
Principal methodology	Differences in price to sales ratios

Source: Developed by author

Damodaran (1996) proposes a valuation model based primarily on differences in price to sales ratios. According to the author, one of the benefits of strong brands is that they can

---

[36] Estimated based on the first brand valuation example presented by Damodaran (1994) in his book *Damodaran on Valuation*, pp. 256–257 (as cited by Fernández, 2001).

charge higher prices for the same products, which in turn generates higher profit margins and higher price to sales ratios. The higher the company's price premium, the greater its brand value. Therefore, the Damodaran model expresses the value of a brand in terms of the value of its shares as:

$$\text{Brand Value} = \left[\left(\frac{P}{S}\right)_b - \left(\frac{P}{S}\right)_u\right] * \text{Sales} \qquad (5.5)$$

where:

$\left(\dfrac{P}{S}\right)_b$ = Price to sales ratio for the company with brand

$\left(\dfrac{P}{S}\right)_u$ = Price to sales ratio for the company without brand

Damodaran (1996) calculates the price to sales ratio based on the following equation (p. 340):

$$
\frac{P_0}{S_0} = \text{Profit Margin} * \left\{ \frac{\text{Payout Ratio} * (1+g)\left(1 - \dfrac{[1+g]^n}{[1+r]^n}\right)}{r-g} \right.
$$

$$
\left. + \frac{\text{Payout Ratio}_n (1+g)^n (1+g_n)}{(r_n - g_n)(1+r)^n} \right\} \qquad (5.6)
$$

With the inputs of the equation, Damodaran calculates the price to sales ratio for the branded company. Then, by looking at private manufacturers producing generic products, he estimates the necessary parameters for computing the price to sales ratio for the unbranded company, such as after-tax operating margin or return on assets.

Damodaran model critique

Pablo Fernández (2001) points out two general problems with the Damodaran[37] model:

1. *Difficulty involved in estimating the parameters of the generic product.* The brand value yielded by this model is very sensitive to changes in assumptions about growth and profit margins for the company without brand. Upon increasing the generic product's growth and profit margin, the value of the brand notably diminishes, such that special attention needs to be paid to how the parameters of the private label are determined.

2. *The Damodaran model assumes the same level of current sales revenues for the branded and unbranded company.* However,

    1.1. The company with a brand may have higher cash flow and higher volume than the unbranded company. Such would be the case for packaged goods companies like Kellogg's, Coca-Cola, etc.

    1.2. It may also be that the company has higher cash flow but a lower volume than the company with a generic product. This would generally be the case for luxury brands such as Rolex, Mercedes, etc.

---

[37] Pablo Fernández (2001) also presents critiques of specific valuations of Kellogg's and Coca-Cola performed by Damodaran that refer to specific assumptions adopted during the corresponding valuations, and not to the model itself. They are therefore not included in the critique provided for this model.

Fernández writes that to account for different levels of sales revenues, equation (5.5) should be re-written as:

$$\text{Brand Value} = \left(\frac{P}{S}\right)_b * S_b - \left(\frac{P}{S}\right)_g * S_g \qquad (5.7)$$

where:

S_b = Sales for company with brand

S_g = Sales for company without brand

5.11   Financial World

Table 5.12   Financial World model

Model name or ownership	Interbrand
Year of development	1988 (model); 1992 (first publication)
Author	J. Murphy
Country	United Kingdom
Approach	Income
Principal methodology	Capitalization of historical income by multiples based on P/E and brand strength analysis

Source: Developed by author

Financial World began publishing brand value estimates in 1992, in a ranking called "The World's Most Valuable Brands" (Kerin and Sethuraman, 1998). Because at that time Financial World published the brand value ranking developed by Interbrand, existing literature on Financial World's methodology actually describes Interbrand's original model.

The model treats brand value as the capitalized profit or cash flow differential between established branded products and generic products. Brand value is calculated based on public information (annual reports, chamber of commerce publications, etc.) and interviews with analysts and company executives.

In using "brand cash flow" and "profit" interchangeably, this approach implies that capital expenses are identical to amortization (Kerin and Sethuraman, 1998: 263).

Determination of brand-related earnings

Financial World (FW) calculates brand value as the differential value between brand earnings for a given year and the earnings which would be obtained by an equivalent unbranded product; this figure represents *brand-related earnings*. Then, FW calculates the two-year weighted average annual brand-related earnings. To yield brand value, FW applies a *multiple* based on brand strength to this figure (Walker, 1995).

Brand strength multiple

In this model, the *multiple applicable to brand earnings* is a function of brand strength. Given that Financial World's methodology rests on data provided by Interbrand, the process used for calculating the *brand strength multiple* was modified in 1995 to reflect the change in Interbrand's methodology:

- *Prior to 1995*, Financial World calculated brand strength based exclusively on the following five dimensions: leadership, stability (customer loyalty), internationality, continuity of the brand's importance within its sector, and security of the brand's legal ownership (Meschi, 1995 as cited in Kerin and Sethuraman, 1998; Fernández, 2001).

- *After 1995*, brand strength was determined by analyzing seven brand dimensions that are assigned different weighting factors (Andrew, 1997; Birkin, 1994 as cited in Kerin and Sethuraman, 1998):

1. Leadership (Maximum score: 25)

2. Geographical extension (Maximum score: 25)

3. Stability (Maximum score: 15)

4. Market (Maximum score: 10)

5. Trend (Maximum score: 10)

6. Support (Maximum score: 10)

7. Protection (Maximum score: 5)

The greater the score earned by the brand according to the above criteria, the higher the multiple applicable to earnings, and thus, the higher the brand value. In this scoring system, a brand can earn a score anywhere between 0 and 100 points. According to Kerin and Sethuraman (1998), the theoretical range of multiples is circumscribed by the P/E (price to earnings) ratio – the price of the share divided by earnings per share – for companies competing within a determined sector or category. The multiple for Financial World brand valuations ranges from 4.4 to 19.3. A high brand multiple indicates confidence that brand earnings will remain stable. Therefore, a high score translates into a high multiple for current earnings. A low score suggests less confidence in brand earnings stability, and translates into a low multiple.

We will now look at an application of this process in a detailed case study.

Application of Financial World methodology: Gillette case study

To calculate brand value, Financial World multiplies:

(a) The brand's two-year average pre-tax net earnings, after deducting the earnings that a generic product would ostensibly generate.

(b) The brand strength multiple.

Table 5.13 shows how Financial World applies the procedure to value the Gillette brand.

Financial World model critique

- The portion of cash flow or earnings attributable to the brand is determined by comparing them against the analogous values that a product without a brand might generate. However, unlike other models, the Financial World model does not explain the generation of this differential.

- The determination of the differential is arbitrary, as the equation assumes that all generic products will have a 5% return on capital employed.

Table 5.13 Financial World valuation methodology – Gillette brand value estimate (1995)

Gillette operating earnings 1995	$961.00	million
Less: Earnings estimated for an equivalent generic product[a]	−49.40	million
Gillette adjusted operating earnings 1995	$911.60	million
Gillette adjusted operating earnings 1994 (calculated as above)	$830.57	million
Weighted two-year average operating brand earnings (the most recent year counts twice as much as the previous year)	$884.57	million

Year	Weight	Adjusted earnings
1995	2	$911.60
1994	1	$830.57

Less: American tax rate @ 35% (0.35 × $884.57)	−309.60	million
Average weighted Gillette earnings after taxes	$574.97	million
Multiplied by: Gillette "brand strength" multiple[b]	×17.9	
Brand value estimated for Gillette (1995)	$10.292	million

Source: Kerin and Sethuraman (1998)
Notes

a. The operating earnings of an equivalent generic razor is given as follows:

- The median ratio of capital employed to sales in the category of personal care products is 0.38; in other words, it takes $0.38 in capital to generate $100 in sales.

- As Gillette razor sales in 1995 were at $2.6 billion, the required capital investment to generate $2.6 billion sales for an equivalent generic razor was $998 million: 0.38 × $2.6 billion = $988 million.

- A generic product should have a 5% return on capital employed or $49.4 million: 0.05 × $988 million = $49.4 million. Although not evident in Kerin and Sethuranman's 1998 article, other authors imply that the 5% return on capital is assumed for all kinds of generic products (c.f. Hope and Hope, 1997: 185; Keller, 1998: 502; and Motameni and Shahrokhi 1998).

b. The brand strength multiple of 17.9 assigned to Gillette is based on the evaluation of its brand strength and P/E ratio in the personal care product category.

- The model excludes behavioral measures of "brand equity" (Kerin and Sethuraman, 1998).

5.12 FutureBrand

Table 5.14 FutureBrand model

Model name or ownership	FutureBrand
Year of development	1999
Author	FutureBrand
Country	USA
Approach	Income
Principal methodology	Demand driver analysis

Source: Developed by author

FutureBrand uses a discounted cash flow model to estimate brand value. The model consists of three principal components that closely resemble those used in the Brand Finance model, presumably due to the collaborative efforts between both companies between 1997 and 1999, during which time Brand Finance was the economic financial valuation unit of FutureBrand:

1. Financial analysis

2. Analysis of brand contribution

3. Analysis of brand-specific risk.

We describe them in detail in the following paragraphs.

Segmentation is usually a pre-stage to the main body of work with the financial, brand driver and brand strength analysis

(J. Carrier, personal communication, 24 November 2008). FutureBrand considers segmentation a key part in the process and it is determined up front. Valuation is generally done on a segmented basis, and total brand value results from adding up the segmented brand values.

1. *Financial analysis*

The financial analysis is based on different measures, such as cash flow, CFROI®[38] or EVA® (Marketing Leadership Council, 2003). Return on tangible assets is removed to identify earnings attributable to the "business processes" and five-year forecasts are made for the client's EVA or cash flow.

2. *Analysis of brand contribution*

This stage focuses on determining the percentage of business economic added value that corresponds to the brand. To arrive at this figure, analysts calculate how much the brand contributes to the generation of demand for its goods and services. Ideally, this process is based on quantitative market research data. Firstly, factors that drive demand within each business segment are defined and ordered by relative importance. Then the brand's role in influencing consumer purchase decisions is measured, using statistical techniques like conjoint analysis and structural equations (Marketing Leadership Council, 2003). The result is a "brand contribution index" that represents the portion of future business earnings, Economic Value Added or cash flows that can be reasonably attributed to the brand.

---

[38] Cash Flow Return on Investment, a proprietary methodology of Credit Suisse Holt. Cf. http://www.csfb.com/institutional/csfb_holt/index.shtml.

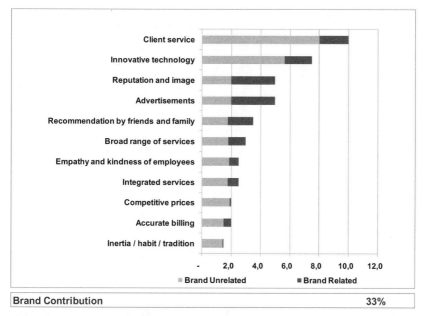

Brand Contribution	33%

Figure 5.20 Analysis of brand contribution.
Source: Based on Marketing Leadership Council (2003: 8) and Binar (2005)

Figure 5.20 illustrates a typical brand contribution analysis carried out for a hypothetical telecommunications company in the residential segment.

3. *Analysis of brand-specific risk*

In this stage, a risk indicator is estimated for future brand earnings through a competitive analysis among all relevant market competitors. This analysis involves a competitive comparison of brand performance by examining factors like time in the market, loyalty, distribution, price premium, brand awareness, sales growth and advertising awareness. A series of key attributes (generally 10) are identified in each case, and the study effectively compares selected competitors

Table 5.15 Benchmarking analysis

	Time in the Market	Distribution	Sales Growth	Market Share	Price Premium	Marketing Investment	Brand Awareness	Advertising Awareness	Satisfaction	Loyalty	**Total Score**
Brand A	10	4	10	5	1	4	10	8	8	10	**70**
Brand B	1	10	2	1	10	4	2	10	10	10	**60**
Brand C	6	1	4	7	5	2	4	7	1	3	**40**
Brand D	4	5	3	10	6	7	4	9	3	6	**57**
Brand E	1	1	2	4	6	10	1	3	8	9	**45**
Brand F	2	3	1	2	8	4	1	1	3	2	**27**

Source: Based on Marketing Leadership Council (2003: 8) and Binar (2005)

in function of these attributes. Each competitor receives a score between 1 and 10 for each attribute, using interpolation. Table 5.15 shows a visual representation of competitive comparison.

The brand risk indicator is given by the total score obtained by each competitor. The conversion of the brand strength score to the brand discount rate is done through an algorithm not disclosed by the company.

The graphic in Figure 5.21 below illustrates the relationships between the various components of the FutureBrand valuation model.

Valuation is generally done on a segmented basis, and total brand value results from adding up the segmented brand values.

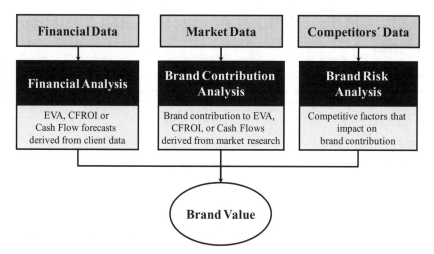

Figure 5.21 FutureBrand methodology.
Source: Developed by the author based on Marketing Leadership Council (2003) and Binar (2005)

FutureBrand model critique

- This model is based on the secondary BVA® model by Brand Finance, but operates differently, particularly in its determination of demand drivers.

- FutureBrand uses CFROI®, EVA® and discounted cash flow indistinctively in the financial analysis stage and later applies a percentage yielded by demand driver analysis on income determined through either of these three methodologies. Due to this inconsistency, and the absence of any clear guidelines for applying one method or another in order to estimate cash flow or operating performance, the results yielded by this model are not comparable.

5.13　GfK-PwC-Sattler: Advanced Brand Valuation model

Table 5.16　GfK-PwC-Sattler model

Model name or ownership	Advanced Brand Valuation model (GfK – PWC – Sattler)
Year of development	2002
Authors	GfK – PWC – Sattler
Country	Germany
Approach	Income
Principal methodology	Demand driver/brand strength analysis

Source: Developed by author

The Advanced Brand Valuation model (ABV) developed by GfK – PWC – Sattler consists of five modules (Sattler, Högl and Hupp, 2002; Mussler, Hupp and Powaga, 2004):

Module 1: Determination of the brand potential index

The ABV model begins by measuring brand strength based on a Brand Potential Index (BPI®) developed by GfK that includes 10 aspects of consumer psychology:

1. buying intention

2. brand allegiance/loyalty

3. acceptance of premium pricing

4. quality

5. brand awareness

6. uniqueness

7. empathy with brand

8. trust in brand

9. brand identification

10. willingness to recommend brand.

These psychological variables include emotional and rational evaluations, and assess the way in which consumers behave with regard to competitors. A brand's BPI index may fall anywhere between zero (weak) and 100 (strong). According to Mussler et al. (2004), the BPI is strongly correlated to market share and buyer loyalty, which in turn are correlated to brand earnings.

Module 2: Isolation of brand-specific earnings

In the ABV model, brand value is calculated as the net present value of the brand's future earnings. Assuming that brand- and non-brand-related factors exert a key influence on all consumer decisions, the model separates the portion of income and expenses attributable to the brand from earnings deriving from non-brand-related factors such as price promotions or distribution.

- **Phase 1: Quantification of the brand's impact on sales.** The brand's impact on company sales is quantified in terms of price as well as quantity. The brand's *price effect* is measured by the price premium that the consumer is willing to pay in excess of the price of a functionally and technically comparable unbranded product. The brand's *volume effect* measures the impact of brand strength in terms of additional sold units that can be reasonably attributed to brand presence. Both the price effect and the volume effect may be

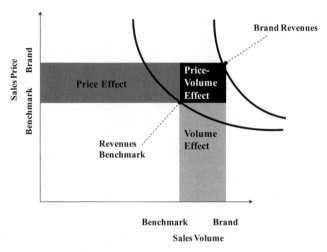

Figure 5.22 Revenue effect attributable to brand.
Source: Mussler et al. (2004)

derived from ad hoc research surveys and statistical techniques such as conjoint analysis or a causal regression model
that links brand strength (BPI) and the strength of other
non-brand-related factors with the brand's volume share or
price premium. The causal model results in an index that
shows the relative weight of brand strength in comparison
to other non-brand-related factors. This index is then used
to calculate the total portions of volume and price premium
attributable to the brand – see Figure 5.22.

- **Phase 2: Determination of brand costs.** Brand management
  expenses related to high-quality products, design, communications, customer service, distribution, etc. must all be
  identified in order to isolate earnings attributable to brand.

- **Phase 3: Determination of brand earnings.** Earnings attributable to brand are calculated as the differential between
  incremental brand revenues and incremental brand costs.

Module 3: Future brand forecast model

This three-step module is based on the long-term brand earnings forecast produced through exhaustive data analysis:

- **Phase 1: Business Plan Analysis.** The company's business plan is assessed in order to forecast future earnings attributable to brand. Linking the planning horizon included in the business plan with the results of the isolation yields the basis of valuation for this period.

- **Phase 2: Determination of the brand's economic useful life.** Unless factors indicate otherwise, this model assumes an indefinite or undefined economic useful life for the brand.

- **Phase 3: Determination of the long-term growth rate.** This module also forecasts long-term growth rates in order to determine long-term brand earnings (terminal value). The estimations for long-term growth are based on socio-demographic and technological trends that affect the sector. The brand's psychological strength is used to evaluate the viability of the business plan and the growth hypothesis. Brands with strong BPIs are expected to grow more rapidly, while those with low BPIs are expected to grow at a slower rate than the market.

Module 4: Determination of brand-specific risk

The ABV model assumes that the brand's risk premium is different from the company risk premium and can be determined independently of it. The calculation of brand-specific risk involves a two-phase process:

- **Phase 1: Determination of category risk (risk premium range):** Through empirical observation, different *beta values* corresponding to firms operating within the category and reflecting different risk structures are obtained. A range of risk premiums is yielded by multiplying the betas of various companies (with different risk structures) by the market risk premium (differential between market returns and risk-free rate).

- **Phase 2: Determination of brand-specific risk within the range yielded in Phase 1:** Once the risk premium range has been determined, the brand-specific risk premium is calculated using the brand risk score. Brand risk score is estimated based on six "risk drivers" used in a model proposed by Sattler in 1997 (cf. Section 5.26) and based on an empirical study carried out among 78 experts (mostly marketing executives of firms operating in packaged goods sectors). The result of the study was an empirical weighting factor for each risk driver. The task of the appraiser is to determine a score between 0 (high risk) and 10 (low risk) for each driver. Later, each driver score is multiplied by its weighting factor. The sum total of weighted scores is the brand-specific risk. As shown in Figure 5.23, the brand's psychological potential (measured through the BPI) shows the strongest influence on the brand risk index. Once the brand's risk score is established, the brand-specific risk premium is determined within the range for the category, according to a function whereby brands with higher risks obtain higher risk premiums.

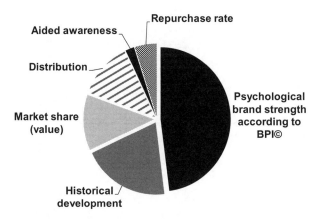

Figure 5.23 Importance of risk drivers.
Source: Sattler et al. (2002). Reproduced by permission of Henrik Sattler, University of Hamburg

Module 5: Determination of brand value and analysis of strategic options

To determine brand value, a capital charge for the cost of capital of the other assets employed by the firm is deducted from the brand-specific earnings. The differential (termed "brand cash flows" in Table 5.17) is then discounted using a discount rate that reflects the brand-specific risk premium calculated in Module 4. Table 5.17 shows an example of a calculation performed by Mussler et al. (2004).

In their analysis of fair value, the authors recognize that the brand's potential buyer could amortize it over its useful fiscal life, generating tax savings. This effect is known as "Tax Amortization Benefit" or TAB.

According to the authors, the value calculated in this manner then represents "fair value" and assumes that there will be no important strategic decisions that affect the valuation, as

Table 5.17 ABV valuation model

Valuation of the brand Euro max using Advanced Brand Valuation	2004 €m	2005 €m	2006 €m	2007 €m
Brand earnings	361.4	384.7	387.1	392.9
Brand costs	−310.0	−330.2	−328.7	−333.6
Brand earnings before taxes	51.4	54.5	58.4	59.3
Taxes (40.8%)	−21.0	−22.2	−23.8	−24.2
Brand earnings after taxes	30.5	32.3	34.6	35.1
Capital charge	−11.8	−12.2	−12.0	−12.3
Brand cash flow	18.7	20.1	22.6	22.8
Discount factor	0.9587	0.8812	0.8099	0.7444
Present value of cash flow	17.9	17.7	18.3	17.0
Terminal value				236.0
Sum of present values	306.9			
Tax benefit of amortization	93.0			
Brand value	399.8			
Brand capitalization rate	8.80%			
Growth rate in perpetuity	1.50%			

Source: Mussler et al. (2004). Reproduced by permission of Dr. Oliver Hupp, GFK Custom Research

well as no brand extensions, new entries or repositioning. A brand could generate value beyond the "base" value by taking advantage of strategic options. The total brand value is comprised of the "base" value plus the value of strategic options. Therefore, the module incorporates an analysis of strategic options for the brand that are not foreseen in the business plan. The module also includes a simulation analysis in order to understand the risks to which brand earnings are subject. Therefore, the brand value yielded by the model will depend on the values taken on by various key factors (interest rates, growth, pricing, etc). The Monte-Carlo simulation method is employed to calculate future brand value probabilities, based on occurrence probabilities for various key variable values.

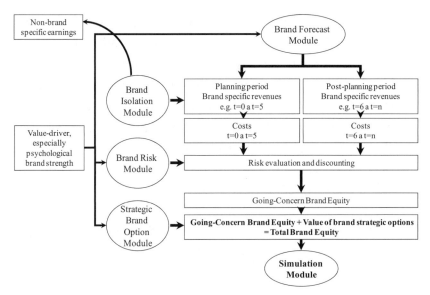

Figure 5.24 Model for measuring brand equity GfK – Pricewaterhouse-Coopers – Sattler.
Source: Sattler et al. (2002). Reproduced by permission of Henrik Sattler, University of Hamburg

Figure 5.24 illustrates the relationships between the model's various components.

GfK-PwC-Sattler model critique

- There is no single procedure for quantifying the brand's impact on earnings; it may be determined via research data, conjoint analysis, or a causal regression model that links BPI and non-brand-related factors.

- The calculation of brand costs involves high levels of subjectivity. There is evidence to suggest that the definition of brand management expenses varies greatly between companies (cf. "Hirose Report," Hirose et al., 2002).

- To determine brand cash flow, corresponding taxes and capital charges are deducted from brand earnings. It remains unclear exactly how this capital charge is calculated; whether it corresponds to the capital employed by the company in general, or if it represents a sub-set of the concept of capital employed. If the charge is calculated as the total capital employed multiplied by the weighted average cost of capital (WACC) it would not be sound to deduct it from brand earnings.

- The applicable discount rate includes a specific correction based on brand strength in order to account for brand-specific risk.

- The risk drivers are based on qualitative research carried out in the packaged goods sector.

5.14 Herp's model

Table 5.18 Herp's model

Model name or ownership	Herp
Year of development	1982
Author	Herp
Country	Germany
Approach	Income
Principal methodology	Price premium/conjoint analysis

Source: Developed by author

The Herp valuation model is based on the conjoint analysis method.[39] Its primary objective is to isolate incremental income generated exclusively by the brand. To arrive at this

---

[39] For a more detailed description of conjoint analysis, see Chapter 4, Section 4.3.1.a.

figure through conjoint analysis, all brand-specific elements are isolated as a proportion of sales, providing information on the price and revenue effects directly attributable to the brand. To perform the conjoint analysis and obtain utility values and relative prices, the branded product attributes to be valued are not compared with those of a generic product, but rather with those of benchmark brands (Zimmermann et al., 2001). To calculate brand value, relative utility is multiplied by the total sold quantity of the product.

Herp model critique

This model is subject to the general critique of the conjoint analysis approach discussed in Chapter 4, Section 4.3.1.a. Zimmermann et al. (2001) note two additional methodological flaws:

- *Relativity of brand value:* This method does not yield an absolute brand value, but rather a relative value, primarily because its comparison does not consider the price of a generic product but rather that of a benchmark brand. Brand value calculated in this fashion can only represent a "floor" or minimum value of the true brand value. The lower the absolute value of the benchmarks, the closer the floor moves to the real value.

- *Category limits:* This approach can only be applied when the brands studied pertain to the same category.

5.15　Hirose model

This model is based on what it defines as the three brand functions:

Table 5.19 Hirose model

Model name or ownership	"Hirose" model; developed by the Brand Valuation Committee of the Ministry of Economy, Trade and Industry of Japan
Year of development	2002
Authors	Hirose et al.
Country	Japan
Approach	This approach cannot be classified under any approach. The authors consider the method as "income."
Principal methodology	Application of proprietary formulas based on accounting data

Source: Developed by author

- price advantage, referred to as Prestige Driver (PD)

- customer loyalty, referred to as Loyalty Driver (LD)

- brand expansion power, referred to as Expansion Driver (ED).

Based on the definitions of these brand functions and the variables that determine brand value, the Committee proposes a valuation methodology expressing brand value as:

$$BV = f(PD, LD, ED, r)$$

where:

r = the discount rate, in this model, equivalent to the risk-free rate.

Prestige driver (PD)

A price premium indicates the ability to sell a product at prices consistently higher than those charged by competitors. The value of this component of the "total brand value" is calculated as:

$$PD = Excess\ profit\ ratio * Brand\ attribution\ rate * Cost\ of\ sales$$

and is expressed mathematically as:

$$PD = \frac{1}{5} \sum_{i=-4}^{0} \left\{ \left(\frac{S_i}{C_i} - \frac{S_i^*}{C_i^*} \right) * \frac{A_i}{OE_i} \right\} * C_o \qquad (5.8)$$

where:

$S_i/C_i - S_i^*/C_i^*$ = the excess profit ratio, calculated as the differential between the ratio of sales to cost of goods sold by the branded company being valued vs. a benchmark company

A_i / OE_i = the brand attribution rate, calculated as the ratio of promotion and advertising expenses to total operating expenses

$i = (-4,0)$ an index that represents years and assumes values of the past five years

S = sales pertaining to the branded company being valued

C = the cost of sales pertaining to the branded company being valued

S^* = sales pertaining to the benchmark company

C^* = the cost of sales pertaining to the benchmark company

A = promotion and advertising expenses pertaining to the branded company being valued (brand management expenses)

OE = the total operating expenses pertaining to the branded company being valued

Calculation of PD

1. *Selection of a benchmark company in the same industry*
To establish a price advantage, the model refers to a benchmark company that, in theory, produces a generic product with the same qualities and features as the branded product. In practice, the Committee selects the company within the same industry without price advantage, i.e., *the company with the smallest unit price index.*

2. *Calculation of excess profitability*
Excess profitability is calculated as the past five-year average of the unit price index differential, i.e., the sales-to-cost of goods sold ratio for the company vs. that of a benchmark. This presupposes identical quality and function for the cost of sales per unit. The Committee chose a five-year time frame to calculate the average excess profitability, as between calculating brand value in time periods of three, ten and five years, the latter has the highest correlation with recent market capitalization.

3. *Calculation of the brand attribution rate:*
brand management cost ratio
According to the Committee, as excess profitability may include not only product price differentials but also advan-

tages generated by non-brand-related factors such as know-how and technology, it is necessary to extract the portion of excess profitability exclusively attributable to the brand. To do this, the Committee proposes using a "Brand Attribution Ratio," which represents the proportion of brand creation, development and management expenses (brand management expenses) relative to the company's total operating costs. As there is no consensus on which costs should be included in the "brand management expenses," the Committee opted to use advertising and promotion costs, given that they play a vital role in brand awareness. Therefore, the ratio of advertising costs to total operating costs, or the "advertising expense ratio," represents the brand attribution ratio.

Loyalty driver (LD)

The grounding logic of the Loyalty Driver calculation is that the presence of highly loyal customers ensures a stable sales figure over time. Mathematically, the Loyalty Driver is expressed as:

$$LD = \frac{\mu_c - \sigma_c}{\mu_c} = 1 - \frac{\sigma_c}{\mu_c} \tag{5.9}$$

where:

μ_c = the 5-year average cost of sales[40]

σ_c = the 5-year standard deviation of cost of sales

σ_c/μ_c = the volatility coefficient of cost of sales

---

[40] μ_c or average *Cost of Sales* during the past five years is obviously not a reliable indicator of brand stability or loyalty. These and other critiques of the model may be found in the "Hirose model critique" section.

If the amount of cost of sales is stable, the standard deviation should be small (the coefficient of volatility approaches 0) and the loyalty driver value approaches 1.

The Committee ruled out quantitative research in the calculation of the Loyalty Driver, due to the investment this would require, and instead evaluates other options, such as the possibility of quantifying market share stability through various alternatives such as market shares per quantity sold, sales, or cost of sales. The Committee decided to use "stability of cost of sales" as a loyalty indicator, as that value is given in financial statements. The Committee also considered the possibility of using stability of sales, but this value reflects the effect of the Prestige Driver and therefore cannot be referenced as an independent parameter.

Expansion driver (ED)

The Expansion Driver is founded on the assumption that a strong brand is able to expand into similar or different industries, markets and geographic regions. It is comprised of two principal indicators:

1. *Measure of geographical expansion capacity:* growth rate of overseas sales.

2. *Measure of expansion capacity into non-related industries:* growth rate of sales in non-core segments, the core segment being the company's largest business segment.

Therefore, the Expansion Driver is defined as the average growth rate of overseas sales and of sales in non-core segments.

$$ED = \frac{1}{2}\left\{\frac{1}{2}\sum_{i=-1}^{0}\left(\frac{SO_i - SO_{i-1}}{SO_{i-1}} + 1\right) + \frac{1}{2}\sum_{i=-1}^{0}\left(\frac{SX_i - SX_{i-1}}{SX_{i-1}} + 1\right)\right\} \quad (5.10)$$

where:

SO = overseas sales

SX = sales of non-core business segments

$\frac{1}{2}\sum_{i=-1}^{0}\left(\frac{SO_i - SO_{i-1}}{SO_{i-1}} + 1\right)$ The average annual growth rate of overseas sales for the past two years; assumes values greater than 1

$\frac{1}{2}\sum_{i=-1}^{0}\left(\frac{SX_i - SX_{i-1}}{SX_{i-1}} + 1\right)$ The average growth rate of sales in the non-core segment of the company for the past two years; assumes values greater than 1

$i = (-1,0)$ represents years and assumes values for the current and past year

In cases in which there is no growth or when the growth rate is less than 1 for overseas sales and sales in non-core segments, the Expansion Driver is not contributing to the brand value, and therefore set at 1.

Brand valuation model

If we combine the three components of the model, the brand valuation equation may be expressed as:

$$BV = f(PD, LD, ED, r) = \frac{PD}{r} * LD * ED$$

$$= \frac{\left[\frac{1}{5} \sum_{i=-4}^{0} \left\{ \left(\frac{S_i}{C_i} - \frac{S_i^\star}{C_i^\star} \right) * \frac{A_i}{OE_i} \right\} * C_o \right]}{r} * \left(\frac{\mu_c - \sigma_c}{\mu_c} \right)$$

$$* \frac{1}{2} \left\{ \frac{1}{2} \sum_{i=-1}^{0} \left(\frac{SO_i - SO_{i-1}}{SO_{i-1}} + 1 \right) + \frac{1}{2} \sum_{i=-1}^{0} \left(\frac{SX_i - SX_{i-1}}{SX_{i-1}} + 1 \right) \right\}$$

$$(5.11)$$

where:

PD = Excess profit ratio * Brand attribution rate * Cost of sales = 5-year average of {[[(Sales of company / Cost of sales of company) – (Cost of sales of a benchmark company)] *Advertising and promotion cost ratio (Cost of brand management)} * Cost of sales of the company today

LD = [5-year average cost of sales – standard deviation of cost of sales (calculated on the basis of data from the past 5 years)] / 5-year average cost of sales

ED = Average of overseas sales growth rate and sales growth rate of non-core business segments

S = sales of the branded company being valued

C = cost of sales of the branded company

S^* = sales of the benchmark company

C^* = the cost of sales of the benchmark company

A = the advertising and promotion expenses of the branded company

OE = the total operating costs of the branded company

SO = overseas sales

SX = non-core business segment sales

r = the discount rate, or the risk-free rate

μ_c = the 5-year average of cost of sales

σ_c = the standard deviation of cost of sales for the past 5 years

Application

The "Hirose Report" provides an example of its application, reprinted in Table 5.20.

The example presented by Hirose leaves out two essential pieces of data that make its calculation inconsistent with the Expansion Driver equation. The equation for calculating the ED in the above example strays from that shown in equation (5.10), and is expressed as:

$$ED = \frac{1}{2}\left\{\left(\frac{SO_0 - SO_{-1}}{SO_{-1}} + 1\right) + \left(\frac{SX_0 - SX_{-1}}{SX_{-1}} + 1\right)\right\} \quad (5.12)$$

where:

0 = the current period and −1 is the most recent past period

Table 5.20 Original example presented in the "Hirose Report"

PD	Data		Company	Benchmark
	Sales		¥100m	¥9m
	Cost of sales		¥80m	¥8m
	Operating costs		¥90m	
	Advertising and promotion expenses		¥9m	
LD	5-year average cost of sales		¥70m	
	Standard deviation of cost of sales		¥5m	
ED	Overseas sales	Current period	¥45m	
		Past period	¥40m	
	Non-core business sales	Current period	¥30m	
		Past period	¥25m	
r	2%			

"Hirose Report" Original Example

PD	Sales	100.00
	(-) Cost of Sales	80.00
	Sales / Cost of Sales	**125.00%**
	Sales / Cost of sales	125.00%
	(-) Benchmark sales / Cost of benchmark sales	112.50%
	Excess profit ratio	**12.50%**
	Excess profit ratio	12.50%
	(*) Brand attribution rate	10.00%
	Excess profit ratio attributable to brand	**1.25%**
	(*) Cost of sales for current period	80.00
	PD = Excess profit ratio attributable to brand * Cost of sales	**1.00**
LD	Five-year standard deviation of cost of sales	5
	(%) 5-year average cost of sales	70
	Coefficient of volatility	7.14%
	LD = 1 – Coefficient of volatility	**92.86%**
ED	Growth rate of non-core segment sales	120.00%
	Growth rate of overseas sales	112.50%
	ED = Average growth rate of overseas and non-core business sales	**116.25%**

Table 5.20 *Continued*

Brand Value = PD*LD*ED/r	
PD	1.00
*LD	92.86%
*ED	116.25%
*r	2%
Brand Value (¥m)	53.97

Source: Hirose et al. (2002: 16)

Below, in Table 5.21, there is an additional example that applies the Hirose approach and incorporates the data that equation (5.10) calls for, as it was originally conceived in the "Hirose Report."

Hirose model critique

This model has various conceptual problems:[41]

1. *General problems*

    1.1. The model treats the brand as a "perpetual bond" and assumes that the interests that derive from it (INT = PD*LD*ED) will not grow in the future. This is one of the model's weak points, because it reduces the growth expectations for any brand to 0.

    1.2. The risk-free rate is applied in the calculation used in discounted cash flow. The Committee justifies this application because it considers risk in cash flow calculations: "The Prestige Driver and Loyalty Driver

---

[41] The Hirose Committee has recognized many of these problems.

Table 5.21 Modified example for a company with sustained growth

PD	Data		Company	Benchmark
	Sales		¥100m	¥9m
	Cost of sales		¥80m	¥8m
	Operating costs		¥90m	
	Advertising and promotion expenses		¥9m	
LD	5-year average cost of sales		¥70m	
	Standard deviation of cost of sales		¥5m	
ED	Overseas sales	2006	¥45m	
		2005	¥40m	
		2004	¥35m	
	Non-core business sales	2006	¥30m	
		2005	¥25m	
		2004	¥20m	
r	2%			

Example with sustained growth

PD	Sales	100.00
	(-) Cost of Sales	80.00
	Sales / Cost of Sales	**125.00%**
	Sales / Cost of sales	125.00%
	(-) Benchmark sales / Cost of benchmark sales	112.50%
	Excess profit ratio	**12.50%**
	Excess profit ratio	12.50%
	(*) Brand attribution rate	10.00%
	Excess profit ratio attributable to brand	**1.25%**
	(*) Cost of sales for current period	80.00
	PD = Excess profit ratio attributable to brand * Cost of sales	**1.00**
LD	Five-year standard deviation of cost of sales	5
	(%) 5-year average cost of sales	70
	Coefficient of volatility	7.14%
	LD = 1 – Coefficient of volatility	**92.86%**
ED	Growth rate of non-core segment sales	122.50%
	Growth rate of overseas sales	113.39%
	ED = Average growth rate of overseas and non-core business sales	**117.95%**

Table 5.21 *Continued*

Brand Value = PD*LD*ED/r	
PD	1.00
*LD	92.86%
*ED	117.95%
*r	2%
Brand Value (¥m)	54.76

Source: Developed by author based on Hirose et al. (2002: 16)

both ... reflect price and quantity effect of the cash flows generated by the brand in its relationship with customers. Therefore, by multiplying Loyalty Driver with Prestige Driver, one can calculate the most stable and certain portion of the present and future cash flows generated by brands" (p. 72). Multiple accounting and financial texts reference the consideration of risk in cash flow rather than discount rates, but the process necessitates working consistently with expected cash flows or "certainty equivalents," accounting for the probability of various scenarios linked to different cash flows (cf. Statement of Financial Accounting Concepts 7; Brealey and Myers, 1993; Beccacece et al., 2006). This is not exactly the process followed by the Committee.

1.3. Beccacece et al. (2006) point out the inconsistency between the structural form that the brand value function assumes in the Hirose model and the correlation between the factors used to explain it: "The product of the factors proposed in the model as brand value function ... is valid when the factors are thought of as uncorrelated" (p. 8).

2. *Problems with the Prestige Driver*

    2.1. The fact that not all companies have price advantages does not indicate that their brands have no value.

    2.2. The "excess profit ratio or differential" assigned to the brand is calculated through the ratio of advertising and promotion costs to total operating costs. This approach presents several problems:

        2.2.1. The portion of costs that a brand represents does not necessarily correlate with its contribution to the generation of profits.

        2.2.2. The advertising costs ratio may vary from sector to sector. For example, in B2B companies, this ratio is generally small, and would therefore yield low brand values under this approach.

3. *Problems with the Loyalty Driver*

    3.1. The measurement of loyalty via stability of cost of sales is unfounded.

4. *Problems with the Expansion Driver*

    4.1. The "representation of growth" in this model is reduced to the Expansion Driver, which looks only at historical data.

    4.2. The "representation of growth" is specious, because it determines discounted cash flow as if it were dealing with a perpetuity without growth.

5.16 Houlihan Advisors

Table 5.22 Houlihan Advisors model

Model name or ownership	Houlihan Advisors
Year of development	1986
Author	n.a.
Country	USA
Approach	Income
Principal methodology	Present Value of the Company's Free Cash Flow less the required return on other non-brand-related employed assets

Source: Developed by author

For Houlihan Valuation Advisors (HVA), a company's value may fall under the various types of assets that comprise it (monetary, tangible and intangible) – see Figure 5.25.

In this manner, brand value is established residually (Angberg, n.d.):

$$V_{tr} = V_e - V_{ma} - V_{ta} - V_{oia} \qquad (5.13)$$

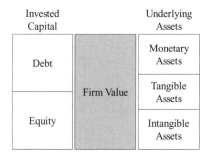

Figure 5.25 HVA Asset taxonomy.
Source: Kam and Angberg (n.d.)

Table 5.23 Houlihan Valuation Advisors brand value calculation ($000 USD)

Assets Employed	Required return	2000	2001	2002	2003	2004	2005
Working Capital Requirements	6.0%	90.0	91.8	93.6	95.5	97.4	99.4
Net Fixed assets	9.0%	225.0	229.5	234.1	238.8	243.5	248.4
Intangible assets	14.0%	75.0	76.5	78.0	79.6	81.2	82.8
Patents	14.5%	10.0	10.2	10.4	10.6	10.8	11.0
Proprietary technology	20.3%	15.0	15.3	15.6	15.9	16.2	16.6
Company's free cash flow		44080	44887	46956	49112	51361	53705
– Assets employed * required return		–40645	–41458	–42291	–43133	–43995	–44875
Free cash flow attributable to brand		3435	3429	4665	5979	7366	8830
Brand value	**50.34**	= Present value (brand's free cash flow, 16%). Growth after 2005 = 4%					

Source: Kam and Angberg (n.d.), Fernández (2001: 669)

where:

V_{tr} = brand value

V_e = company value

V_{ma} = value of monetary assets

V_{ta} = value of tangible assets

V_{oia} = value of intangible assets.

In this model, brand value is given by the present value of the company's free cash flow less the return on other non-brand-related assets (Fernández, 2001). Table 5.23 shows an example of a valuation carried out under this methodology.

HVA model critique

In this model, cash flow attributable to the brand is similar to EVA, but cash flow attributable to a company with a generic product is substituted by the required return on the non-brand-related assets employed by the branded company (Fernández, 2001). For this reason, the HVA approach has been harshly criticized by various authors (Roos, 2005; Fernández, 2001).

5.17 Intangible Business

Table 5.24 Intangible Business model

Model name or ownership	Intangible Business
Year of development	2001[42]
Author	S. Whitwell
Country	United Kingdom
Approach	Mixed (income/market)
Principal methodology	Royalty savings

Source: Developed by author

[42] Cf. http://www.intangiblebusiness.com/sitestyle/modules/feature/right_brochure/Intangible-Business-web.pdf.

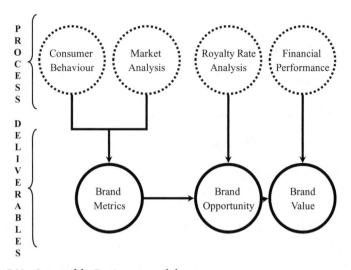

Figure 5.26 Intangible Business model.
Source: Whitwell (2005). Reproduced by permission of Intangible Business Ltd.

Intangible Business Ltd. has developed a brand valuation methodology based on the "royalty savings" method. Figure 5.26 illustrates the model's processes and deliverables.

The model portrayed in Figure 5.26 includes the components listed in Table 5.25.

The method involves four steps:

Step 1: Analysis of relative brand strength

According to Intangible Business, it is the consumers who ultimately decide which brands they'll buy, most often based on preferences and availability. Brand strength in any given market is defined by the brand's performance, relative to that

Table 5.25 Intangible Business model components

Component	Process	Source
Brand strength	Consumer research	Brand strength analysis
Royalty rate	Operations/margin	Profitability and brand analysis
Sales forecast	GDP/market sector/brand	Market analysis
Brand earnings	Calculation	Valuation model
Taxation	Application	Current rates
Discount rates	Evaluation of risk	Future weighted average cost of capital

Source: Intangible Business (2004). Reproduced by permission of Intangible Business Ltd.

Table 5.26 Analysis of relative brand strength: selecting a benchmark

Competitor Set	Recognition	Relevance	Satisfaction	Differentiation	Loyalty	Brand Score
Our brand	63	70	56	63	40	**58**
Competitor 1	50	60	80	52	45	**57**
Benchmark	85	90	80	65	62	**76**
Competitor 2	73	65	50	50	35	**55**
Competitor 3	80	90	75	62	50	**71**

Source: Intangible Business (2004). Reproduced by permission of Intangible Business Ltd.

of competitor companies, from the consumer's point of view. Tables 5.26 and 5.27 show how Intangible Business measures brand strength.

From among the competitors, a benchmark is chosen against which to compare data and obtain an intelligible index of relative brand strength. The benchmark is selected on the grounds of its comparability and relevance as well as its

Table 5.27 Analysis of relative brand strength: calculation of the BSA Index

#	Brand drivers	Brand performance	Weighting multiple	Benchmark position	Brand performance
1	Recognition	63	1	85	63
2	Relevance	70	1	90	70
3	Satisfaction	56	1	80	56
4	Differentiation	63	1	65	63
5	Loyalty	40	1	62	40
				76	58
	BSA Index	76.3%		100%	

Source: Intangible Business (2004)

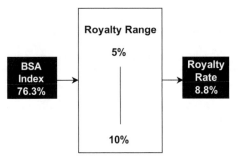

Figure 5.27 Determination of the royalty rate.
Source: Intangible Business (2004). Reproduced by permission of Intangible Business Ltd.

capacity to indicate measures of profitability and consumer preference.

Step 2: Brand premium analysis (royalty rate determination)

An applicable range of royalty rates is determined on the basis of public information and internal or external market data that reveal comparable commercial agreements in the sector and the economic sustainability of the royalty rates – see Figure 5.27.

According to Intangible Business (2004: 4), "licensing and brand valuation are naturally interlinked as the royalty rate reflects a profit-sharing mechanism between a brand owner (licensor) and an operator of the brand in the market (licensee). The stronger the brand the more the brand can earn and command in license fees."

Step 3: Market analysis

Once the royalty rate has been set via benchmark and profitability analysis, the revenues to which the royalty rate will be applied are determined. A market analysis is performed in order to forecast revenues. The objective of this analysis is to assess competitive environment, industry trends, and sector outlook, taking into account the factors in Table 5.28.

Step 4: Valuation

Once the revenues are forecasted, the royalty rate is applied to yield a brand profit or cash flow from which taxes are then

Table 5.28 Market analysis in the Intangible Business model

Variable	Historic	Current	Future outlook
Macro economic	GDP value	GDP value	+3%
Sector growth	4%	3%	+2.5%
Share of market	5%	5.5%	3%
Share of voice	4%	6%	4%
Average pricing	€85	€87	€93
Turnover	€100m	€110.6	€136m

Source: Intangible Business (2004). Reproduced by permission of Intangible Business Ltd.

Table 5.29 Application of the Intangible Business model

Brand premium royalty					8.8%
Discount rate					7.2%
Tax rate					30.0%
Growth rate to 2007					5.4%
EVA growth rate post 2007					2.5%

All amounts in £000's	2003	2004	2005	2006	2007
Net turnover	110500	116493	122746	129270	136074
Brand Premium royalty rate	8.8%	8.8%	8.8%	8.8%	8.8%
Brand profit/Cash flow	**9724**	**10251**	**10802**	**11376**	**11975**
Taxation	(2917)	(3075)	(3240)	(3413)	(3592)
Profit after taxes	**6807**	**7176**	**7561**	**7963**	**8382**
Discount factor	1.072	1.149	1.232	1.321	1.416
	6350	**6241**	**6135**	**6030**	**5927**

Brand value calculation	
Brand value to 2004	30683
Perpetuity calculation	129260
Total brand value	**159942**

Source: Intangible Business (2004). Note: The author corrected the growth rate to 2007, changing it from 3.0% to 5.4%. Reproduced by permission of Intangible Business Ltd.

deducted. Brand profits after tax are discounted at present value using the appropriate discount rate. Table 5.29 provides an example of a brand valuation carried out in accordance with the Intangible Business model.

Intangible Business model critique

This model is subject to the general criticism of royalty savings methods.

5.18 Interbrand

Table 5.30 Interbrand model

Model name or ownership	Discounted cash flow/multiplier model
Year of development	1988 (multiplier model); 1993 (DCF model)
Author	J. Murphy
Country	United Kingdom
Approach	Income
Principal methodology	Capitalization of multiples based on P/E; strength and demand driver analysis

Source: Developed by author

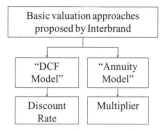

Figure 5.28 Interbrand's alternative brand valuation models.
Source: Developed by author

Interbrand has developed at least two different brand valuation models (see Figure 5.28): the original multiplier model cited unremittingly in the academic literature, and a more recent model based on demand driver analysis quite similar to the FutureBrand model developed later on. Both models are described in detail below.

While Interbrand affirms that it developed the first model in 1988 and later revised it in 1993, suggesting that the second model replaced the first, Haigh (1994) makes reference to the parallel application of both approaches (p. 196). He writes that

Interbrand calculates brand value at certain times by using a discounted cash flow method (the second model), and on other occasions applies a multiplier to historical brand earnings (the first model). Although this may have been true at some point, Interbrand has confirmed that it no longer uses the Annuity model in its valuations (Interbrand, personal communication, 21 January 2009).

5.18.1   Interbrand's multiplier model ("Annuity" model)

Earnings attributable to brand and the brand strength multiplier constitute the two principal elements in this model (Motameni and Shahrokhi, 1998).

Earnings attributable to brand

The model uses the three-year weighted average earnings attributable to the brand in order to avoid distortions caused by short-term industry variations. Values are typically weighted three times for the current period, twice for the previous period and once for the period immediately preceding. Then the sum of the earnings is divided by the sum of the weighting factors; in this case, six. If projected future profits are expected to be above average, the weighting process is revised (Haigh, 1994). In this case, it may be that historical earnings have been low due to factors previously out of the company's control, and that the changes to the situation allow recent profits to be weighted more heavily.

For Seetharaman et al. (2001), the calculation of brand earnings within the framework of this model should only consider factors related to brand identity. However, this condition is rather restrictive, as it is difficult to separate certain functions from the brand. For example, even when a distribution system is not a component of a brand's identity, it supports the brand by contributing to its success.

According to Haigh (1994), the following are the factors that Interbrand considers in its calculation of brand earnings:

- *Brand profits:* The profits used in the calculation of brand value are those attributable to the brand after allocating overheads and before interest. Because different capital structures (different combinations of debt and equity) do not affect brand performance, interest expenses are ignored.

- *Elimination of profits generated by private labels:* The monetary base onto which the earnings multiplier is applied must be related exclusively to the brand. All profits attributable to any other good produced by the brand owner, but not sold under the brand name, must be ignored.

- *Capital remuneration:* The return on capital that would have been used for the production of a private label or "commodity" is deducted from the profits attributable to brand. This enables the calculation of the brand's residual profits.

- *Taxation:* The multiplier is applied to profits after taxes.

- *Re-expression of profits at present value:* The framework of the model requires that historical profits are expressed at present value, by adjusting for inflation.

- *Provision for loss of future earnings.*

Brand strength indicator

Interbrand's multiplier approach is based on the assumption that brand strength determines the multiplier applied to profits attributable to brand, to arrive at brand value. A strong brand lessens uncertainty associated with future cash flow, and thus results in a higher multiplier. The inverse situation is given by a weak brand.

The multiplier, therefore, derives from the brand strength analysis, which, in turn, demands a thorough review of the brand's position within the market in which it operates, as well as a close look at its performance and future strategic plans. In the Interbrand model, brand strength is calculated based on seven weighted factors (see Table 5.31).

Determination of the multiplier

Brand strength determines the brand earnings multiplier through a functional relationship, or an S-curve that links brand strength to the multiplier. As the multiplier is applied to brand earnings, it resembles the Price Earnings Ratio (P/E ratio), with brand earnings as the denominator and brand value as the numerator. According to Torres Coronas (2002), to determine this value, Interbrand reviewed the P/E ratios yielded by numerous transactions effected in the market, or P/E ratios for companies with brands comparable to those being assessed. Interbrand also calculated the brand strength scores for these companies. The relationship between the brand strength score and the P/E ratio yielded an S-curve. The multiplier's maximum value is 20 (Haigh, 1994; Zimmermann et al., 2001). Figure 5.29 presents a generic "S-curve." Interbrand equates the x-axis with the brand strength score (0–100) and the y-axis with the multiplier value (0–20).

The S-curve is explained by the fact that unknown or new brands are weak for a certain period of time until their aware-

Table 5.31 Brand strength analysis in the Interbrand model

Factor	Definition	Maximum Score
Leadership	The greater the ability of the brand to function as a market leader and hold a dominant market share, the higher the score it will receive on this factor.	25
Stability	The greater the ability of the brand to retain its image and consumer loyalty over long periods, the higher the score it will receive for this factor.	15
Market	Brands in growing and stable markets with strong entry barriers are more valuable than brands in markets more exposed to changes in technology or fashion.	10
International image	An international brand is considered stronger than a regional or domestic brand.	25
Trend	The greater the ability of the brand to remain relevant and consistent to consumers, the higher the score it will receive on this factor.	10
Support	Brands that receive support and are consistently managed earn higher scores than those without any organizational investment. In order to evaluate this factor, amount and quality of brand investment is taken into account.	10
Protection	The stronger and broader the legal trademark's protection, the higher the score it will receive on this factor.	5
Brand strength		100

Source: Based on Seetharaman et al. (2001), Kerin and Sethuraman (1998) and Haigh (1994). Reproduced by permission of Emerald Group Publishing Ltd.

ness increases and their market position improves (Haigh, 1994). The brand's value is positively affected as the brand grows stronger, and once it reaches a dominant position, the rate of growth will slow.

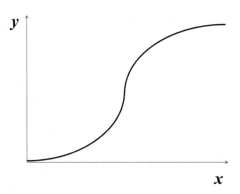

Figure 5.29 "S-curve" and the determination of brand multiplier in the Interbrand model.
Source: Based on Henry C. Co. (n.d.)

Table 5.32 Brand value calculation in the Interbrand model

Profits from branded product		A
Less:	Profits from unbranded line produced in parallel with the branded product	−B
Less:	Profits from assets that do not contribute to the strength of the brand	−C
Net profits from branded product		D
D × multiplier = Value of brand		

Source: Seetharaman et al. (2001: 250). Reproduced by permission of Emerald Publishing Group Ltd.

Calculation of brand value

The multiplier is later applied to brand profits in order to arrive at brand value, as shown in Table 5.32.

Interbrand multiplier model critique

1. *General critique:*

    (a) According to Pablo Fernández (2001), "valuing a brand using this method is highly subjective, not only because of the parameters used, but also because of the methodology itself" (p. 668, own translation).

2. *Critique of the quantification of the profit differential:*

(a) The quantification of the brand's profit differential and brand strength multiplier are very subjective processes (Fernández, 2001: 668; Tollington, 1999).

3. *Critique of the determination of the brand multiplier:*

(a) According to Tollington (1999), "where a prudent P/E multiplier or similar multiplier is applied to a brand's profits after eliminating, first the profits from unbranded goods such as own label products, which are often produced in parallel to the brand and, second, the profits from assets which do not contribute to the brand's strength ... there is an underlying and perhaps unjustified assumption that the brand profits can be valued in the same way as the business as a whole" (Section "Problem of valuation methods," para. 3).

(b) The way in which Interbrand has introduced the S-curve suggests the presence of a mathematic function and implies that there is no variance, when in fact it is likely for a single brand score to correspond to various multiples (Torres Coronas, 2002). This relationship therefore introduces several statistical problems, exacerbated by the fact that the final value is highly sensitive to slight variations in the multiplier.

4. *Critique of the determination of the Brand Strength Index:*

   (a) The brand strength analysis presents complications
       from a statistical point of view (Torres Coronas, 2002),
       as the score is given by the subjective weighting of
       very often redundant or inter-related factors, and is
       therefore likely to yield a biased total score.

   (b) The method assumes identical factors and weighting
       processes for all industrial sectors, regions and product
       categories. However, the weight of each factor, the
       factors themselves and the amount of key factors nec-
       essary for determining brand strength may vary by
       sector, product, region or industry/product life cycle.

5.18.2   Interbrand's discounted cash flow model

This model differs from the previous model in its:

- application of a future discounted cash flow model, rather
  than a historical earnings capitalization model;

- method of determining earnings attributable to brand
  through demand drivers, rather than comparison with
  theoretical profits yielded by a generic product;

- determination of a discount rate instead of a multiplier.

To calculate brand value, Interbrand uses a five-stage process
(Interbrand, 2008; Interbrand, 2006; Interbrand Zintzmeyer
& Lux, n.d.; Interbrand Zintzmeyer & Lux, 2003; Lindemann,
2003):

1. *Segmentation:* This stage consists of determining the main homogenous client groups on which the financial and demand analyses are based.

2. *Financial analysis:* Through this analysis, the model attempts to establish "economic earnings" or EVA (Economic Value Added), also referred to here as "intangible earnings."

3. *Demand analysis:* In this step, Interbrand establishes the "Role of Brand Index (RBI)" or the percentage of "intangible earnings" attributable to brand, referred to as "brand earnings."

4. *Brand strength analysis:* Through competitive analysis, Interbrand analyzes brand strength, which is in turn related to the discount rate (analogously to the brand strength-multiplier relationship seen in the previous model).

5. *Brand value calculation:* In this stage, the discount rate is applied to "brand earnings." The sum of the present value of "brand earnings" represents brand value.

Stage 1: Segmentation

According to Interbrand, as consumer attitudes and behaviors towards brands vary from sector to sector depending on product type, distribution and other market factors, brand value can only be accurately determined through the separate evaluation of the individual segments that represent a group of homogenous consumers.

Stage 2: Financial analysis – Estimation of "economic earnings," EVA or "intangible earnings"

To isolate earnings specifically attributable to the brand, Interbrand determines EVA or Economic Value Added, which indicates if a company is capable of generating returns that exceed the cost of capital employed (Interbrand Zintzmeyer & Lux, n.d.: 1). The model uses five-year EVA forecasts for the individual segment being evaluated.

"Intangible earnings" and "EVA" are used synonymously in Interbrand's commercial literature. Occasionally, Interbrand has used the term "economic profit" as a synonym of "intangible earnings" too (cf. Interbrand Zinztmeyer & Lux, n.d.: 90). Interbrand rejects this, privately stating that "economic value added is not equal to intangible earnings" (Interbrand, personal communication, 21 January 2009). But this formal declaration is not accompanied by a consistent use in their commercial literature. Let us review a couple of examples:

- The Best Global Brands Annual Ranking, Country Best Brands and Sectorial Rankings have alternatively used the terms "economic earnings," "intangible earnings" and EVA to refer to the same concept: the output of the financial analysis of the Interbrand model and the basis for calculating brand earnings. While the Best Global Brands Annual Ranking for the year 2001 used the term EVA, the Best Global Brand Annual Rankings from 2004 to 2007 use the term "intangible earnings," the Best Global Brands Annual Ranking in 2008 uses "economic earnings" and finally the Best US Retail Brands refers again to "intangible earnings." For more examples, on alternative uses of these terms, cf. Interbrand (2001, 2001b, 2002, 2003, 2004, 2005, 2006, 2007, 2008, 2008b, 2008c, 2009), Interbrand Design Forum (2009), Interbrand Zintzmeyer & Lux (n.d., 2003, 2007), Frampton (2008) and Lindemann (2003, 2004).

- In Interbrand Zintzmeyer & Lux (2003: 119) and in Interbrand Zintzmeyer & Lux (n.d.: 3), we can observe two examples of the application of the Interbrand model, one published in 2003 and another some time around 2004. Both demonstrate how Interbrand utilizes EVA and "intangible earnings" interchangeably to refer to the NOPAT less Cost of Capital.

Although it employed the concepts of EVA and "intangible earnings" interchangeably in the past, the "Best Global Brands" ranking publication from 2006 states: "The concept of intangible earnings is similar to value-based management concepts, such as economic profit or EVA (Economic Value Added is Stern Stewart's branded concept) (cf. "Interbrand Best Global Brands 2006"). Obviously, Interbrand's characterization of the relationship between these two concepts has been unsteady, which has in turn generated confusion surrounding these two terms. For a more thorough look at EVA, its advantages and limitations, cf. Pablo Fernández (2001).

Stage 3: Demand analysis or Role of Brand Index (RBI) – Determination of brand earnings

The Role of Brand Index (RBI) is "a measure of how the brand influences customer demand at the point of purchase" (Interbrand, 2006: 10). The result of this analysis, expressed as a percentage, is applied to "intangible earnings" in order to calculate brand earnings (Interbrand, 2006, 2009).

In its brand ranking publication from 2006, Interbrand states: "Since intangible earnings include the returns for all intangibles employed in the business, we need to identify the earnings that are specifically attributable to the brand. Through our proprietary analytical framework, called 'role of brand,' we can calculate the percentage of intangible earnings that is entirely generated by the brand" (Interbrand, 2006: 21).

Interbrand holds that in certain industries, such as the fragrance or packaged goods industries, the role of the brand is very high, as the brand represents the predominant factor in the consumer's purchase decision. However, in other sectors (particularly in B2B), brand is just one of many factors, rendering its role much smaller.

"Role of brand" is determined via a three-step process:

1. Firstly, Interbrand *identifies the demand drivers or the factors that motivate consumers to purchase a particular brand.* Interbrand finds that Microsoft customers are conscious not only of the brand in itself, but also of its market domination, its presence in 80% of the market, and the difficulty associated with transferring files to a new software platform. In the case of Shell, in addition to the brand alone, customers are aware of the location of its gas stations.

2. Step 2 determines the *relative importance* of the specific attributes identified in step 1.

3. Lastly, Interbrand determines the *role that the brand plays in each of these drivers.* This step is the most subjective part of the process.

Figure 4.2 in Chapter 4 shows an example of a "role of brand" determination that operates in the same way as the Interbrand Role of Brand Index. The total length of each bar indicates the driver's importance; the area shaded black represents the brand's role or influence on the perception of the driver.

The Role of Brand Index is expressed as a percentage, such that if RBI is 30%, 30% is extracted from intangible earnings or EVA as brand earnings. If it is 50%, 50% of intangible earnings or EVA is extracted as brand earnings.

Stage 4: Brand strength analysis – Determination of brand risk and discount rate

As in the previous model, brand strength represents the brand's relative capacity to "guarantee demand," and in this way sustains future earnings. This analysis yields the brand risk which is later expressed as a discount rate. The determined discount rate is then applied to earnings attributable to brand in order to arrive at the brand value.

Stage 4.1: Brand strength analysis
In this stage, the brand strength is compared with that of its competitors for each of the seven brand strength factors cited in Interbrand's original model. Table 5.33 shows how Interbrand analyzes these attributes as a function of other sub-attributes or sub-criteria. For example, the "market" factor is analyzed based on "industry concentration" and "market growth" criteria.

Stage 4.2: Determination of the discount rate
A discount rate that adequately reflects the brand risk profile is used to calculate the present value of future brand earnings.

Table 5.33 Brand strength specific attributes or evaluation criteria by factor

Factor	Evaluation Criteria	Maximum Score
Leadership	Market share, market position, market segment, brand awareness	25
Stability	History, current position, satisfaction, customer loyalty	15
Market	Competitive structure (concentration), market growth, volume, sales	10
International image	Presence in foreign markets, export history	25
Trend	Consideration, attractiveness	10
Support	Quality, consistency, share of advertising, identity	10
Protection	Date of registration, legal coverage and monitoring	5

Source: Developed by author based on Zimmermann et al. (2001) and Interbrand Zintzmeyer & Lux (n.d.)

The model assumes a relationship between brand strength and discount rate: *ceteris paribus*, the higher the brand strength score, the lower the discount rate. The brand strength index calculated in Stage 4.1 is translated into a discount rate using the S-curve (Interbrand Zintzmeyer & Lux, n.d.). Thus, a brand with an average strength score will be discounted at the industry WACC, and a leading brand with a maximum brand strength score of 100 will be discounted at a risk-free rate (Interbrand Zintzmeyer & Lux, n.d.). Haigh (1994) shows a relationship between the Brand Strength Index (BSI), the Multiple and the Discount Rate. As illustrated in Table 5.34, according to this author, the discount rate is equivalent to the inverse of the multiplier.

Table 5.34 Relationship between Brand Strength Index, Multiples and Discount Rates in the Interbrand model

Brand Strength Index	Discount Rate	Multiple
100	5%	20,0X
75	7.1%	19,1X
50	10%	10,0X
0	34.1%	2,9X

Source: Based on D. Haigh (1994)

Stage 5: Calculation of brand value

The present value of brand earnings is inversely related to brand risk. To calculate brand value for a particular segment, future brand earnings are discounted at present value and an annuity or perpetuity is calculated as a terminal value. The sum of the value of the individual segments yields the total value of the brand.

The model's various components and their interrelations can be summarized as follows:

- the financial analysis stage is used to determine intangible earnings;

- the RBI module is used to determine the ratio of brand earnings to total intangible earnings; and

- the brand strength analysis module is used to determine the discount rate required for re-expressing future brand earnings at present value.

Interbrand discounted cash flow model critique

1. *Critique of the quantification of "intangible earnings"*

   The examples shown earlier in this chapter demonstrate that Interbrand refers to the basis on which the RBI is applied as EVA or "intangible earnings" interchangeably. In Chapter 7, we shall see that the conflation of intangible earnings and EVA is a widespread quandary in the discipline of brand and intangible asset valuation.

2. *Critique of the determination of "role of the brand"*

   The determination of the number of demand drivers, their relative importance and the role of the brand in each one, is rather subjective, even when based on statistical analysis of market research data. The process of grouping various research variables into one factor (even with the help of a hierarchical analysis tool), deciding on the number of variables that influence buying decision, establishing the scale against which their relative importance is determined, and assessing the brand's role or contribution for each demand driver, is altogether very subjective.

3. *Critique of the determination of the brand strength score:* subject to the same criticism suffered by the previous model:

   (a) Brand strength factors may be interrelated, which can ultimately yield a biased total score (Torres Coronas, . 2002).

   (b) Uniform factors and weights are used across all sectors, regions and categories.

4. *Critique of the determination of the discount rate:* Because of the clear relationship between brand strength, discount rate and multiplier (as shown in Table 5.34), this model is subject to the same criticism we saw with the multiplier model. In addition, the discount rate is calculated as the inverse of the multiplier (see equation (5.14)).

$$\text{Brand Discount Rate} = \frac{1}{\text{Multiplier}} \qquad (5.14)^{43}$$

The configuration of this equation invites the following critiques:

(a) According to Tollington (1999), applying a P/E multiplier to brand earnings unfoundedly assumes that the brand can be valued in the same way as the business as a whole.

(b) The form in which the S-curve appears suggests the presence of a mathematical function in which there is no variance, when in fact it is likely for a single brand score to correspond to various multipliers (Torres Coronas, 2002).

(c) Observing the relationship shown in equation (5.14) and Table 5.34, it becomes clear that Interbrand is confusing discount rates and capitalization rates. Pratt (2002) masterfully distinguishes between the two concepts in his succinct description: "a capitalization rate is a yield rate used to convert a single payment or measure of economic income into present value (as opposed to a discount rate, which is used to convert

---

[43] The reader may observe that the multiple is the inverse of the discount rate with the data provided in Table 5.34.

all expected future payments to present value)" (p. 12). This definition makes it quite evident that the multiplier can be calculated as the inverse of the capitalization rate and not as the inverse of the discount rate; in other words, the inverse of the multiplier is equivalent to the capitalization rate, and not to the discount rate, as suggested in equation (5.14) and Table 5.34. The confusion surrounding the way in which the multiple was derived indicates a deeper misunderstanding of the nature and relationships of the P/E ratio with the required return on equity. The P/E ratio is equivalent to the inverse of the required return on equity only if the expectation of growth for the firm is zero. Otherwise, this equivalence does not hold.[44]

5.19 Kern's x-times model

Table 5.35 Kern's x-times model

Model name or ownership	Kern x-times model
Year of development	1962
Author	W. Kern
Country	Germany
Approach	Income
Principal methodology	Capitalization of decreasing royalties

Kern's model calculates brand value by capitalizing future earnings attributable to the brand. But earnings attributable to the brand are estimated based on a set of contestable assumptions. Zimmermann et al. (2001) describe the model's principal assumptions as follows:

[44]For more on the relationship between price earning ratios and discount rates, check Copeland, Koller and Murrin (2000).

$$BV = \sqrt[3]{R^2} * L * \frac{q^n - 1}{q^n * (q-1)}$$

BV = Value of the brand

R = Average expected annual revenues

L = Normal royalty rate in the industry

n = number of years' duration for the expected revenue stream (the brand's economic useful life)

q = 1 + p/100 (annuity present value factor), where p = the normal imputed interest rate for the country concerned

$$c = \frac{q^n - 1}{q^n * (q-1)} \quad \text{(capitalization factor)}$$

Figure 5.30 Kern's model.
Source: Zimmermann et al. (2001)

- Brand value is a growing function of revenue. This is represented by a curve with a decreasing positive slope (Square Root Function).

- The return on sales that could be achieved is in line with the industry average (4–6%).

- The royalty rate used should reflect the "brand strength," that is, the brand position in the market and the level of brand protection provided by intellectual property law.

- Brands have limited useful lives. Proper estimation is required to apply the equation described in Figure 5.30.

Kern model critique

Zimmermann et al. (2001) point out several flaws in the Kern model:

- There is no empirical evidence to support the assumed functional relationship (a curve with a decreasing positive slope) between growth in brand value and growth in revenues.

- The determination of normal royalty rates in the industry through experts' opinions gives the model a very subjective quality.

- The determination of the brand's economic useful life (variable n in Figure 5.30) is wholly arbitrary.

5.20   Lev's Intangibles Scoreboard

Table 5.36   Intangibles Scoreboard model

Model name or ownership	Knowledge Capital Scoreboard; Intangibles Scoreboard
Year	1999; 2002
Authors	B. Lev; F. Gu and B. Lev
Country	USA
Approach	Income
Principal methodology	Excess earnings

Source: Developed by author

Baruch Lev, professor of Accounting and Finance at the Stern School of Business at NYU, has developed a series of methods for valuing intangible assets. In 1999 he created the Knowledge Capital Scoreboard which he improved with the help of Feng Gu, and re-introduced three years later as the Intangibles Scoreboard (cf. Andriessen, 2004: 321). The purpose of this method is to calculate the financial value of a set of intangible assets (not one intangible asset in particular) based on publicly available information (Andriessen, 2004).

Module 1: Calculation of annual normalized earnings

This value is calculated by averaging the historical earnings for the past three years with future earnings for the next three years, as forecasted by analysts. Forecasted earnings receive a greater weight than historical earnings (Mintz, 1999).

Module 2: Calculation of "intangible-driven earnings"

The contributions of physical and tangible assets (or their adjusted book values, multiplied by average historical return thereon) are deducted from normalized earnings. Lev uses 7% for physical assets and 4.5% for financial assets as average historical rates of return after taxes (Hofmann, 2005). Thus, the residual value obtained represents the intangible assets' contribution to the company's normalized earnings. Lev refers to this value as "intangible-driven earnings" (IDE).

Module 3: Forecasted growth of intangible earnings

In this module, Lev applies a three-stage valuation model. According to Andriessen (2004), from year 1 to year 5, growth forecasts for aggregate earnings developed by analysts are applied. During year 6 to year 10, the long-term macroeconomic growth forecasts are used. From year 11 onwards, the model applies the economy's long-term growth rate.

Module 4: Calculation of the net present value of intangible earnings

Forecasted intangible earnings are discounted back to present value using a discount rate that reflects the intangible earnings-specific risk. The sum of discounted intangible earnings is the total value of the company's intangible capital.

Lev's model critique

- Lev's model is not useful for calculating the discrete value of different intangible assets, but rather for valuing a set of a company's intangible assets. Although this model cannot assess brand value discretely, it is included here as an academic example of the excess earnings method cited in Chapter 4.

- The method of determining the return on physical and financial assets is arbitrary.

- According to Andriessen (2004), this method calculates "a fair return on the tangible and financial resources used [which is] not the same as the contribution of these resources to earnings [as] the actual contribution can be lower or higher" (p. 325).

- Hofmann (2005) shows that this method can generate only a rough approximation of the real value of the intangible assets, as its "determination of intangible capital is based on analysts' estimates of future aggregate earnings to which (...) the company's intangible assets generally tend to make a rather unsystematic contribution" (p. 8).

5.21 Millward Brown Optimor

Table 5.37 Millward Brown Optimor model

Model name or ownership	Millward Brown Optimor
Year of development	2005
Authors	A. Farr and J. Seddon
Country	UK/USA
Approach	Income
Principal methodology	Capitalization of brand earnings based on a growth multiple and brand-consumer relationship analysis

Source: Developed by author

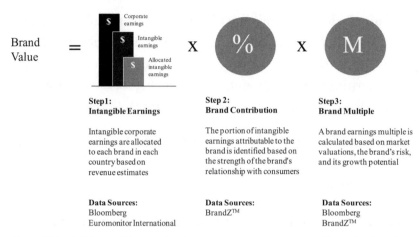

Figure 5.31 Millward Brown Optimor: three components of brand valuation. Source: Millward Brown Optimor (2006). Reproduced by permission of Millward Brown Optimor

Millward Brown Optimor (MBO) is a division of Millward Brown, the market research company owned by WPP Group. This division, founded in 2005, has developed a proprietary brand valuation model in which consumer perception is an essential component of brand value, as "brand success involves a combination of business performance, product delivery, clarity of positioning and leadership" (Millward Brown Optimor, 2007: 26).

The MBO valuation model (Millward Brown Optimor, 2006, 2007) is comprised of three steps, as shown in Figure 5.31:

1. **Calculation of intangible earnings** based on market and consumer information, together with financial data deriving from various sources (Bloomberg, Euromonitor International, etc.).

2. **Calculation of brand contribution**, or the brand's effectiveness in generating business earnings. This measure takes regional differences into account and "reflects the share of earnings from a product or service's most loyal consumers or users" (Millward Brown Optimor, 2007: 4).

3. **Calculation of the brand multiple**, based on an index of short-term expected brand growth, also known as "Brand Momentum."

Step 1: Calculation of "intangible earnings" attributable to brand

According to Andy Farr (2006), Millward Brown Optimor allocates the company's "sales" to each particular brand, business and region. Operating costs, relevant taxes, and a charge for capital employed are then deducted from these "sales,"* as shown in equation (5.15).

$$IE_t = S_t - CoS_t - GE_t - Amort_t - T_t - CCE_t \qquad (5.15)$$

where:

IE_t = intangible earnings for period t

S_t = net sales for period t

CoS_t = the cost of goods sold in period t

GE_t = general expenses for period t

---

*While the source of this information, an article authored by Andy Farr and published in the UK *Financial Times* on 5 April 2006, refers explicitly to "earnings," this appears to be a misprint, as deducting operating costs from earnings would imply a double deduction. We assume that, in fact, MBO is referring to sales and not income.

Amort$_t$ = the amortizations for period t

T$_t$ = taxes on earnings before interest for period t

CCE$_t$ = the Cost of Capital Employed for period t. This may also be expressed as CCE$_t$ = WACC$_t$ *CI$_t$, where CI$_t$ is capital invested in period t and WACC$_t$ is the weighted average cost of capital

Equation (5.15) may be re-expressed as:

$$IE_t = NOPAT_t - CI_t * WACC_t \qquad (5.16)$$

The resulting value, according to MBO, represents intangible earnings derived from the branded business. This concept is very similar to EVA. Both concepts will be studied in depth later on.

For Pablo Fernández (2001), EVA is no more than NOPAT less the company's book value ($D_{t-1} + Evc_{t-1}$) multiplied by the weighted average cost of capital (WACC):

$$EVA_t = NOPAT_t - (D_{t-1} + Evc_{t-1}) * WACC \qquad (5.17)$$

NOPAT, in turn, is synonymous with the company's unlevered profits or profits before interest after taxes.

$$NOPAT_t = EBIT_t - Taxes \qquad (5.18)$$

The reader may have noticed that the last member of equations (5.16) and (5.17) are rather similar. In fact, replacing CI$_t$ with ($D_{t-1} + Evc_{t-1}$) effectively yields EVA, which Millward Brown Optimor refers to as "intangible earnings."

When we address common errors in intangible asset and brand valuation, we will see that the erroneous belief that EVA is identical to the "creation of intangible value" constitutes a popular misconception in the discipline. EVA is not synonymous with value creation nor with intangible earnings.

Step 2: The brand's effectiveness in generating earnings: calculation of "brand contribution"

Once the business' wrongly-named "intangible earnings" have been calculated, MBO uses its *BrandZ*™ database to ascertain the proportion of intangible earnings that can be attributed to the brand and not to other factors, such as price, availability and performance.

The result of this analysis is termed "brand contribution" and it is expressed as an index that can range from one to five, where five indicates the strongest brand contribution. The score is determined on the basis of three *BrandZ*™ components (Farr, 2006):

1. The degree of commoditization in the market.

2. The influence of various factors, such as distribution or switching costs.

3. The strength of the clients' relationship with the brand.

Farr (2006) indicates that, according to the MBO's method, the brands that earn the highest scores are those for which:

(a) the barriers to switching are low;

(b) the perceived differentiation is high;

(c) the image is distinctive and relevant.

Detailed description of the brand contribution calculation

1. *Deduction of sales generated by non-brand-related factors:* According to MBO (2006), brand preference may originate in factors that are unrelated to the brand promise, such as price and functional criteria. The sales deriving from non-brand-related factors are removed.

2. *Segmentation of the target market based on the strength of the brand relationship:* The criteria to segment consumers and customers is given by the strength of their relationship with the brand. The degree of strength of the customer-brand relationship is determined by the BrandDynamics™ Pyramid (see Figure 5.32).

3. *Calculation of brand contribution:* The portion of earnings deriving from the top two tiers of the pyramid in Figure 5.32 represents the brand contribution – i.e., the proportion of earnings deriving from the most committed consumers or customers.

Brand contribution is measured country by country. Millward Brown Optimor (2006) provided an example for Nokia

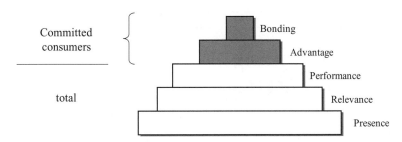

Figure 5.32 Calculation of brand contribution with the BrandDynamics™ Pyramid.
Source: Millward Brown Optimor (2006). Reproduced by permission of Millward Brown Optimor

(Figure 5.33) to illustrate how brand contribution for multinational brands can vary substantially between countries. MBO indicates that Nokia's strength in Germany and Italy reflects its nearly iconic status in these countries, while in other parts of the world, a lower contribution index indicates a stronger competitive landscape (in Japan) or growth potential (in the USA).

As shown in Figure 5.33, while brand contribution is originally valued on a scale from 1 to 5, it is later converted into a percentage through an algorithm undisclosed by MBO.

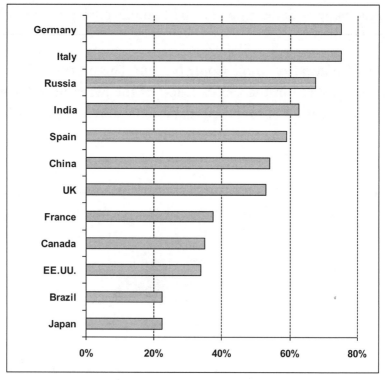

Figure 5.33 Regional variations in brand strength: brand contribution metric for Nokia.
Source: Millward Brown Optimor (2006). Reproduced by permission of Millward Brown Optimor

Step 3: Calculation of the brand multiple based on "Brand Momentum"

In this step, three brand risk factors are used to calculate short-term growth index and project future earnings:

- "Brand Voltage" per country. According to Farr (2006), Brand Voltage is a "validated research-based estimate" that predicts the brand's capacity to increase its market share in the future.

- Growth rates in the categories in which the brand operates.

- Growth rates in the countries in which the brand operates.

"Brand Momentum," defined by Millward Brown Optimor (2007) as "an index of a brand's short-term growth rate (one year) relative to the average short-term growth rate of all brands in the *BrandZ*™ ranking" (p. 25), is yielded by an undisclosed algorithm that links the three variables listed above. Millward Brown Optimor (2006) explains that:

- Brands with growth rates in the top 10% earn Brand Momentums of 10.

- Brand Momentums for other brands are calculated linearly in accordance with the short-term growth rate. Therefore, a brand with an average growth rate would earn a Brand Momentum of 5. Brands with above-average growth rates earn momentums between 5 and 10, while those with below-average growth rates earn momentums from 0 to 5.

The "Brand Momentum Index" yielded by this process is then converted into a brand multiple through an undisclosed algorithm.

Application

The numerical example in Table 5.38 illustrates the application of MBO's valuation equation.

As Table 5.38 shows, brand value is given by the product of intangible earnings, brand contribution and the brand multiple.

Table 5.38 Application of Millward Brown Optimor brand valuation methodology

	Intangible Earnings ($m)	Brand Contribution (%)	Brand Multiple (x)	Brand Value ($m)
US	$585	71%	15.7	$6550
Japan	$8	32%	10.8	$28
Germany				–
UK	$89	63%	16.8	$937
France	$1	57%	12.5	$10
China	$16	57%	13.3	$118
Italy	$6	66%	12.1	$50
Spain	$6	80%	13.5	$69
Canada	$83	65%	16.7	$898
Russia				–
India				–
Brazil				–
Global Brand Value =				**$8661**

Source: Millward Brown Optimor (2006). Reproduced by permission of Millward Brown Optimor

General overview of Millward Brown BrandZ™ research methodology: BrandDynamics™ Pyramid, BrandVoltage™ and BrandSignature™

In 1998, Millward Brown introduced the *BrandZ™* system, a global brand survey based on BrandDynamics™ research, and based on three "basic" components:

- The *BrandDynamics™ Pyramid*, which establishes the nature and depth of the consumer-brand relationship.

- *Brand Signature™*, which identifies the brand's strengths and weaknesses relative to other brands in the category.

- *Brand Voltage™*, a metric that numerically expresses the brand's strengths and weaknesses and quantifies the brand's potential for maintaining or increasing sales.

The *BrandDynamics™ Pyramid* symbolizes the relationship between the brand and its customers (Millward Brown, n.d.). It consists of five tiers (Haigh, 1999; Clarke, 2001), each of which represents a different degree of closeness to the brand (see Figure 5.34):

1. *Presence:* Consumers who show a certain degree of familiarity with the brand, but are not necessarily loyal to the brand and who do not always consider the brand during the purchase process. Brand presence or awareness is understood as a preliminary step in the path to brand loyalty.

2. *Relevance:* Customers who can afford to buy the brand's products, and for whom the brand's promise is relevant.

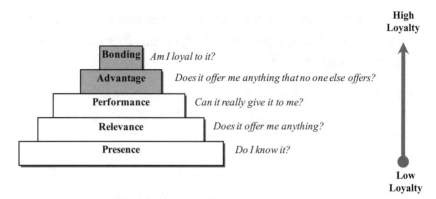

Figure 5.34 BrandDynamics™ Pyramid.
Source: Adapted from D. Haigh (1999); K. Clarke (2001). Reproduced by permission of Millward Brown Optimor

3. *Performance:* Performance is measured with category-specific attributes, and refers to product performance. Consumers who find that the brand does not perform acceptably will not ultimately represent committed consumers.

4. *Advantage:* Many brands may have acceptable product performance, but for the brand to have added value, consumers need to perceive a differential and positive (emotional or rational) advantage relative to other brands in the category.

5. *Bonding:* Consumers who feel that the brand is the only one that offers key advantages in the category generate a stronger connection to the brand and are highly likely to be loyal to it.

The *BrandDynamics™ Pyramid* attempts to graphically describe the "consumer's path to loyalty." Those on the bottom of the pyramid have a weak relationship with the brand; the brand enjoys stronger bonds as it moves its customers to the top of the pyramid. The amount spent on the brand is expected to increase as consumers climb the pyramid (Millward Brown, n.d.).

According to BrandZ's website, *Brand Signature*™ identifies the brand's *strengths and weaknesses* relative to other brands in the category. In other words, it measures "how well a brand converts people from one level up to the next in the pyramid when compared against the average brand performance for the category" (Clarke, 2001: 162).

Brand Voltage™ is a synthetic measure of a brand's ability to retain consumers in the various levels that lead to brand loyalty. In this sense, it provides a measure of the brand's vulnerability. It sums up the *Brand Signature*™ in a single number and expresses the brand's capacity to maintain, increase or diminish its market share in the near future. For MBO, this number is crucial for brand valuation because it predicts a brand's potential for growth.

Recall that the consumers on the top tier of the pyramid have more brand loyalty (and spend more on the brand). It follows, then, that this consumer group largely accounts for earnings and sales. The *Brand Voltage*™ calculation considers not only the brand's ability to keep consumers on a given tier (i.e., negative or positive deviations) but also the average amount that consumers on this tier spend on the brand.

According to Clarke (2001), after verifying this measure on 150 brands, Millward Brown was able to prove that those brands with positive Brand Voltages had higher probabilities of increasing their market share during the following year.

Millward Brown holds that there is a "proven link between Brand
Voltage™ and Market Share"

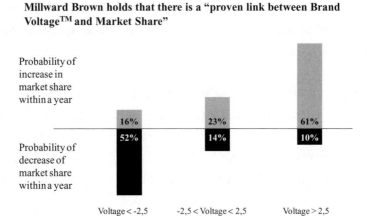

Figure 5.35 Voltage™ and changes in market share.
Source: Castanheira, J. (2008)

Brands with negative Brand Voltages had higher probabilities
of decreasing their market share (see Figure 5.35).

However, this indicator should not be read literally; competitive context, market conditions, and various factors of brand
positioning must also be taken into account. For example, for
leading brands like Coca Cola or McDonalds, positive voltage
does not indicate a capacity to increase market share in mature
markets, but rather a capacity to maintain a dominant position. Similarly, new brands can only increase market share
and this scenario is not necessarily connected with a healthy
brand.

Millward Brown Optimor model critique

1. *Critique of the calculation of the financial basis*

Like Interbrand and BrandEconomics, MBO confuses EVA
with intangible earnings.

2. *Critique of the calculation of brand contribution*

(a) In calculating brand contribution as the ratio of committed consumers to total consumers, MBO does not consider the brand's ability to attract consumers. The brand's contribution to total value should include its ability to attract new customers, and not only reflect its capacity to retain committed ones.

(i) Under this approach, a new or recently launched brand could not be valued, or would be valued at zero, as it could not yet have a solid base of loyal consumers. Therefore, even if the base of the pyramid were wide and many consumers were deciding to try the new product (although its novelty would impede this from entering into the realm of consumer loyalty), the MBO model would assign it a low brand contribution value.

(ii) Similarly, a declining brand may have many loyal customers (for example, mature customers and an older consumer base) but very low capacity for attracting new demand (entering new segments, or increasing presence in current segments). In the case of a declining brand, the pyramid's base would be small and its top would be bigger, yielding a high brand contribution index, despite its low ability to attract new customers.

(b) The scale from 1 to 5 established to measure brand contribution is completely arbitrary. MBO does not reveal how this number is converted into a brand contribution value.

3. *Critique of the calculation of Brand Momentum and Brand Multiple:*

   (c) This metric is a "short-term index," effectively barring any long-term elements from the model. Considering this "short-term growth index" alone, the method can easily lead to under- or overvaluations, where the expected long-term growth index is different from the Brand Voltage value.

   (d) The scale from 0 to 10 established to measure Brand Momentum is completely arbitrary. MBO does not reveal how it converts Brand Momentum into a Brand Multiple.

5.22 Motameni and Shahrokhi's Global Brand Equity Valuation model

Table 5.39 Motameni and Shahrokhi model

Model name or ownership	Global Brand Equity Valuation model
Year of development	1998
Authors	R. Motameni and M. Shahrokhi
Country	USA
Approach	Income
Principal methodology	Income capitalization based on P/E ratios and brand strength analysis

Source: Developed by author

Motameni and Shahrokhi (1998) define Global Brand Equity (GBE) as the product of the brand's net earnings and a brand multiple based on brand strength. The model may be expressed symbolically as:

$$GBE = \left\{ M \left[\left(\sum_{i=1}^{n} \sum_{j=1}^{m} W_{ij} * CBPF_{ij} \right) \middle/ 30 + \left(\sum_{i=1}^{n} \sum_{j=1}^{m} W_{ij} * CPF_{ij} \right) \middle/ 30 + \right.\right.$$

$$\left.\left. \left(\sum_{i=1}^{n} \sum_{j=1}^{m} W_{ij} * GPF_{ij} \right) \middle/ 30 \right] \right\} * BNE \qquad (5.19)$$

where:

GBE = Global Brand Equity or Capital Brand Global

M = the function that determines the multiple applicable to brand net earnings

W_{ij} = importance of factor j in country i

$CBPF_{ij}$ = the value of customer base potency factor in country i

CPF_{ij} = the value of competitor potency factor j in country i

GPF_{ij} = the value of the j global potency factor in country i

BNE = brand net earnings

The model encompasses three modules:

- Determination of brand strength

- Determination of the brand strength multiple

- Determination of brand net earnings.

Module 1: Determination of brand strength

The brand being valued must be audited following a series of criteria in order to predict its potential future. The brand's general profile with respect to these criteria indicates its strength. The model assesses three criteria in its determination of brand strength:

1. *Customer base potency factor (CBPF$_{ij}$):* The following factors are analyzed in order to estimate this value:

    (a) *Brand image and loyalty:* According to Motameni and Shahrokhi (1998), loyalty is a key factor for brand equity. A strong positive image plays a major role in the creation of brand loyalty. There are two alternative methods of measuring loyalty:

    (i) *Price premium* can serve as a very effective measure of brand loyalty. For Aaker (1996), a basic indicator of loyalty is given by the sum that a customer would pay with respect to another brand that offers similar benefits.

    (ii) *Customer satisfaction* can be an indicator of brand loyalty, particularly in the service sector.

    (b) *Brand awareness:* This brand equity component can affect perception and attitudes, and also drives purchase decisions and loyalty.

    (c) *Brand extension possibilities:* This criterion is closely tied to the brand's potential for diversification through entry into new markets. There are various indicators for measuring this potential; among them, current brand awareness in markets in which it is not present.

(d) *Brand association:* The key components of brand equity association involve a brand's unique or differentiating attributes.

(e) *Value perception:* This component measures the brand's level of success in creating a valuable image. It may be determined by asking customers if the brand provides good value for the money or if there are reasons for buying from this brand rather than from its competitors (Aaker, 1996).

(f) *Organizational association:* Corporation support and reputation are key for the success of many brands. Organizational associations may be measured through corporate communication expenses (ex. advertising share or SOV).

(g) *Differentiation:* This attribute is key to brand survival. Motameni and Shahrokhi (1998) recommend measuring this criteria through surveys that explore whether or not customers view the brand as distinctive.

(h) *Perceived quality:* Perceived quality is among the key dimensions of brand equity (Aaker, 1996) and should be measured relative to that of competitors. Motameni and Shahrokhi (1998) suggest measuring perceived quality through surveys that explore whether the brand is perceived as being of higher, equal or lower quality than its competitors.

2. *Competitive potency (CPF$_{ij}$):* This measure involves the analysis of the following factors:

(a) *Brand trend:* This criteria assesses if a brand is adapting well to changes in consumer needs and lifestyles.

(b) *Brand support:* This criteria assesses the level and consistency of marketing and advertising investment to support the brand.

(c) *Brand protection:* This criteria assesses the degree of legal protection of the brand name and other distinctive brand-associated characteristics, such as design, packaging and logo.

(d) *Competitive strength:* Evaluated based on criteria such as:

    (i)   brand stability or time in the market (assuming that an established brand has been able to build a loyal and satisfied customer base);

    (ii)   market share;

    (iii) profitability;

    (iv) R&D expenses.

3. *Global potency (GPF$_{ij}$):* In light of the significant differences between domestic and external markets, brand equity may vary from one country to the next. Restrictions on marketing strategy globalization must be taken into account when evaluating a brand's global performance.

The brand is assessed in each of the three factors or potencies and assigned a score between −10 (the lowest possible score) and +10 (the highest possible score). The score earned in each factor is later multiplied by the weighting factor W_{ij} which is in turn determined through consumer or manager surveys, depending on the relevance of each factor. The sum of the weighted factor scores yields a total brand strength score, which is then divided by 30 (the maximum brand strength score attainable in this scale), and expressed as a percentage.

Module 2: Determination of the brand strength multiple

In line with the Interbrand approach, and based on the multiples resulting from recent brand transactions, the model assumes a relationship in the form of an S-curve between the brand multiple and the brand strength score. The brand multiple is calculated in light of the brand strength score, and using this S-curve, whose shape will vary between product categories for each brand.

Module 3: Determination of brand net earnings

In order to calculate earnings differentials between the branded and the generic product, this model employs a method similar to that used by Financial World. A sum representing earnings derived from an equivalent unbranded product is deducted from brand-related earnings. Generic earnings are estimated as the product of the capital required to generate the branded product sales and the generic return on capital employed. The capital required to generate branded sales is estimated as the product of the median ratio of capital employed to sales in the category and the branded sales. The generic product return on capital employed is set at 5%. After deducting generic earnings from the branded business earnings, taxes are discounted. This final value then represents brand net earnings. Figure 5.36 shows an application of the Global Brand Equity model.

1. Determine the values and weights of the brand strength factors	2. Determine the multiple	3. Determine the sales / generic equivalent differential (BNE)
1.a. Customer base potency (CBPF$_{ij}$) Brand awareness = 10 Brand association = 8 $\}$ = 26/3 = **8.67** Perceived quality = 8 $\quad$ Wij = 0.33	By adding the values of the weighted factors 8.67 + 9.00 + 8.50 = **16.17**	Year 1 2 Operating earnings 30.00 35.00 Estimated earnings from equivalent generic (1) (12.05) (15.50) Brand Operating Earnings 17.94 19.50
1.b. Competitive potency (CPF$_{ij}$) Brand trend = 8 Brand support = 9 $\}$ = 36/4 = **9.00** Brand protection = 9 Competitive strength = 10 $\quad$ Wij = 0.25	Then by dividing by 30 to obtain the index for calculating the multiple via the S-curve 16.17/30 = **87.2%**	Weight 2 1 Weighted brand earnings 18.46 Taxes (@ 35%) (6.46) After tax brand earnings 12.00 Multiplied by x 19.1 **Brand Value** **$ 229.2m**
1.c. Global potency (GPF$_{ij}$) Market factors = 7 Promotional factors = 7 Distribution factors = 10 Product factors = 9 $\}$ = 55/6 = **8.50** Price factors = 10 $\quad$ Wij = 0.17 Regulation factors = 8	Multiple 19.1X Brand Strength 87.2 **M = 19.1**	**Estimated earnings from equivalent generic (1)** Branded product sales = $ 500 Median ratio (capital employed / sales) in the sector = 0.482 Required investment to generate $500 in sales for an equivalent generic product = $241 Return on capital employed for the unbranded product (5%) = 12.05 (= 241 x 0.05)

Figure 5.36 Application of the Global Brand Equity model.
Source: Developed by author based on "A Proposal for Measuring Brand Equity," Hand Out Session 9, Rice MBA[45]
Note: For the sake of simplicity, this chart includes only some factors of the Consumer Base Potency (CBPF$_{ij}$).

Motameni and Shahrokhi model critique

- In this model, "brand equity" is synonymous with "brand economic value."

- Motameni and Shahrokhi's model is somewhat reminiscent of the multiple-based methodology used in Interbrand's original model, published one decade earlier. It is therefore subject to the same critique of the calculation of brand net earnings and the S-curve-based determination of the multiple (cf. Section 5.18.1).

[45] Cf. www.ruf.rice.edu/~aperkins/HTML%20files/classes/mgmt684/ Session9Handout.ppt.

- Motameni and Shahrokhi (1998) caution that "since the weights [for each potency factor, W_{ij}] are determined by management or customer surveys, there is room for slippage, there is room for manipulation, if managers are compensated by value of brand equity" (Brand Multiple Section, para. 1).

5.23   Prophet

Table 5.40   Prophet model

Model name or ownership	Prophet
Year of development	2003
Author	S. Kumar
Country	UK/USA
Approach	Income
Principal methodology	Demand driver/brand strength analysis

Source: Developed by author

Prophet defines brand value as the net present value of expected cash flows attributable to the brand (Kumar and Hansted Blomqvist, 2004).

The Prophet valuation methodology encompasses three steps and five main components (as shown in Figure 5.37).

Step 1: Segmentation

Brand value can be generated or destroyed at any consumer touchpoint. The influence of the brand will vary depending on the client, product or service category, channel, and reason for purchase. It is therefore necessary to consider these different segments in the brand valuation exercise. The purpose of segmentation is to identify groups that manifest similar buying behaviors; Kumar and Hansted Blomqvist (2004) exemplify

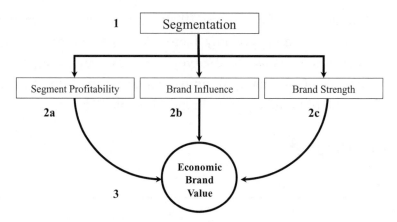

Figure 5.37 Prophet brand valuation process.
Source: Kumar and Hansted Blomqvist (2004). Reproduced by permission of Emerald Group Publishing Ltd.

this with a hypothetical scenario in the airline business: a passenger who flies for pleasure in economy to a nearby destination will have a different set of priorities than that of a business passenger in first class on a transatlantic flight. In this case, proper segmentation would be given by class of travel (economy, business or first class) and flight distance.

Step 2a: Segment profitability

Once the business segments have been established, segment-related cash flows are determined based on a financial analysis.

Step 2b: Brand influence

Brand value is a function of the cash flows that the brand can generate. To identify and separate brand-related cash flow, demand drivers relevant for the customers in each segment are analyzed. This step delineates the factors that lead consumers to choose one brand over another. Brand, along with price, comfort and quality, is one of the drivers that consumers consider during the buying process. These drivers are ranked based on their relative importance for the customer decision process. Then the role of the brand in influencing the perception of each driver is determined. Multiplying each driver's "importance" by its "brand influence" yields an average weighted index that measures the brand's influence on demand generation. Finally, the segment brand influence index is multiplied by the segment cash flows to obtain the cash flows attributable to the brand for each segment.

Step 2c: Brand strength

In this model, brand strength is determined as an index yielded by comparing the brand's performance with that of its competitors, based on a series of brand metrics. The criteria for comparison will depend on the industry and the market, but will most often include factors such as market share, market share trend, customer quality (length of relationship and income per customer), loyalty, and customer satisfaction. Brand strength is later used to determine the appropriate discount rate for brand-related cash flow.

Step 3: Economic brand value

The brand-related cash flow calculated in step 2b is discounted by the discount rate determined in step 2c, in order to obtain brand value for each segment. Total brand value is given by the sum of the present values of each segment.

Prophet model critique

Perhaps because its author, Shailendra Kumar, began his career at Interbrand and served as Head of Brand Valuation at

FutureBrand, this model is very similar to those proposed by the two cited entities. It is therefore prone to the same criticism that the Interbrand and FutureBrand models have received in terms of subjective drivers analysis and its uselessness for the calculation of a brand's fair value. In this model, the result of the drivers analysis, the brand influence index, is applied to brand-related cash flow, but it remains unclear why it is not applied to revenue, gross profits, net profits or any other financial bases. There is no empirical study or theoretical justification for linking this index with one financial basis over another. Additionally, this model does not define how brand-related cash flow is calculated.

5.24   Repenn's brand valuation model (System Repenn)

Table 5.41   System Repenn

Model name or ownership	Enterprise Value
Year of development	1998
Author	W. Repenn
Country	Germany
Approach	Mixed (Income/cost)
Principal methodology	Creation and development expenses plus 10% of average annual revenues in the past 5 years

Source: Developed by author

Repenn's model (illustrated in Figure 5.38) conceives brand value as the sum of:

• The cost of brand creation, maintenance, development, etc. – referred to as "underlying value."

Potential Saleable Value of a Brand = |Underlying Value| + |Operating Value|

Cost to create, maintain and develop the brand (Dev. costs, patent fees, etc.)

10% of average annual revenues in past 5 years ("Repenn Factor")

Where:

$$\text{Operating Value} = 10\% * \left(\sum_{i=1}^{5} \frac{R_i}{5} \right)$$

Where:
10% is the constant "Repenn Factor" and
R_i is the annual revenue for period i

Figure 5.38 Saleable value according to System Repenn.
Source: Developed by author based on Zimmermann et al. (2001)

- The value generated by the ongoing use of the brand – referred to as "operating value," and calculated as 10% of average annual revenues within the past five years (Zimmermann et al., 2001: 34).

System Repenn critique

The "Repenn Factor," used to estimate brand revenues, and calculated at 10% of total revenues, is an arbitrary figure devoid of any supporting empirical evidence or theoretical justification. According to Zimmermann et al. (2001), this component implies a 10% "brand-induced price premium" for all brands valued under this methodology, when, in fact, price premiums differ substantially from brand to brand.

5.25   Sander's Hedonic brand valuation method

Table 5.42   Sander's Hedonic brand valuation method

Model name or ownership	Sander's Hedonic Method
Year of development	1995
Author	Sander
Country	Germany
Approach	Income
Principal methodology	Hedonic price analysis

Source: Developed by author

Sander's brand valuation method (illustrated in Figure 5.39), based on the hedonic pricing method, is considered a variation on price premium-based valuation models (Raboy and Wiggins, 1997; Zimmermann et al., 2001). The hedonic price method is generally used to measure variations in real estate pricing that reflect changing values of environmental attributes such as water, air pollution, views, proximity to city center and highway access (Boos, 2003).

The hedonic price theory assumes a functional relationship between product prices and characteristics. This function is expressed as a standard regression function:

$$y_i = \beta_0 + \beta_1 * x_1 + \beta_2 * x_2 + \ldots + \beta_n * x_n + \varepsilon \qquad (5.20)$$

where:

y_i = the product price

β_0 = a constant that represents the price not explained by the individual characteristics present in the equation

β_i = the coefficients of the individual characteristics

x_i = the individual characteristics

ε = is a random error term

When β_i is positive, the corresponding attribute is desirable and has a positive influence on price. Thus, the coefficient β_i can be interpreted as a measure of the economic return on characteristic x_i (Boos, 2003). This is a variation of one unit in characteristic x_i and will generate a variation in the price of β_i.

In brand valuation, the hedonic approach statistically isolates the revenue associated with the specific product characteristics and treats the brand as one of these characteristics. Because the hedonic function is able to predict the changes in price that would transpire if the product characteristics were different,[46] the final product price may be calculated both with and without the brand. The difference between the product price with and without the brand represents the unit revenue generated by the brand and is determined through multiple regression analysis.

Total brand revenues are determined by multiplying the hedonic price for the brand (i.e., unit revenue attributable to the brand) by the total quantity sold. Then, the brand-specific expenses (those that would not have been incurred in the absence of the brand) are deducted from total brand revenues to derive brand-specific earnings.

Sander's model critique

Although at first it may seem as though this model, like other quantitative and statistical techniques, is free of the subjective dimension inherent to other methods, it is rather complex

---

[46] In fact, *hedonic prices* refers to incremental price changes deriving from alterations in certain product characteristics.

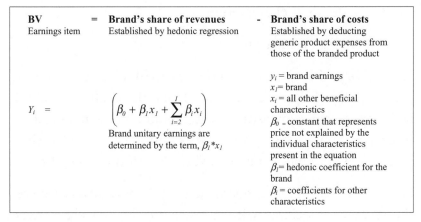

BV	=	Brand's share of revenues	-	Brand's share of costs
Earnings item		Established by hedonic regression		Established by deducting generic product expenses from those of the branded product

$$Y_i = \left(\beta_0 + \beta_1 x_1 + \sum_{i=2}^{I} \beta_i x_i \right)$$

Brand unitary earnings are determined by the term, $\beta_1 * x_1$

y_i = brand earnings
x_1 = brand
x_i = all other beneficial characteristics
β_0 = constant that represents price not explained by the individual characteristics present in the equation
β_1 = hedonic coefficient for the brand
β_i = coefficients for other characteristics

Figure 5.39 Sander's Hedonic brand valuation method.
Source: Adapted from Zimmermann et al. (2001). Reproduced by permission of Schmindt Axel/BBDO Consulting GmbH

theoretically as well as practically. The major flaws of this model include:

- *Restrictive assumptions regarding principal variables:* Boos (2003) writes that from a theoretical standpoint, the model assumes that there is a linear relationship between dependent and independent variables, that coefficients are constant during the data collection stage, and other assumptions that are not easily fulfilled in practice.

- *Identification of the product's individual characteristics:* The final outcome of the model depends on the identification of the product's characteristics; however, the construction of the statistic model is usually based on a series of hypotheses and assumptions regarding market conditions, products and prices. While wholly different than that present in other brand valuation methods, there is still a troublesome degree of subjectivity in this analysis (Boos, 2003).

- *Narrow definition of brand costs:* According to Zimmermann et al. (2001), in defining brand-specific expenses so narrowly, Sander's method considers only the cost of brand development, protection, design, etc., and excludes other marketing investments such as advertising, sponsorship, public relations, product promotions, etc., which obviously also have an effect on brand value.

- *Practical complexity:* The application of this model calls for detailed information necessary for modeling the extant relationship between product price and individual characteristics. As the method requires the identification of a sufficient number of relevant competitors (brands that sell the same product, but with different characteristics), the market in which the product operates must be well-developed for the approach to be properly applied. Where there is insufficient data on product characteristics, or when variations in competitor product prices or characteristics are not substantial enough, hedonic price methods will produce poor results (Boos, 2003).

5.26 Sattler's model[47]

Table 5.43 Sattler's model

Model name or ownership	Sattler's Model
Year of development	1997
Author	Sattler
Country	Germany
Approach	Income
Principal methodology	Demand driver/brand strength analysis

Source: Developed by author

[47] Sattler later developed another model collaboratively with GfK and PwC which shares no methodological qualities with the model presented in this section, except the utilization of this model's brand strength coefficients for the calculation of brand risk in the second model, as described in Section 5.13.

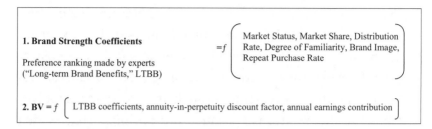

Figure 5.40   Principal elements of Sattler's Model.
Source: Zimmermann et al. (2001). Reproduced by permission of Schmindt Axel/BBDO Consulting GmbH

Sattler's brand valuation model (see Figure 5.40 above) consists of five steps (Zimmermann et al., 2001):

1. The *first step* involves the identification of *brand value indicators* through a survey of experts. This process produces a set of criteria for the long-term brand value, including market position during the past five years, market share in value terms, weighted distribution rate, prompted awareness, image advantages relative to the competition according to brand surveys, and repeat purchase rate.

2. In the *second step*, experts calculate the long-term value of the selected brands, expressing them as brand strength coefficients, and ranking them by their long-term value.

3. The *third step* determines the relative importance of the brand strength coefficients in terms of their influence on long-term brand value, by employing conjoint analysis and regression, and utilizing data provided by experts.

4. In the *fourth step*, the coefficients are used to calculate each brand's long-term benefits.

5. In the *fifth step*, a linear function is used to re-express long-term brand benefits as monetary brand value. The conversion requires the presence of at least two points of reference; that is, the long-term brand benefits for at least two brands must be translated into brand value. Finally, the long-term brand value is calculated based on the long-term brand benefits, the brand's contribution to earnings within the past year and the discount factor for an annuity in perpetuity.

Sattler's model critique

In general, this model is rather subjective, as it is based exclusively on expert surveys. According to Zimmermann et al. (2001), "the monetary conversion of the calculated benefit values is accompanied by a significant level of uncertainty; the estimated parameters permit only an inexact forecast of real brand value and the generalization of results makes sense only for product groups with the same structure as those analyzed" (p. 65).

5.27 Semion

Table 5.44 Semion model

Model name or ownership	Semion Brand Broker GmbH
Year of development	1996
Author	Semion Brand Broker GMBH
Country	Germany
Approach	Income
Principal methodology	Demand driver/brand strength analysis

Source: Developed by author

Semion® Brand-Broker GmbH is a German company special-izing in brand brokerage, closing the gap between parties who require already-registered trademarks and trademark owners who want to sell their trademark rights.

The Semion approach defines the following four brand value drivers or evaluation criteria to determine brand value:[48]

- brand protection

- financial value

- brand strength

- brand image.

Figure 5.41 shows the sub-components that the abovemen-tioned criteria encompass.

According to Zimmermann et al. (2001), the Semion model has four stages:

1. *Determine a value for each driver* based on its sub-criteria. The indicators for each driver are aggregated to yield a single driver value.

2. The resulting values are *added* to give a *weighting factor*.

3. Next, average *pre-tax earnings* are calculated for the past five years as the financial basis on which to value the

---

[48] Cf. http://www.branding.de/value/value2004e.html.

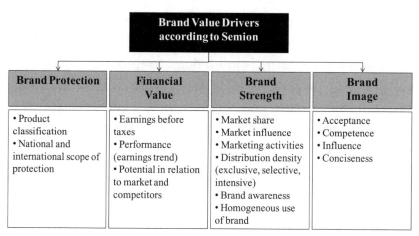

Figure 5.41 Semion brand value outline.
Source: Adapted from Zimmermann et al. (2001) and Semion's website

trademarks being used. Those trademarks not being used are valued based on the "average investment in the creation of a new brand."

4. Finally, *average pre-tax earnings are multiplied by the weighting factor* to produce brand value.

Equation 5.21 shows a mathematical expression of the model.

$$BV = \frac{\text{Average}}{\text{earnings}} \times \begin{bmatrix} \text{Financial} & \text{Brand} & \text{Brand} & \text{Brand} \\ \text{value} & +\text{protection} + \text{strength} + \text{image} \\ \text{driver} & \text{driver} & \text{driver} & \text{driver} \end{bmatrix}$$

(5.21)

Source: Adapted from Zimmermann et al. (2001)

Semion model critique

Semion discloses very little information about its model. It remains unclear whether the driver values and their individual components are calculated on the basis of market surveys, expert opinions, or the range of values that these entities could possibly assume. Semion does not provide any empirical evidence to justify the seemingly arbitrary relationship between brand value and the four factors proposed for estimating the weighting factor. The indicators for the four brand value drivers are not clearly defined.

Zimmermann et al. (2001), present further criticism of this model:

- The criteria used introduce potential correlations.

- The model does not include sufficient measures of future brand potential or development.

5.28 Simon and Sullivan's stock price movements model

Table 5.45 Simon and Sullivan model

Model name or ownership	Stock Price Movements
Year of development	1990[49]
Authors	Simon and Sullivan
Country	USA
Approach	Other
Principal methodology	Structural analysis of brand value determinants

Source: Developed by author

[49]This year marks the first reference to this methodology in the literature found by the author: Simon, C. and Sullivan, M. (1990), "The measurement and determinants of brand equity: A financial approach," Working paper #197, The University of Chicago, as cited in Kahle and Kim (2006: 23 and 29) and Aaker (1991:, 25).

In this model, developed by Professors Simon and Sullivan (1993), "brand equity" is synonymous with "brand value," and is defined as "the incremental cash flows which accrue to branded products over and above the cash flows which would result from the sale of unbranded products" (p. 29).

This model assumes "market efficiency," wherein share prices will reflect at any time all information available. The stock price is used as a basis from which to determine brand value. To do so, the brand value is isolated from the value of other company assets. First, the company value is divided between tangible and intangible assets; later, the brand value is extracted from the total value of the intangible assets (Motameni and Shahrokhi, 1998).

The model involves two phases of analysis (Aaker, 1991; Motameni and Shahrokhi, 1998; Torres Coronas, 2002):[50]

Phase 1: macro-analysis – determination of brand value and its relationship to its determinants

First, the macro-analysis estimates an objective value for the company's brands, and relates this value to the brand equity determinants.

According to this model, from a financial market perspective, the brand's value may be calculated on the basis of the company's market capitalization or market value.

$$MV = V_{TA(cost)} + V_I \qquad (5.22)$$

---

[50]In reality, these may be best understood as potential uses, and not phases, of the model. The author has chosen the latter term for the sake of consistency.

where:

MV = the market value of the company's assets

$V_{TA(cost)}$ = the total value of the tangible assets at replacement cost

V_I = the total value of the intangible assets

Once the value of the intangible assets has been calculated, it is divided into three components:

$$V_I = f(VB, V_{NoM}, V_{ind}) \qquad (5.23)$$

where:

VB = brand value

V_{ind} = the value of industry-related factors that allow monopoly profits (regulation, concentration, etc.)

V_{NoM} = the value of the non-brand-related factors that reduce company costs relative to its competitors (R&D, patents, etc.)

Based on equation (5.23), in the case of a monobrand,[51] brand value will consist of the market value of the company's assets less the value of the remaining tangible and intangible assets.

$$VB = MV - (V_{TA(cost)} + V_{ind} + V_{NoM}) \qquad (5.24)$$

---

[51] In the case of a multi-brand company, this calculation is prorated in light of the total profits or earning share that each brand represents.

But equation (5.24) is merely a conceptual construct. To calculate brand value, the authors use a structural equation that links brand determinants with brand value. Brand value will depend on the following brand value determinants, as designated by the authors:

- *advertising expenses* (current and historical);

- *age of brand* (the brand's survival time is believed to be positively correlated with the company's ability to consistently offer high-quality product and services that satisfy consumers and generate consumer loyalty);

- *order of entry* (deemed positively correlated with strategic position and consumer loyalty/risk perception);

- *current and historical advertising share* (deemed positively correlated with consumer perception).

Phase 2: micro-analysis – measuring the brand value's response to changes in marketing policy

The micro-analysis isolates the changes that occur in the individual value of each brand by measuring the brand equity's reaction to important marketing decisions. Simon and Sullivan find that financial markets do not ignore marketing factors, and recognize that stock prices indeed reflect marketing decisions.

Simon and Sullivan model critique

This method has several *weaknesses:*

- It assumes market efficiency, whereby all available information and events relevant to brand image are easily identifiable for all market actors and incorporated into share prices. However, as Zimmermann et al. (2001) point out, if the process of diffusion of brand information is slow or imperfect, it would be impossible to attribute changes in stock price to changes in brand value. This assumption goes against the logic of the model.

- This approach is more appropriate for monobrand corporations, as the proration that divides brand value among various brands is merely an approximation (Zimmermann et al., 2001).

- Limiting brand strength to four factors may be too restrictive in some cases (Torres Coronas, 2002).

Torres Coronas (2002) cites some of the model's *strong points:*

- It considers the brand's ability to generate earnings and lower costs.

- It uses objective market-based valuation metrics.

5.29   The Nielsen Company: Brand Balance Sheet and Brand Performance

Table 5.46   The Nielsen Company model

Company name/ownership	Brand Balance Sheet and Brand Performance
Year of development	1989; 2001
Authors	Shulz and Brandmeyer; AC Nielsen[52]
Country	Germany
Approach	Income
Principal methodology	Brand strength/drivers analysis

Source: Developed by author

[52] The firm has been renamed as The Nielsen Company recently.

5.29.1 The Nielsen Company: Brand Balance Sheet

This model, developed by Schulz and Brandmeyer, encompasses four modules:

- determination of brand value criteria

- determination of brand income

- discount factor

- brand value estimation.

Module 1: Determination of brand value criteria

This module involves a system of brand value indicators based on 19 criteria, grouped into six categories, as shown in Figure 5.42 below.

Because the values of these criteria are measured in different units, they are scaled to allow for comparability, and then added, such that the total value may earn a maximum score of 500.[53] A brand value factor is determined based on the total score. This brand value factor is, in turn, a benchmark for the brand's future potential.

Module 2: Determination of brand income

Brand-related income is calculated based on total industry sales, estimated market share and the average return for the sector.

---

[53] The Nielsen Company's procedure for scaling and weighting this information is not disclosed.

1.	Market Attractiveness: What is the market situation?
	1. Market value (potential for market development)
	2. Market development
	3. Market value creation

2.	Market Share: What is the size of the brand share in the market?
	4. Market share in value terms
	5. Relative market share
	6. Development of market share
	7. Share of profits earned in the market

3.	Strength in Distribution: How do wholesalers and retailers assess the brand?
	8. Weighted distribution
	9. Commercial appeal of the brand

4.	Brand Management: What Does the company do for the brand?
	10. Product quality
	11. Brand price
	12. Share of voice

5.	Brand Loyalty: How strong is consumer loyalty to the brand?
	13. Brand loyalty
	14. Brand confidence
	15. Share of mind (unaided brand awareness)
	16. Advertising recall
	17. Identification with brand

6.	Brand Scope: How large is the area of influence?
	18. International reach of brand
	19. International brand protection

Figure 5.42   Brand Balance Sheet brand value criteria.
Source: Adapted from Zimmermann et al. (2001). Reproduced by permission of Schmindt Axel/BBDO Consulting GmbH

Module 3: Determination of the discount factor

The discount factor – a function of the long-term capital market yield plus risk premium – is used to discount brand income at present value. The discount factor and the risk premium dimension therein included are both derived from the score yielded in the first module. A higher score generates a lower discount factor and a higher brand capacity for income generation (and vice versa).

Module 4: Brand value calculation

The income attributable to the brand is discounted assuming a perpetual annuity with no growth. The discounted value of brand income then constitutes the brand's economic value. Figure 5.43 illustrates this model.

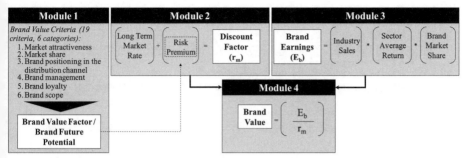

Figure 5.43 Modules of The Nielsen Company's "Brand Balance Sheet" model.
Source: Developed by author

"Brand Balance Sheet" model critique

The "Brand Balance Sheet" model has the typical problems of all scoring systems, as well as the following flaws:

- Subjective determination and weighting of the brand strength criteria, as well as interdependence among the brand value criteria (Zimmermann et al., 2001).

- Aligned with the general critiques that Smith and Parr (2005) make on scoring systems, Zimmermann et al. (2001) question the validity of the corrclation between the brand score (obtained as a result of the analysis performed in Module 1) and risk premiums.

- In assuming a perpetual annuity with no growth, the model assumes that the brand's income will not increase as well as an unlimited lifespan for any brand.

5.29.2   The Nielsen Company's Brand Performance

Having realized that the "Brand Balance Sheet" had several problematic issues, The Nielsen Company developed a more

1.	Market attractiveness (15%)
	1. Market volume
	2. Market growth
2.	**Market acceptance (35%)**
	3. Market share (volume and value)
	4. Market share growth (volume and value)
3.	**Consumer acceptance (40%)**
	5. Brand awareness
	6. Brand presence within the relevant set
4.	**Weighted distribution (10%)**
	7. Distribution

Figure 5.44 Brand Monitor: "Brand Performance" brand value criteria. Source: A.C. Nielsen GmbH (2006). Reproduced by permission of The Nielsen Company

advanced model called "Brand Performance." This model also involves four modules, as described below.

Module 1: Brand Monitor

The objective of this module is to determine a brand strength index through a scoring system based on seven brand value indicators grouped into four categories, as illustrated in Figure 5.44.

The weighted values yielded in this module are added and set to scale. A brand can earn a maximum score of 1000 points. Absolute brand strength is then determined as a percentage of the points obtained by the brand through the scoring system. Next, relative brand strength is determined by comparing the brand's absolute brand strength with that of its relevant competitors.

Module 2: Brand value share or brand earnings

In this module, the brand's earnings are determined through the following process:

- Market earnings potential is determined as the product of the estimated market volume and the average net operating margin for the sector.

- The brand value share for the current fiscal year is determined by multiplying the market earnings potential by the relative brand strength.

Module 3: Determination of the appropriate discount rate

In this module, the value of the "interest" or discount factor is determined based on sector risk ratings. Unlike the analogous step in the "Brand Balance Sheet" model, this process does not make any adjustment for brand-specific risk.

Module 4: Brand value calculation

In this stage, brand value is determined by assuming a perpetual annuity and discounting future brand earnings using the interest factor calculated in module 3.

Figure 5.45 and equation (5.25) demonstrate the modules that comprise this model, as well as the culminating equation for calculating brand value.

$$
BV = \begin{pmatrix} \text{Annual} \\ \text{Sales of} \\ \text{respective} \\ \text{brands} \end{pmatrix} * \begin{pmatrix} \text{Net} \\ \text{Operating} \\ \text{Margin} \end{pmatrix} * \begin{pmatrix} \text{Relative} \\ \text{Brand} \\ \text{Strength} \end{pmatrix} * \begin{pmatrix} \text{Perpetual} \\ \text{Annuity} \\ \text{NPV Discount} \\ \text{Factor} \end{pmatrix}
$$

$$(5.25)$$

Source: Zimmermann et al. (2001)

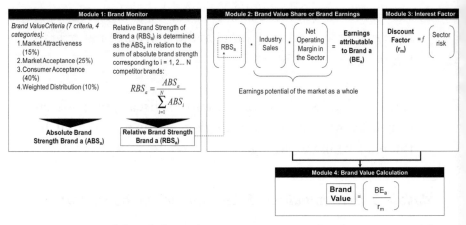

Figure 5.45 Modules of The Nielsen Company's "Brand Performance" model. Source: Developed by author

The Nielsen Company's Brand Performance model critique

This model has several flaws:

- Unrealistic and arbitrary assumptions: the model assumes the same net operating margin and a perpetual lifespan for any brand.

- The process of determining brand earnings is arbitrary.

- This model assumes a perpetual annuity with no growth – which does not necessarily make sense for all brands – and applies it uniformly to new, mature, rising and declining brands alike.

5.30   Trout & Partners[54]

Table 5.47   Trout & Partners model

Model name or ownership	Trout & Partners
Year of development	2000
Author	J. Trout
Country	USA
Approach	Income
Principal methodology	Price premium capitalized by P/E-based multiple

Source: Developed by author

In December 2001, the AASB released a document summarizing a host of valuation models. Among the models discussed was that proposed by Trout & Partners, which assumes that brand names will have value only if their market share is higher than that of a generic substitute selling at the same price, and/or if its price premium is greater than that of a generic substitute. Thus, Trout & Partners defines BEV (brand economic value) as:

$$BEV_i = VC * CM_i * PP_i * t_c * M_i \qquad (5.26)$$

where:

BEV_i = economic value of brand i

VC = value of the category in monetary terms

---

[54] All data presented in this section derive from the document presented by AASB in December 2001 under the title, "For consideration by the AASB at its 12 & 13 December 2001 meeting," AASB 2001, Agenda Paper 9.4.

CM_i = the market share of sales expressed as a percentage

PP_i = the price premium expressed as a percentage

t_c = the corporate tax rate

M_i = the capitalization multiple

M_i is then calculated as:

$$M_i = (P/E)_s * RA \qquad (5.27)$$

where,

$(P/E)_s$ = the price/earnings ratio for the sector

RA = the risk adjustment

The abovementioned document cites an example that illustrates the process, by applying the model to the valuation of Coca-Cola (p. 64):

($730 m)	× (0.824) ×	(0.77) ×	(0.35)	= $162 m
(Grocery Category Value, September 1999)	(Market Share)	(Price Premium)	(Tax Rate)	

"$162m represents the incremental net cash flow value for grocery distribution only, which represents approximately 33% of total distribution" (AASB, 2001: 65). Therefore, assuming the same factors for all other channels, relevant net cash flow for the Coca-Cola brand is calculated as:

$$BEV = \frac{\$162\,m}{0.33} = \$491\,m$$

$$BEV = \$491\,m * M_i$$

$$BEV = \$491m * (P/E)_s * RA$$

$$BEV = \$491\,m * 17.9 * 0.46$$

$$BEV = \$4043\,m$$

According to Trout & Partners, the earnings multiple risk adjustment should be based on measures derived from customer loyalty surveys, such as brand longevity (AASB, 2001). Trout & Partners recognize that the calculation of the capitalization multiple is highly subjective, but they argue that the primary goal of their model is to provide a measure of marketing performance, and that therefore emphasis should not be laid on the capitalization multiple.

Trout & Partners model critique

The Trout & Partners model is one of the few models to bring *no technical or management-oriented advantages*. Rather, it presents the following *disadvantages:*

- The utilization of the sector PER is arbitrary and subjective.

- The utilization of the 35% tax rate multiplied by brand-related earnings is wholly unfounded. Were such a calculation reasonable in any way, a 65% rate should be used to calculate after-tax brand-related income. Where this is not the case, the higher the tax rate, the greater the brand value yielded.

5.31   Villafañe & Associates' Competitive Equilibrium model

Table 5.48   Villafañe & Associates model

Model name or ownership	Competitive Equilibrium Model
Year of development	2002
Authors	E. Moreno and I. Rivilla
Country	Spain
Approach	Income
Principal methodology	Competitive equilibrium analysis

Source: Developed by author

This model conceptually and methodologically determines the market share obtainable by each product (or service) in function of its global competitiveness index, derived from the set of its attributes – both objective and subjective (image) – and from the rest of the company's basic marketing mix factors (Rivilla, 2005).

The model (see Figure 5.46) consists of six well-defined steps or modules:

1. **Calculation of competitive equilibria deriving from objective attributes.** The model's initial step consists of gathering and consistently evaluating the relevant *objective information* on perceived value. This process implies determining a set of sector-specific variables. Villafañe & Associates holds that brand valuation models should be sector-specific, given that the objective market factors will vary between them. For

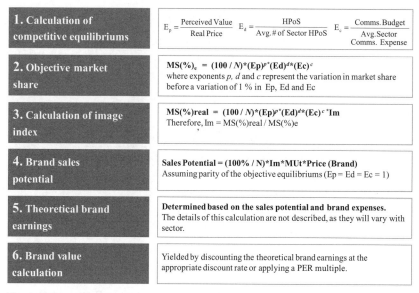

1. Calculation of competitive equilibriums	$E_p = \dfrac{\text{Perceived Value}}{\text{Real Price}}$ $E_d = \dfrac{\text{HPoS}}{\text{Avg. \# of Sector HPoS}}$ $E_c = \dfrac{\text{Comms. Budget}}{\text{Avg. Sector Comms. Expense}}$
2. Objective market share	**MS(%)$_e$ = (100 / N)*(Ep)^{p*}(Ed)^{d*}(Ec)^c** where exponents *p, d* and *c* represent the variation in market share before a variation of 1 % in Ep, Ed and Ec
3. Calculation of image index	**MS(%)real = (100 / N)*(Ep)^{p*}(Ed)^{d*}(Ec)$^{c\,*}$Im** Therefore, Im = MS(%)real / MS(%)e
4. Brand sales potential	**Sales Potential = (100% / N)*Im*MUt*Price (Brand)** Assuming parity of the objective equilibriums (Ep = Ed = Ec = 1)
5. Theoretical brand earnings	**Determined based on the sales potential and brand expenses.** The details of this calculation are not described, as they will vary with sector.
6. Brand value calculation	Yielded by discounting the theoretical brand earnings at the appropriate discount rate or applying a PER multiple.

Figure 5.46   Villafañe Competitive Equilibrium Model.
Source: Developed by author

example, objective information on perceived value may be represented by prices, technical characteristics and performance of each product, as well as quantifiable factors of distribution (coverage and penetration) and advertising/promotional activities (budgeted or real advertising investment). Based on this data, the model calculates what it refers to as a "global equilibrium of forces." In the example, this global equilibrium is composed of product, distribution and communication equilibria, which may be considered indices of the relative strength of non-brand-related attributes that influence a product's or service's expected market share, and are calculated as follows:[55]

---

[55]The definition of the variables for each equilibrium will vary by industry.

$$\text{Equilibrium of Product}(E_p)$$
$$= \frac{\text{Perceived (or Theoretical) Value}}{\text{(Retail Price)}} \qquad (5.28)$$

Equilibrium of Distribution (E_d)
$$= \frac{\text{Number of Comparable Points of Sale (CPoS)}}{\text{Average Number of CPoS in Sector}} \qquad (5.29)$$

Equilibrium of Communication (E_c)
$$= \frac{\text{Brand Advertising/Promotion Budget}}{\text{Average Advertising/Promotion Budget in the Sector}}$$
$$(5.30)$$

2. **Calculation of the objective market share.** The equilibria calculated in Module 1 allow for the determination of a "theoretical objective market share;" the market share that would be obtained by the company, if the product, distribution and communication equilibria were the only determinants of market share. Equation (5.31) shows how the objective market share is calculated.

$$(\%)\, MS_e = (100\%/N) \cdot (E_P)^p \cdot (Ed)^d \cdot (Ec)^c \qquad (5.31)$$

where:

MS = Market share percentage (applicable to total market units, Mt)

N = Number of market competitors

p, d, c = Substitution elasticities that represent variation in market share before 1% variations in Ep, Ed and Ec

Ec, Ed and Ep = Communication, distribution and product equilibria

3. **Calculation of the image index or adjustment factor.** The difference between the "theoretical market share" and the "real market share" is given in this model by the set of subjective or emotional (intangible) values. This set of values justifies the relative real position of a company-brand's sales, by explaining the differences in sales between products that a priori offer the same price characteristics and objective factors subject to direct, consistent and comparable quantification using conventional criteria. Therefore, the real market share is simply the theoretical market share adjusted for an image factor:

$$(\%)\,MS_{real} = (\%)\,MS_e \cdot (Im)\,; \; Im = (\%)\,MS_{real}/(\%)\,MS_e$$

The real market share may be formulated fully as:

$$MS(\%)_{real} = (100\%/N)\cdot(E_P)^p \cdot (Ed)^d \cdot (Ec)^c \cdot (Im) \qquad (5.32)$$

where:

MS = market share

N = number of market competitors

P, d, c = substitution elasticities that express the percentage in which the brand's MS would vary for each 1% variation in the corresponding competitive equilibrium

Im = adjustment factor, interpreted as a coefficient that represents the different set of factors or circumstances other

than objective basic equilibrium, fundamentally brand efficiency and brand/product image, if the determination of
Equilibrium of Product (Ep) had only considered objective
and quantifiable measures; and only brand efficiency if the
calculation of perceived value had treated brand as a perceived value.

Logically, under the premise that all competitors operate
with the same competitive equilibria, image and brand-
company efficiency, the market would be divided evenly
among all participants:

$$MS(\%) \ of \ global \ parity = 100\%/N$$

4. **Brand sales potential.** Using the *Im* ratio as a **comparative
index of the set of subjective/image factors** between brands,
the first step in the valuation system for each derives from
the **calculation of the brand sales potential at objective equilibrium parity** *(Ep = Ed = Ec = 1).*

Sales Potential
$$= (100\%/N) \cdot \textbf{\textit{Im}} \cdot MUt \cdot Price(Brand) \rightarrow (at \ Brand \ Price)$$

Actually, the Villafañe & Associates model does no more than
outline the brand's contribution to total company sales. That
is, it calculates how much the brand contributes or has contributed to sales within a determined time period and market,
but does not calculate the "economic" value by discounting
cash flow. Were an appraiser to calculate a brand value based
on this model, he should take two additional steps:

5. **Theoretical brand earnings.** Determined based on the
brand's sales potential and expenses.

6. **Calculation of brand value.** Given by discounting the theoretical brand profits or applying a PER[56] multiple.

Villafañe & Associates model critique

- This model distinguishes between the concepts of "commercial communication" (considered objective and measured through advertising budget and expense) and "brand," (which encompasses all the factors unexplained by the product, distribution and communication equilibria). The model considers that the brand can fully account for the proportion of real market share unexplained by product, distribution and communication equilibrium factors.

- The model's principal objective is not to calculate the brand's economic value, but rather to determine its contribution to sales within a determined market and time period. This is why the literature on the model is not precise on its method of calculating present value of theoretical brand profits, and indicates that this value may be calculated either by discounting future earnings or by applying a PER multiple to brand-related profits in a determined year. This last assumption is subject to Tollington's critique of Interbrand's multiple method regarding the determination of the brand multiple (cf. Section 5.18.1).

5.32 Other brand valuation providers and models

There are many other companies that provide brand valuation services, but do not publish their detailed methodology.

---

[56] These comments are based on personal meetings with Eduardo Moreno of Villafañe & Associates, who generously dedicated time to thoroughly explain the company's methodology to me.

Additionally, certain agencies and academics have published some information on their methodologies, but it is so scarce or confusing that its in-depth description was withheld from this chapter. Below the reader can find a list of providers with undisclosed methodologies as well as methodologies proposed by academics or other institutions on which information is rather scarce or incomplete:

1. American Appraisal

2. Appraisal Economics

3. Beacon Valuation Group

4. Bekmeier-Feuerhahn[57]

5. Bradley Elms Consultants

6. BrandSync

7. Chicago Partners

8. Cogent Valuation

9. Deloitte

10. Equilibrium Consulting

11. Ernst & Young

---

[57] The author decided not to include a description of this methodology, as its procedure and formulation, as described by Zimmermann et al. (2001), was found to be obscure and confusing.

12. Eurobrand

13. Fischer Valuation model (Fischer, 2007)

14. GfK

15. GravitasPartners

16. Inflexion Point

17. InteCap, Inc. (now CRA International)

18. Intellectual Capital Partners, Inc.

19. IPMetrics

20. IP-Valuation

21. KLM, Inc.

22. KPMG

23. Mentor Group

24. Mintz & Partners

25. Morar Consulting

26. MR Valuation Consulting

27. Ocean Tomo

28. ONR 16800[58]

29. Predictiv

30. PwC

31. TATA Economic Consultancy Services

32. Valuation Consulting

33. Vivaldi Partners

34. Willamette Management Associates

From the previous list, we can identify at least three clearly distinct brand valuation models: Bekmeier-Feuerhahn, Fischer and ONR 16800. The rest of the providers listed use methods that could not be determined from the literature. Without considering providers such as AUS Consultants or Houlihan Advisors (who seem to apply general methodologies rather than proprietary methods) or absoluteBRAND (who applies the methodology developed by Intangible Business) or the Residual Approach proposed by Anson (2005) which seems to be quite general, we can conclude that at least 39 proprietary brand valuation methodologies have been developed up to the present day.

---

[58] This refers to the brand valuation standard issued by the Austrian Standards Institute on 1 March 2006, under the name "Method for the valuation of the intangible asset 'brand'." Cf. http://www.on-norm.at/publish/2518. html?&L=1.

The reader should note that multiple citations of GfK, Ernst & Young and PwC models are not redundant. While these firms have developed models jointly with scholars or with other companies in joint venture contexts (cf. Sections 5.3.3 for Ernst & Young and 5.13 for GfK-PwC-Sattler), they are included in the above index primarily because:

- they are independent valuation providers, despite having developed a model in collaboration with a scholar or another company.

- there is no evidence to suggest that the models developed collaboratively and presented earlier in this chapter represent the company's principal valuation methods.

5.33   Conclusions

This chapter has reviewed 40 valuation models that apply to product or service brands, but not to corporate names. Most of the reviewed models are proprietary. A total sum of 63[59] providers, scholars and authors of commercial brand valuation models, and 39 different proprietary brand valuation models have been identified. Of these models, some have been modified and are no longer applied as they were originally conceived, and at least five are no longer actively in use.

[59] Not counting Financial World, which is simply a magazine that often published Interbrand's rankings.

6

A Taxonomy of Brand Valuation Methods

THIS CHAPTER PRESENTS AN ANALYSIS OF CONVERGENCE and divergence of the various methodologies discussed in Chapter 5. It reviews several different classifications previously proposed in the literature, and then attempts to determine relevant criteria for grouping and classifying the methods outlined in Chapter 5. Finally, these methods are effectively classified and compared on the basis of the criteria established through this analysis.

6.1 By use of financial or non-financial indicators

Myers (2003) classifies brand valuation methods as in Figure 6.1.

Chapter 5 addressed the first group; the methods that Myers deems "consumer-related" do not yield a monetary brand value, but rather represent different methods of "brand *evaluation*" (cf. Chapter 1, Section 1.2).

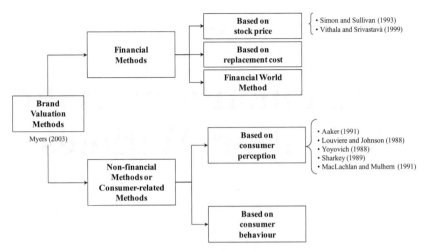

Figure 6.1 Myers' brand valuation model classification.
Source: Developed by author based on Myers (2003)

6.2 By application or possible objectives

Haigh (2000) classifies brand valuation models by distinguishing between:

- **Financially-focused brand valuation models:** This group includes static models that attempt to estimate brand value at a determined moment in time. In general, these models yield aggregate (and not segmented) valuations, and typically consider current use.

- **Strategically-focused brand valuation models:** Dynamic and predictive valuation models fall under this category. These models typically consider market segmentation and potential uses.

Figure 6.2 shows the characteristics of both groups of models.

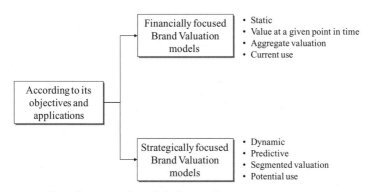

Figure 6.2 Classification of models by applications.
Source: Adapted from Haigh (2000). Reproduced by permission of Brand Finance PLC

6.3 Classification proposed by BBDO

Zimmerman et al. (2001) propose the following four groups for the classification of brand valuation methods:

- Financial models

- Psychographic or behavioral models

- Financial-behavioral models

- Portfolio or "input/output" models

Figure 6.3 summarizes the characteristics of the four groups of models.

The "Psychographical/Behavioral" models are not models of brand "valuation" but rather of "*evaluation*" (cf. Chapter 1, Section 1.2). The same may be said of "Portfolio" or "Input/Output" methods, which can only yield relative (and not absolute) values. Figure 6.4 shows many of the methods we have described, classified in accordance with the taxonomy proposed by Zimmerman et al. (2001).

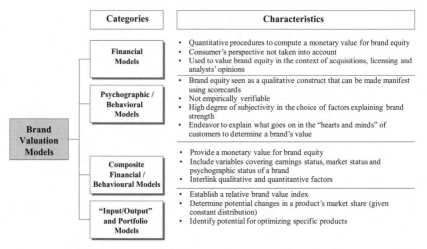

Figure 6.3 Characteristics of different categories of brand valuation models according to BBDO.
Source: Zimmermann et al. (2001). Reproduced by permission of Schmindt Axel/BBDO Consulting GmbH

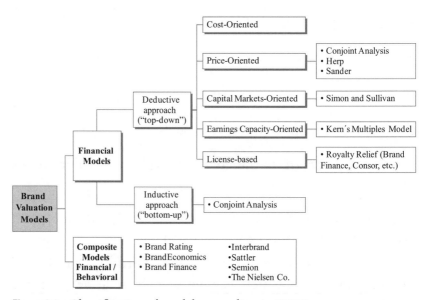

Figure 6.4 Classification of models according to BBDO
Source: Developed by author based on Zimmermann et al. (2001)

6.4 Classifications based on mixed criteria

Some authors have developed classification systems that are based on complex criteria. For example, Motameni and Shahrokhi (1998) propose a hybrid classification of brand valuation models centered on two criteria:

- use of financial and non-financial indicators

- type of approach employed.

The authors cite six general "brand equity valuation" methods proposed by Aaker (1991: 22–27) and Kapferer (1992: ch. 11):

1. *Valuation based on marketing and R&D expenses*: According to the authors, this method values the brand based on the aggregate advertising, marketing and R&D expenses invested in it over a given period of time. The logic behind this model is that brand value originates from this type of investment.

2. *Valuation based on price premiums*: This method values the brand based on the extra revenue yielded by price differentials. Under this approach, the price premium may be determined through simple market observation, or measured through market research.

3. *Valuation at market value*: This approach uses objective market measures, thereby allowing for comparisons between companies over time.

4. *Valuation based on consumer factors*: This approach involves factors such as loyalty, awareness, memorability,

and other features measured through surveys designed to track consumers' preferences and attitudes.

5. *Valuation based on future earnings potential*: By discounting future earnings at present value, this approach may conceivably avoid the disadvantages of the historical cost approach.

6. *Valuation at replacement cost*: This method seeks to overcome the flaws of the historical cost approach.

Sattler, Högl and Hupp (2002) distinguish between three categories of brand valuation methodologies:

- Those *based on cost*, such as System Repenn.

- Those based on *evaluations of analogous licenses*. The authors note that this method of valuation is only valid when the benchmark brand and the brand being valued are more or less identical. They cite the Andersen, KPMG and System Repenn models as examples.

- *Indicator models*, such as Interbrand's or Semion's.

6.5 By intended universality of the calculated value

Roos (2005) classifies brand valuation methods by distinguishing those that yield a single universal value for all viewers from those that yield a specific value for the viewer – see Figure 6.5.

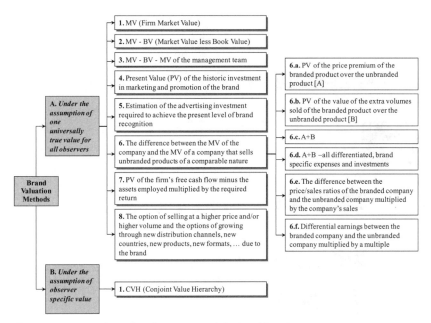

Figure 6.5 Roos' brand valuation model classification.
Source: Roos (2005), Fernández (2001). © ICS Ltd 2005. Reproduced by permission of ICS Ltd.

Although Göran Roos does not cite specific examples, these methods correspond to those we reviewed in Chapter 5; the procedure described in 6.f. is that used by Interbrand, method 7 is that of Houlihan Valuation Advisors and AUS Consultants, etc.

6.6 By its nature or origin (academic vs. commercial)

In order to arrive at an analysis of convergence and divergence of the methods developed within the academic world and those devised by corporations or smaller marketing divisions thereof, we have grouped the models reviewed in Chapter 5

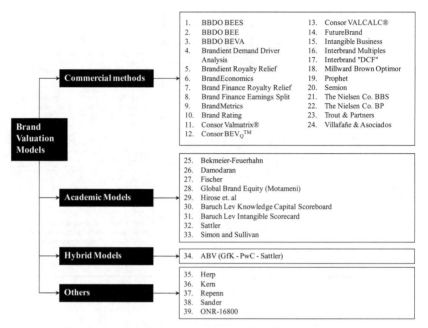

1.	BBDO BEES	13.	Consor VALCALC®
2.	BBDO BEE	14.	FutureBrand
3.	BBDO BEVA	15.	Intangible Business
4.	Brandient Demand Driver Analysis	16.	Interbrand Multiples
		17.	Interbrand "DCF"
5.	Brandient Royalty Relief	18.	Millward Brown Optimor
6.	BrandEconomics	19.	Prophet
7.	Brand Finance Royalty Relief	20.	Semion
8.	Brand Finance Earnings Split	21.	The Nielsen Co. BBS
9.	BrandMetrics	22.	The Nielsen Co. BP
10.	Brand Rating	23.	Trout & Partners
11.	Consor Valmatrix®	24.	Villafañe & Asociados
12.	Consor BEV$_Q$™		

25.	Bekmeier-Feuerhahn
26.	Damodaran
27.	Fischer
28.	Global Brand Equity (Motameni)
29.	Hirose et. al
30.	Baruch Lev Knowledge Capital Scoreboard
31.	Baruch Lev Intangible Scorecard
32.	Sattler
33.	Simon and Sullivan

34.	ABV (GfK - PwC - Sattler)

35.	Herp
36.	Kern
37.	Repenn
38.	Sander
39.	ONR-16800

Figure 6.6 Academic, commercial and hybrid methodologies.
Source: Developed by author

by the context of their development (see Figure 6.6). They are thus classified as academic, commercial or hybrid, or mixed (as in the case of those methods developed collaboratively by scholars and providers).

The above figure effectively categorizes a total of 39 proprietary brand valuation models, excluding those that involve largely opaque or undisclosed methodologies (cf. Chapter 5, Section 5.32).

Those methods that could not be classified as academic, commercial or hybrid, have been placed in the "others" category.

6.7 By approach employed (cost, market and income)

As we saw in Chapter 4, there are three basic approaches to measuring brand value (International Valuation Guidance Note 4, Cravens and Guilding, 1999; Seetheraman et al., 2001):

1. cost

2. market

3. income.

An additional category, "mixed," is often included to describe those methods that combine two or more approaches. Therefore, while the royalty relief methodology sometimes falls under the "income" category, it is often considered "mixed," as it combines both income and market perspectives. "Real Option Valuation" may also appear as a separate category in certain classification systems.

Figure 6.7 below shows the methodologies presented in Chapters 4 and 5 classified by approach.[60]

[60] In Figure 6.7 we have included Futurebrand's methodology as non-general. In fact, it could be classified as general since its demand driver analysis module is identical to the RBI module from the Interbrand DCF model and its competitive benchmarking analysis is very similar to Brand Finance's. But as the combination of both modules or procedures is unique, in the context of this work, it will be classified as a non-general methodology.

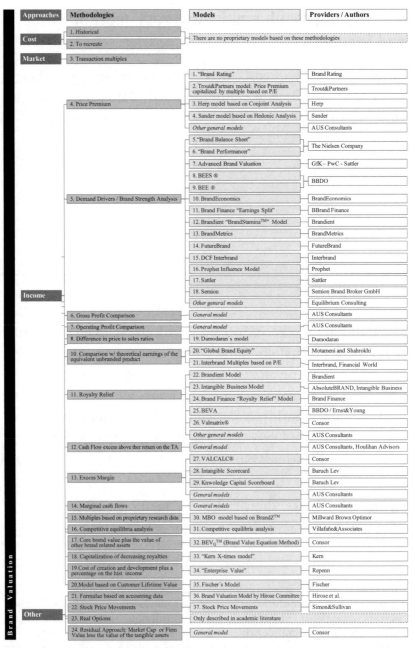

Figure 6.7 Classification of brand valuation methodologies by approach.
Source: Developed by author

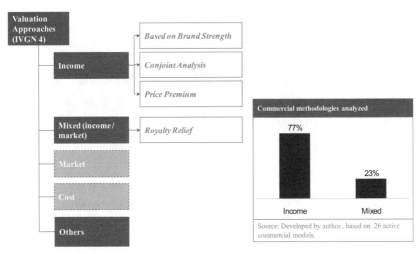

Figure 6.8 Distribution of methods by valuation approach.
Source: Developed by author

Figure 6.8 shows that of the *commercial* methodologies actively employed, 77% are based on the income approach, while 23% apply a mixed approach (mostly royalty relief[61]).

Our analysis shows that the majority of the methodologies reviewed pertain to companies whose services are strikingly marketing-oriented, and that therefore those based on demand driver analysis ("reasons-to-buy") or brand strength (in order to determine earnings attributable to brand) are the most prevalent.

We have not identified any companies that use the market, cost or real options approach as their principal methodology. But in practice, many companies use market- or cost-based techniques as secondary methods whose results may be

---

[61] Many authors find that the royalty relief method, here classified as "mixed," more accurately falls under the "income" approach.

effectively compared with those yielded by the primary methodology.

Among the mixed and income-based methodologies, we have observed great diversity in estimation models and high levels of consistency in the application of the royalty savings approach.

The very fact that the majority of commercial methodologies subscribe to the income approach leads us to carefully consider the two key variables in this approach:

- income attributable to brand;

- appropriate discount rate for discounting cash flow or profits attributable to brand.

The following two secondary variables allow us to analyze in deeper depth the procedural differences between various models:

- designation of the brand's useful life as finite or indefinite;

- representation of growth.

We shall effectively analyze these differences by examining other classifications based on the four variables proposed, and comprehensively comparing the methods on the basis of:

- the techniques used to determine the proportion of income attributable to brand;

- their representation of brand risk;

- their representation of the brand's useful life;

- their representation of growth.

6.8 By method of determining the proportion of income or revenues attributable to brand

This step constitutes the central element for the majority of brand valuation models.

In our review, we have detected at least 16 different procedures for calculating the brand's contribution to earnings, profits or cash flow, as shown in Figure 6.9.

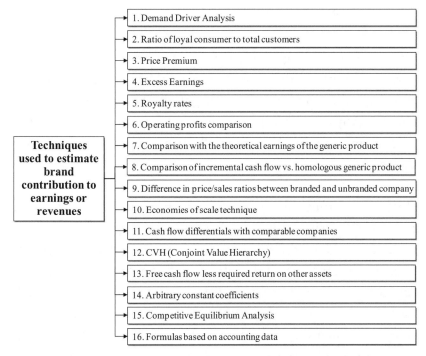

Figure 6.9 Classification of brand valuation models by method of determining the proportion of earnings or revenue attributable to brand.
Source: Developed by author based on Smith and Parr (2000), Pike and Roos (2004), Haigh (2000), Fernández (2001) and Damodaran (1996)

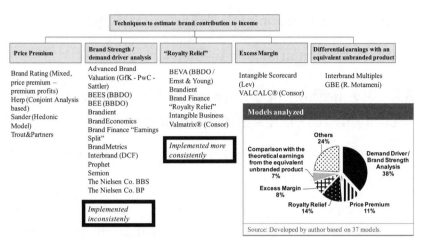

Figure 6.10 Providers and principal methods of calculating brand contribution to income.
Source: Developed by author

Of the methodologies identified in Chapter 5,[62] 38% use brand strength or demand drivers analysis to determine the proportion of earnings or profits attributable to brand; 14% use the royalty savings method, while only 11% use the price premium method, and 8% use excess earnings – see Figure 6.10.

Within the income approach, the methodologies based on royalty relief show high levels of consistency, while the rest evidence widely different methods of calculation, with at least 10 different general methodologies at work. Various differences are also observed within each methodology, as each varies in its basic configuration, components, selection of relevant indicators, method of calculation, assumptions, etc.

---

[62] Here, Bekmeier-Feuerhahn and the methodology proposed by the standard ONR-16800 are not taken into account given the lack of precise information on them.

Six academics who have independently developed brand valuation methods also propose six wholly different models, which again manifests the vast intellectual variation and diversity of brand valuation models developed in the academic arena.

The majority of these models were loosely outlined in Chapter 4; Chapter 5 discussed their commercial applications. In the next section, we will compare different "providers'" and scholars' implementation of each of these methodologies.

6.8.1 Demand driver analysis

Different companies have applied this approach in different ways. In this section, we will describe several models currently implemented by consultants and academics, as well as obsolete models that are no longer used – see Table 6.1.

6.8.2 Ratio of loyal consumers to total consumers

Millward Brown Optimor uses this technique based on a market research tool called BranDynamics, as shown in Table 6.2.

6.8.3 Price premium

Different companies and authors vary in their implementation of this approach based on the determination of the price or utility differential between the brand being valued and that of benchmark brands or products (see Table 6.3). Further discussion of this method may be found in Section 4.3.1.

6.8.4 Excess earnings

This method, originally conceived to value intangible assets, is embodied in Revenue Ruling 68-609, but some authors use modified versions of it, as shown in Table 6.4.

Table 6.1 Different methods of demand driver analysis for the determination of brand profits

Model / company	Indicator / coefficient	Applicable to	Type of analysis	Based on
1. BBDO BEES®	"Weighting factor"	Average pre-tax earnings	"Black Box"	Analysis of brand strength attributes
2. BBDO BEE®	"Weighting factor"	Present value of after-tax cash flow	"Black Box"	Analysis of brand strength attributes
3. Brandient	"Role of Brand"	"Earnings"	"Black Box"	"Market Research Analysis"
4. Brand Economics, LLC	Multiple	Annual Sales	Statistical	Analysis of brand strength attributes and their connection to EVA
5. Brand Finance plc	BVA® percentage (Brand Value Added Index)	EVA	Statistical	Demand driver analysis
6. Brand Metrics	Dilution® percentage	NOPAT	Statistical (Delphi technique)	Demand driver analysis
7. FutureBrand	Percentage	EVA or Free Cash Flow	"Black Box"	Demand driver analysis
8. GfK – PwC – Sattler ("Advanced Brand Valuation Model")	Price premium and incremental units attributable to brand determined through relative brand strength (BPI), less brand-related expenses		• Conjoint analysis • Causal regression analysis (BPI and other factors not related to brand vs. price premium and market share)	Brand strength analysis (BPI)

9. Interbrand ("DCF model")	RBI (Role of Brand Index)	EVA	"Black Box"	Demand driver analysis
10. Prophet	"Brand influence" percentage	Cash flow	"Black Box"	Demand driver analysis
11. Sattler (1997 model)	Brand value indicators	Function coefficients that link indicators with long-term brand profits	Expert survey to determine indicators Regression and conjoint analysis to determine their importance	Analysis of brand strength attributes
12. Semion	Weighting factor	Average pre-tax earnings for the last 3 years	Arbitrary	Analysis of brand strength, image, protection and financial status
13. The Nielsen Company ("Brand Performance")	Relative brand strength factor (RBSi)	Potential market earnings (=industry sales * net operating margin in the sector)	"Black Box"	Analysis of brand strength attributes (Brand Monitor Module)

Source: Developed by author

Table 6.2 Millward Brown Optimor's method of determining income attributable to brand

Model/ company	Indicator/ coefficient	Applicable to	Type of analysis	Based on
1. Millward Brown Optimor	"Brand contribution"	Intangible earnings (= EVA in the context of this model)	MBO's description makes this stage sound rather like a mathematical operation (division), and not a proper "analysis"	Ratio of loyal customers to total customers (based on BranDynamics and BrandZ data)

Source: Developed by author

6.8.5 Royalty rates

Different companies vary in their implementation of this approach based on the analysis of comparable agreements, common practices in the sector, and brand strength attributes – see Table 6.5.

6.8.6 Operating profits comparison

In this method, operating profits are expressed as a sales percentage, compared with the operating profit ratio of a set of comparables, and later multiplied by income from sales associated with the brand being valued, to yield profits attributable to brand. The application of this technique is described in greater detail in Chapter 4, Section 4.3.5.

Table 6.3 Methods of calculating brand profits based on price premium

Model/company	Indicator/coefficient	Applicable to	Type of analysis
1. AUS Consultants	Smith and Parr (2000) propose two ways of performing this calculation:		Direct observation (no analysis). Smith and Parr (2000) suggest that the price of the brand being valued may be compared with that charged by a private label manufacturer
	• The difference in forecasted sales revenues between the branded product and a generic product for a determined period of time, assuming that both companies sell the same volume of the product or service	• In this case, the result is direct, obviating the need for ulterior operations	
	• Unit price differential between both companies	• Forecasted sales volume	
2. Brand Rating	The past 3 years' average price differential relative to a generic product in the same category	Number of units sold	Direct observation (no analysis)
3. Herp	The brand's relative utility compared to that of other non-generic benchmark brands	Number of units sold	Statistical (Conjoint analysis)
4. Sander	Hedonic pricing methods (variation in unit price resulting from a variation in the brand as a product characteristic)	Number of units sold	Statistical (Multiple regression)
5. Trout & Partners	Price premium index	Category value * market share * tax rate	Direct observation (no analysis)

Source: Developed by author

Table 6.4 Variations of the excess earnings method used to determine brand earnings

Model, provider or author	Earnings attributable to all intangible assets	Notes
1. RR 68-609	$$EE_{IA} = E_B - E_{TA}$$ Where: • EE_{IA} is the average annual earnings attributable to the business' intangible asset portfolio • E_B is the average earnings of the business • E_{TA} is the earnings attributable to tangible assets $$E_{TA} = \text{Calculated at} \begin{cases} 8\% \text{ for low risk} \\ 10\% \text{ for high risk} \end{cases}$$	• Arbitrary • Determines the average earnings attributable to the intangible asset portfolio as a whole, not to any one asset in particular
2. "Knowledge Capital Scoreboard" and "Intangibles Scoreboard," Prof. Baruch Lev, NYU	$$EE_{IA} = E_B - E_{FA} - E_{TA} = E_B - 4.5\% * V_{FA} - 7\% * V_{TA}$$ Where: • EE_{IA} is the average annual earnings attributable to the business' total portfolio of intangible assets • E_B is the business' average earnings • E_{FA} is the average earnings attributable to financial assets; the result of multiplying the adjusted book Value of Financial Assets (V_{FA}) by the after tax rate of return, which Lev sets arbitrarily at 4.5% • E_{TA} is the average earnings from tangible assets; the result of multiplying the adjusted book value of Tangible Assets (V_{TA}) by the after-tax rate of return, which Lev sets arbitrarily at 7%	• Arbitrary • Determines the average earnings attributable to all intangible assets, and not that of any one asset in particular
3. AUS Consultants (Smith, 1997)	$$E_b = E_t - (E_{wc} + E_{ta} + E_{ia})$$ Where: • E_b = earnings attributable to brand • E_t = total company earnings • E_{wc} = total earnings attributable to net working capital • E_{ta} = total earnings attributable to tangible assets • E_{ia} = total earnings attributable to intangible assets other than brand	• The determination of returns on tangible assets and on intangible assets other than brand are both arbitrary

Source: Developed by author based on Pratt (2002: 177), Lev (1999), Andriessen (2004), Hofmann (2005) and Smith (1997)

Table 6.5 Methods of calculating brand earnings through royalty relief

Model/company	Indicator/coefficient	Applicable to	Type of analysis
1. AbsoluteBrand	Royalty rate	Net revenue from forecasted sales	• Analysis of comparables in the sector • Demand drivers analysis
2. AUS Consultants	Royalty rate	Net revenue from forecasted sales	• Analysis of comparables when there is an active market
3. Brand Finance	Royalty rate	Net revenue from forecasted sales	• Analysis of comparables in the sector • Brand strength analysis
4. Consor	Average royalty rate as percentage of wholesale product prices	Net revenue from forecasted sales	• Analysis of comparables in the sector
5. Intangible Business	Royalty rate	Net revenue from forecasted sales	• Analysis of comparables in the sector • Brand strength analysis (BSA)
6. BEVA (Ernst & Young and BBDO)	Royalty rate	Net revenue from forecasted sales	• Brand strength analysis (BBDO's 5 level model) • "S-curve" that links strength and royalty rates
7. Kern's x-times model	Normal royalty rate for the industry	Estimation of sales revenue through an increasing function with a decreasing slope, i.e., a rational function	• Royalty rate determined through expert opinions

Source: Developed by author

6.8.7 Comparison with theoretical earnings yielded by a generic product

Three models use this approach based on a comparison between the earnings of the brand being valued and those that would hypothetically be yielded by an otherwise equivalent generic product, as illustrated in Table 6.6. The companies that employ this technique vary in their implementation thereof.

6.8.8 Comparison of the cash flows of branded and unbranded companies

Here, the income attributable to the brand is estimated by considering the brand effect on different value drivers (cf. Chapter 4, Section 4.3.8), as shown in Table 6.7.

6.8.9 Difference in price to sales ratios

Damodaran (1996) proposes valuing brands based on differences in price/sales ratios, shown in Table 6.8.

6.8.10 Economies of scale

In this method, the gross margin of the business being valued is compared with the average gross margin of a group of comparable competitors. The difference yielded is then multiplied by sales revenues attributable to brand, and the resulting figure represents earnings attributable to brand. This technique is discussed in depth in Chapter 4, Section 4.3.4.

6.8.11 Differences in cash flow with a benchmark company

This technique assumes that the difference in net cash flow between the subject company (the company owning the brand

Table 6.6 Methods of calculating brand earnings compared with theoretical earnings of a generic product

Model/company	Brand earnings	Assumptions	Type of analysis
1. Financial World	$E_{FW} = E_b - E_g$ Where • E_{FW} is operating earnings attributable to brand according to Financial World • E_b is operating earnings of the business associated with the brand being valued • E_g is estimated earnings for an otherwise equivalent generic product	In the calculation of earnings for an otherwise equivalent generic product, it is assumed that: • the return on capital employed for the generic product will be 5 % • capital employed will be equal to the product of the branded sales multiplied by the median ratio of capital employed to firm sales in the sector	The assumptions underlying the calculation of the earnings of an equivalent generic product are arbitrary.
2. Motameni and Shahrokhi's "Global Brand Equity" Model	Idem FW	Idem FW	Idem FW
3 Interbrand	$E_{IB} = EBIT_b - EBIT_g - CR - T$ Where: • E_{IB} is earnings attributable to the brand according to Interbrand • $EBIT_b$ is earnings of the business associated with the brand being valued • $EBIT_g$ is earnings estimated for a private label product • CR is the capital remuneration • T is applicable taxes	The difference between this model and the two listed above it is that much like the EVA approach, this method deducts capital remuneration from the EBIT differential	The assumptions underlying the calculation of an equivalent generic product are arbitrary

Source: Developed by author

Table 6.7 Methods of calculating brand cash flow through comparison with theoretical cash flow of a generic product

Model/company	Brand cash flow	Type of analysis
1. AUS Consultants	Comparison of the cash flows of branded and unbranded companies	Comparative

Source: Developed by author

Table 6.8 Methods of calculating brand profits through differences in price/sales ratios

Model/ company	Indicator/ coefficient	Applicable to	Type of analysis
Damodaran	$\left[\left(\dfrac{P}{S}\right)_b - \left(\dfrac{P}{S}\right)_u\right]$ (Difference in price to sales ratio between the branded company and a generic product)	Sales revenues	• Analysis of financial statements to get inputs to calculate the P/S ratio for the branded company and estimation of the generic comparable parameters.

Source: Developed by author

being valued) and a group of comparable companies that have no trademark derives wholly from the brand factor. For further discussion of this approach, see Chapter 4, Section 4.3.7.

6.8.12 CVH (Conjoint Value Hierarchy)

This methodology, developed by ICS (Intellectual Capital Services), measures intangible resources' contribution to value through an empirical system that models the company's intellectual capital, and later creates isomorphic curves to estimate the results – see Table 6.9.

Table 6.9 Methods that apply CVH to calculate profits attributable to brand

Model/ company	Indicator/ coefficient	Applicable to	Type of analysis	Based on
ICS (Intellectual Capital Services)	CVH	"Value of the company"	Statistical (Conjoint analysis). Importance determined by a management board or external stakeholders	Analysis of general attributes

Source: Developed by author

6.8.13 Free cash flow less required return on assets other than brand

At least two companies determine free cash flow attributable to brand and/or intangible assets as free cash flow less return on tangible or intangible assets other than brand – see Table 6.10.

6.8.14 Arbitrary constant coefficients

Repenn estimates the brand's contribution to historical earnings from the past five years as a constant at 10%. This percentage, known as the "Repenn Factor," is added to the costs of creating and maintaining the brand – see Table 6.11.

6.8.15 Competitive equilibrium analysis

Villafañe & Associates apply an "Objective Equilibriums Model" to estimate global values attributable to the differential between competing brands on the basis of their sales in the relevant market.

Table 6.10 Methods of calculating brand profit as free cash flow less return on assets other than brand

Model/company	Free cash flow attributable to brand/intangible assets	Notes
1. AUS Consultants	$FCF_{IP} = FCF_B - RR_{OTA}$ Where: • FCF_{IP} is free cash flow attributable to intellectual property • FCF_B is the business' free cash flow • RR_{OTA} is the required return on other tangible assets	• Determines free cash flow attributable to all intellectual property assets
2. Houlihan Advisors	$FCF_m = FCF_B - RR_{OA}$ Where: • FCF_m is free cash flow attributable to brand • FCF_B is the business' free cash flow • RR_{OA} is the required return on the business' assets other than brand	• According to Houlihan Advisors, this determines free cash flow attributable to brand

Source: Developed by author

Table 6.11 Methods based on arbitrary constant coefficients

Model/company	Indicator/coefficient	Applicable to	Type of analysis
Repenn Model	Brand contribution is set at 10 % ("Repenn Factor") and deemed constant and independent of all brand variables	Historical earnings (past five years)	• Arbitrary • No analysis

Source: Developed by author

This method is very similar to price premium analyses; the primary difference is that instead of assuming variations in pricing, it assumes variations in volume. In this model, the brand's differential value is determined as:

$$S_b = [(MS_R - MS_E) * MU_t] * P_b \qquad (6.1)$$

where:

S_b = the value of sales attributable to brand

MS_R = the real market share

MS_E = the equilibrium market share

MU_t = the size of the market in units

P_b = the current price of the brand

6.8.16 Equations based on accounting data

Hirose et al. (2002) propose an equation based primarily on accounting data for the determination of income attributable to brand, as shown in Table 6.12.

6.9 By method of "representing brand risk"

6.9.1 Comparison of models by representation of brand risk

Various models consider and configure the risk factors for the brand being valued in very different ways, as shown in Table 6.13 below.

Table 6.12 Equations based on accounting data

Model/ company	Indicator/coefficient	Type of analysis
Hirose et al. (2002)	PD * LD * ED = Brand earnings Where: PD = excess profit ratio * brand attribution rate * cost of sales LD = (average cost of sales − standard deviation of cost of sales)/average cost of sales ED = average growth rate of overseas sales and sales in non-core business segments	• Arbitrary • No analysis

Source: Developed by author

6.9.2   Classification by representation of brand risk

Of the 39 commercial and academic methodologies studied, nearly 60% use models of risk based on discount rates (see Figure 6.11 below). Of the 23 models that explicitly consider risk as a discount rate, more than 40% use Weighted Average Cost of Capital (WACC) or the Capital Asset Pricing Model (CAPM) to calculate the discount rate. Of the models that use WACC or CAPM, 70% adjust the discount factor in light of brand-specific risk. Multiples are applied in 15% of the models reviewed. But in most of these models (and especially those in which the multiple is not based on P/E ratio), the multiple is not related to the capitalization rate, and therefore has no grounding in corporate finance theory.[63]

Although the practice of adjusting the discount rate has received recent criticism in academic forums, it is widely accepted in the fields of brand, intangible asset and financial asset valuation.

[63] Strictly speaking, these methodologies should not be included under the "income" approach, given that they apply neither a discount rate nor a capitalization rate to convert future income into present value.

Table 6.13 Classification of methods by their approach to "brand risk"

Model/company	Risk factor	Model	Adjustments	Notes
1. AUS Consultants	Discount rate	• Factor models (CAPM or APT) when the commercial viability of the investment is high • Capital risk models in other cases	No	In CAPM, quantification of risk by comparison: The risk measure to value IP assets and brands is estimated by studying the betas of listed companies that are highly dependent on the same kind of brand as the brand being valued
2. BBDO BEE®	Discount rate	CAPM	Brand-specific risk premium	The method of determining brand-specific risk premium is not disclosed
3. BEVA (BBDO and Ernst & Young)	Discount rate	N/A	Adjusted by brand risk	The method of determining the brand risk adjustment factor is not disclosed
4. Brandient	Discount rate	CAPM, WACC	The company's systematic risk is adjusted by *Brand Stamina*™ (brand earnings risk indicator)	According to Brandient, *Brand Stamina*™ measures the brand's strength and vitality. How exactly this is determined is not disclosed

Table 6.13 *Continued*

Model/company	Risk factor	Model	Adjustments	Notes
5. Brand Finance	Discount rate	CAPM, WACC	Systematic risk is adjusted by βrand βeta®	Quantification of risk by comparison: The βrand βeta®, that represents brand risk, is calculated on the basis of competitive benchmarking or brand strength analysis
6. BrandMetrics	Discount rate	CAPM, WACC	No adjustment; this method uses the company's WACC	
7. Brand Rating	Discount rate	N/A	Adjusted by brand risk	
8. Consor	Discount rate	CAPM, WACC	No adjustment; this method uses the company's WACC	
9. FutureBrand	Discount rate	CAPM, WACC	Systematic risk adjusted by the Brand Risk Index	Quantification of risk by comparison: The Brand Risk Index is calculated on the basis of competitive benchmarking or brand strength analysis
10. GfK – PwC – Sattler ("Advanced Brand Valuation Model")	Discount rate	WACC	Adjusted by brand-specific risk	Brand-specific risk is calculated on the basis of brand strength

11. Hirose et al. (2002)	Discount rate	Risk-free rate	No adjustment; this method simply uses the risk-free rate	Calculated based on performance of the sovereign bond
12. Houlihan Advisors	Discount rate	WACC	No adjustment; this method uses the company's WACC	
13. Intangible Business	Discount rate	CAPM, WACC	No adjustment; this method uses the company's WACC	
14. Intangibles Scoreboard (Lev)	Discount rate	N/A	Adjusted by brand risk	N/A
15. Interbrand DCF	Discount rate	"S-curve" based on P/E ratio		Quantification of risk based on an "S-curve" that links brand strength scores with applicable discount rates
16. Interbrand Multiples	Multiple	"S-curve" based on P/E ratio		Quantification of risk based on an "S-curve" that links brand strength scores with multiples
17. Global Brand Equity (Motameni and Shahrokhi)	Multiple	Idem Interbrand multiples		Idem Interbrand multiples
18. Kern's x-times model	Discount rate	"Normal interest rate for the country"	No brand risk adjustment	

Table 6.13 *Continued*

Model/company	Risk factor	Model	Adjustments	Notes
19. The Nielsen Company Brand Balance Sheet	Discount rate	Risk premium + long-term market rate	Risk premium adjusted by brand-specific risk	The mechanism by which the risk premium is adjusted is not fully disclosed
20. The Nielsen Company Brand Performance	Discount rate	Rate of risk is a function of the sector risk	No	
21. Prophet	Discount rate	CAPM, WACC	Systematic risk is adjusted by Brand Risk Index	Quantification of risk by comparison: The Brand Risk Index is calculated on the basis of competitive benchmarking or brand strength analysis
22. Sattler (1997 model)	Discount rate	N/A	N/A	
23. Trout & Partners	Capital-ization multiple	Based on P/E ratio	Risk adjustment	The risk adjustment is determined on the basis of customer loyalty surveys
24. Villafañe & Associates	Discount rate or Multiple	N/A	N/A	

Source: Developed by author

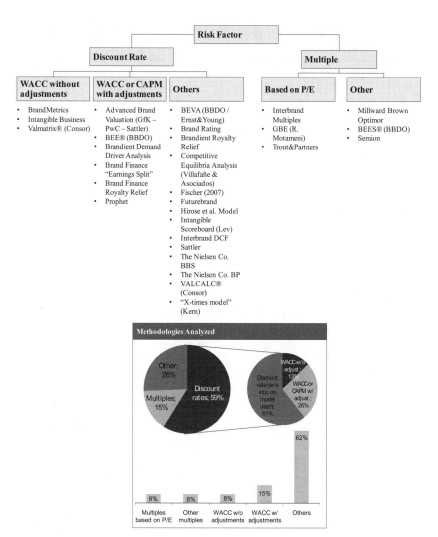

Figure 6.11 Classification by representation of risk.
Source: Developed by author

6.10 By method of "representing the brand's growth and useful life"

These two variables also illustrate convergence and divergence among different approaches used by scholars and providers, as shown in Table 6.14.

Table 6.14 Classification by method of representing long-term brand growth and useful life

Model/Company	Annuity (finite useful life)		Perpetuity (indefinite useful life)		Others
	Without growth	With growth	Without growth	With growth	
1. Brand Finance				✓	
2. BrandMetrics		✓			
3. Brand Rating			✓		
4. Consor Valmatrix®		✓			
5. Futurebrand				✓	
6. GfK – PwC – Sattler				✓	
7. Hirose et al. (2002)			✓		
8. Houlihan Advisors				✓	
9. Intangibles Scoreboard (Lev)				✓	Model of growth in 3 stages
10. Intangible Business				✓	
11. Interbrand DCF		✓		✓	
12. Kern's x-times model					Annuity with a positive decreasing slope for the brand value growth curve
13. Millward Brown Optimor					Brand Momentum: Reflects only short-term growth.

Table 6.14 *Continued*

Model/Company	Annuity (finite useful life)		Perpetuity (indefinite useful life)		Others
	Without growth	With growth	Without growth	With growth	
14. Sattler (1997)					Perpetuity. There is no information on the representation of growth.
15. The Nielsen Company Brand Balance Sheet		✓			
16. The Nielsen Company Brand Performance		✓			

Source: Developed by author

The classification presented in Table 6.14 reflects the ways in which most authors present their models in their commercial literature, and does not indicate the only possible way of applying them. The models used by Consor and Brand Finance, among other providers, are highly flexible regarding the variables of useful life and growth. There may be various reasons behind this flexible approach: sometimes, the brand's remaining useful life may be depicted as finite, based on a genuine analysis of circumstances surrounding the brand, the market, and the category; at other times, this depiction merely reflects a typical accounting situation. Because accountants generally prefer to know with certainty how much they are going to amortize year to year and avoid having to recognize an impairment, accounting practices often involve designating a finite useful life for the brand.

6.10.1 Classification by representation of the brand's useful life and long-term growth

Of the 39 models studied, 14 specifically represent the brand's useful life and expected growth. As mentioned in the previous section, the analysis presented here manifests the way in which providers typically present these variables in their commercial literature, and by no means dictates the manner in which the said variables are to be treated in subsequent applications of the models in which they appear.

Of the 14 models that involve these variables, 50% use the growing perpetuity formula, while 21% use the constant perpetuity formula. Twenty-one percent also tend to represent time and expected growth through an annuity with growth. The rest of the models use other formulas. The classification is shown in Figure 6.12.

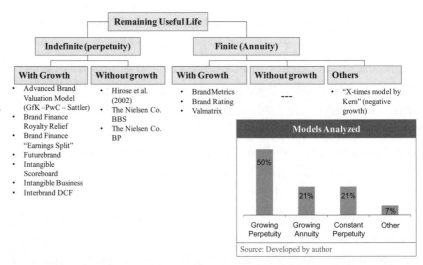

Figure 6.12 Classification by representation of useful life and expected long-term growth.
Source: Developed by author

7

The Current Situation

I N CHAPTER 6, WE COMPARED VALUATION METHODS proposed by various practitioners and reviewed several different classifications thereof. In this chapter, we will analyze the current status of brand valuation by examining how these methods are put into practice. We will begin by reviewing current methodological and industry trends, and outlining common errors made in valuation practices. Finally, we will discuss the most prevalent and notorious problems associated with brand valuation today.

7.1 General trends in brand valuation

In the comparative analysis described in Chapter 6, we identified at least 14 general trends in brand valuation. These trends may be classified into two large groups: *industry trends* and *methodological trends*. *Industry trends* refer to developments observed in the marketing behavior of practitioners. *Methodological trends* refer to changes in the components and modules that constitute the methods we have presented.

Among the *industry trends*, we count:

1. Recent proliferation of proprietary methods and brand valuation firms.

2. Lack of understanding and credibility among users about brand valuation.

3. Concentration of commercial offer and academic developments in Anglo-Saxon countries.

4. Increasing professionalism in the sector and sophistication in valuation techniques.

5. Growing convergence between marketing specialists and corporate finance experts, evidenced in the development of valuation models that involve both areas of knowledge.

6. Widespread use of certain models, i.e. the adoption of popular methods by practitioners.

7. Disparity between models' popularity/commercial success, and their financial validity from a corporate finance theory perspective.

8. Differences between methodologies proposed by scholars and those proposed and applied by practitioners.

9. Proliferation of detrimental "black box" methods.

The *methodological trends* include:

1. Vast inconsistency in the application and execution of similar theoretical models, except in the case of royalty saving methods.

2. Differences in the implementation of income-based models, particularly regarding the techniques used to determine cash flows and discount rates.

3. Substantial divergence of results yielded by different methods.

4. Widespread use of income-based models that assume an indefinite life for the brand.

5. Widespread use of risk models that include WACC adjustments.

We will now address each of these trends individually.

7.1.1 Proliferation of proprietary methods and brand valuation firms

Up until 1995, there were only five companies specializing in brand valuation that had developed at least five different proprietary brand valuation models. At that time, four academics and independent authors had presented their own valuation models. As we have seen, today there are at least 39 different proprietary brand valuation models practiced by different academics, independent scholars and companies "specializing in brand valuation." In total, we have identified 63 authors and providers of brand valuation models. The principal brand valuation practitioners and authors include:

- "Branding" and marketing companies that have ventured into the field of brand valuation (BBDO, Brand Rating, Interbrand, FutureBrand).

- Market research firms that have elaborated valuation methods founded on the results of their quantitative research (The Nielsen Company, Millward Brown, GfK).

- Companies specializing in economic valuation that have expanded their services into intangible asset valuation (AUS Consultants).

- Intangible asset valuation specialists (Brand Finance, Intangible Business, etc.).

- Intellectual property attorneys and agents.

- The "Big 4" and other audit firms.

- Academics with proprietary models (Lev, Damodaran, Sattler, etc.).

Figure 7.1 shows the frequency distribution by provider type, based on those identified in Chapter 5.

In addition, most of these *practitioners use more than one methodology*, not to mention the multiple variations and adaptations of their models. In Chapter 5, we saw that AUS Consultants and Brand Finance both select their approach from among a host of methodologies, in light of the objective of the valuation and the data currently available. Commercial literature on the "Big 4" indicates that these firms also apply

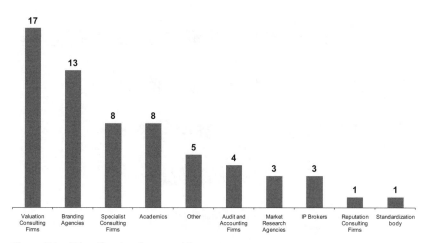

Figure 7.1 Distribution by provider type.
Source: Developed by author. Sample: 63 providers and authors

various methodologies in their brand valuation schemes, depending on the nature and circumstances of the project at hand.

The very fact that most practitioners equip themselves with a "set of methods" is also reflected on the user end of the situation. According to a study carried out in Germany, *63% of all companies that do value brands use two or more different methods* (Günther and Kriegbaum-Kling, 2001: 281).

7.1.2 Lack of understanding and credibility among brand valuation users

Perhaps the most detrimental aspect of the "explosion of brand valuation models and practitioners" has been the tremendous confusion and lack of credibility on the part of valuation users, be they financial officers or marketing specialists. In a 2001 survey of 79 German companies, nearly 40% affirmed that they had not carried out a brand valuation because "there

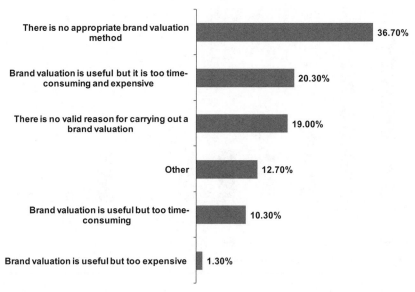

Figure 7.2 Reasons for not carrying out a brand valuation (sample: 79 companies).
Source: Günther and Kriegbaum-Kling (2001). Reproduced by permission of Handelsblatt GmbH

is no suitable method for brand valuation" (Günther and Kriegbaum-Kling, 2001: 279). The reader can see the results of this survey in Figure 7.2.

In a conference hosted by the Institute of the Analysis of Intangible Assets in September 2006, entitled "Valuation of Intangible Assets in the Finance Sector," the Auditor General of one of Spain's largest banks expressed his thoughts on brand valuation: "The issue of intangible asset valuation is very muddied. I don't want the people who look at my balance sheet to have any uncertainty. The fact that an intangible asset can have different values, depending on the method by which it is valued, makes me quite uneasy." He is not alone; many finance executives share his misgivings.

7.1.3 Commercial and academic concentration in Anglo-Saxon countries

The development of brand valuation techniques and models has roused great interest in the academic and professional services communities of Anglo-Saxon countries, in part because of their national accounting standards. Figure 7.3 shows that over three quarters of the providers and academics who developed the methods described in Chapter 5 (excluding those for which the information available was insufficient), are based either in Germany or the USA. The former has recently experienced perhaps the greatest level of intellectual development (in terms of brand valuation models) in the world. Japan showed itself to be rather interested in the development of brand valuation models, through the Hirose Committee's endorsement from the Japanese Ministry of Economy,

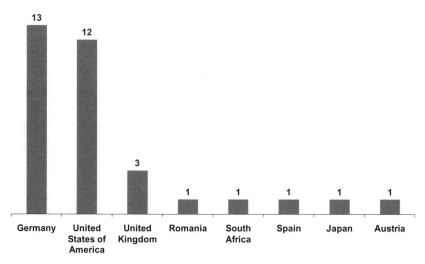

Figure 7.3 Distribution of brand valuation models by country.
Source: Developed by author. Sample: 33 providers. Note: The sample includes only one model per practitioner. The Financial World model has been excluded.

Trade and Industry. Other countries that have developed valuation models include Spain, South Africa and Romania.

7.1.4   Increasing professionalism in the sector and sophistication of brand valuation techniques

Intangible valuation specialists increasingly resort to econometric and statistical techniques to solve the typical deficiencies of brand valuation methods (Boos, 2003). Such recourses include hedonic pricing models and cluster analysis, a multivariate statistical technique.

Despite the complexity and sophistication of these methods, the issue of "subjectivity" remains, but is generally operative at a different level: data requirements are even more important here than in other models, while the problems of allocating earnings and expenses are still prevalent and there is a great deal of subjectivity in the identification and selection of individual attributes (Boos, 2003).

7.1.5   Growing convergence between marketing specialists and corporate finance experts

Audit firms and economic valuation specialists have manifested great interest in developing models jointly with marketing teams:

- E&Y AG collaborated with BBDO to develop their BEVA (Brand Equity Valuation for Accounting) model in 2004.

- PWC uses Sattler's ABV (Advanced Brand Valuation) model, developed jointly with GfK, a market research firm.

- Stern Stewart & Co. developed the Brand Economics® brand valuation model based on its EVA® calculation methodology as well as the BAV (Brand Asset Valuator) brand evaluation methodology developed by Young & Rubicam.

Furthermore, many brand and finance specialists who provide brand valuation services are beginning to feature this aspect of convergence prominently in their taglines and project proposals:

- Brand Finance's corporate image (a bridge) and tagline ("Bridging the Gap Between Marketing and Finance") suggest that its methodology incorporates measures relevant to both areas.

- Equilibrium, a British company specializing in branding that also offers brand valuation services, affirms that it is "balancing the art and science of brands," in many ways fusing the hard science of finance with the softer side of marketing measures.

These are just some examples of the developments that reflect the growing convergence at work in the industry.

7.1.6 Widespread use of certain models among practitioners

Figure 7.4 shows the frequency distribution of the principal models used by brand valuation practitioners.

Where a firm uses more than one model, Figure 7.4 has included its "principal" model, with the exceptions of

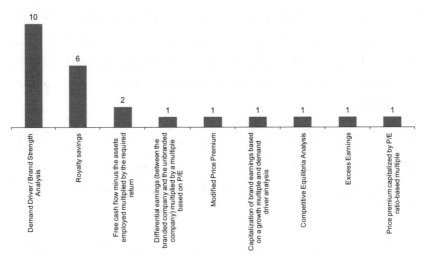

Figure 7.4 Methods most commonly used by practitioners.
Source: Developed by author. Source: 21 practitioners

Interbrand and Consor, for which it remained unclear which model was used most frequently. The Financial World model as well as defunct models developed by The Nielsen Company ("Brand Balance Sheet") and BBDO (BEES and BEE) have also been excluded from this distribution analysis. Thus, it includes a total of nine methodologies applied by 21 practitioners.

As is clearly visible, the majority (50%) of practitioners studied use demand driver analysis as their principal methodology, followed by royalty savings, used by 30%.

"Application" here refers to the adoption of the method by consultancies only; we have not included any empirical data on users' acceptance of any model. The only empirical study to address the application of certain methods on the part of corporations was carried out in Germany by Günther and Kriegbaum-Kling (2001). Their research involved an empirical study of the most commonly used methods among 46 German companies, and found that 10.4% used GfK models, 10.4% applied the Brand Performance model developed by The Nielsen Company and 3% used Interbrand's model. Given the geographical and statistical restriction of this research (particularly the size of the sample), we cannot consider its findings representative of the current situation in the US, UK, Spain or Australia; accordingly, this section addresses the adoption of various models by practitioners, and not by users.

7.1.7 Financial validity vs. widespread usage of models among practitioners

Each method presents different degrees of financial validity and usage. Many models, such as Interbrand's, which has purportedly valued 2500 brands, have received tremendous criticism from scholars as well as from other practitioners.

In Figure 7.5, the extension of the commercial application is calculated on the basis of the findings shown in Section 7.1.6, with the exception of Interbrand, for which a high volume of commercial application is assumed, given the company's market trajectory, brand awareness, media presence and prestigious client list. In all other cases, and without any competitive information, the extension of application is estimated as the adoption of the methods by a greater number of firms, and not based individually on client lists or sales.

The degree of validity depicted in the figure reflects various factors:

- The magnitude of criticism received by each methodology in terms of its theoretical and practical applicability, its

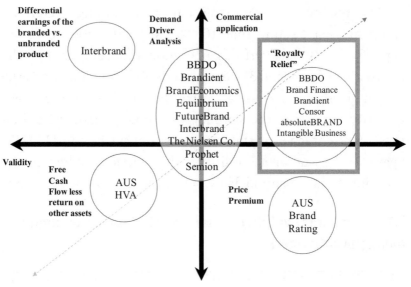

Figure 7.5 Validity vs. widespread commercial usage.
Source: Developed by author

replicability and its intellectual rigor, as described in previous chapters.

• The preference of transfer pricing regulations in the US, Canada, Germany, Australia and Japan, designed to guarantee greater degrees of objectivity (Anson, 1996, as cited in Boos, 2003: 87).

• Valuers' preferences for certain methods (particularly those that value brands for financial reporting purposes), as described by various authors. According to Mard et al. (2002), the royalty relief method is used predominantly for determining the fair value of brands for financial reporting because this method is the most comprehensive and valid option for this purpose (p. 61).

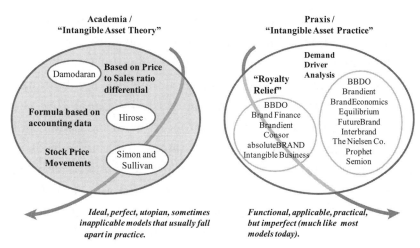

Figure 7.6   The worlds of academics and practitioners.
Source: Developed by author

7.1.8   Worlds apart: the academic and practitioners' realms

There is a large degree of divergence among the methods proposed by academics and those applied by practitioners (see Figure 7.6). The royalty savings method, one of the most popular among practitioners, has been widely criticized by scholars, eager to point out the difficulty associated with identifying relevant comparables (Torres Coronas, 2002; Barwise et al., 1989, as cited in Torres Coronas, 2002: 51; Sinclair, 2007).

7.1.9   The third world: "black box" methods

"Black box" methods are those whose components or modules are not fully disclosed. Unfortunately, these kinds of models seriously jeopardize credibility in the industry and occasionally turn out to be scams. This by no means indicates that all models that for any reason choose not to reveal their procedures in depth are methodologically arbitrary or unsound. But very often, the "black box" is used to obscure parts of the model that may be weak or difficult to justify. I once heard one of the most successful professionals in the branding industry (in terms of sales, of course) tell a client that the brand contribution index (the proportion or percentage of income attributable to brand) was determined on the basis of a "historical database." But if the methodology indeed required such a recourse, how was the database originally conceived? Of course, the mysterious database was a total fabrication; brand contribution was determined arbitrarily. While it is surprising that a client would accept this kind of answer, it's even more surprising that some practitioners would employ tactics so damaging to the industry as a whole.

7.1.10 Vast inconsistency in the application of various brand valuation techniques

While all methodologies analyzed introduce varying degrees of consistency in their implementation, the greatest degree of inconsistency is found in the application of demand driver analysis methods (see Figure 7.7). Such variation derives mainly from the way in which brand is interpreted statistically (as an attribute either separate or related to the other attributes that constitute a product) and from the ways relationships between different variable models are defined.

As we saw in Chapter 6, methodologies that use "Demand drivers/brand strength analysis" to determine the proportion of earnings or profits attributable to brand vary substantially in their approaches to selecting brand attributes, calculating the index and establishing the basis on which to apply it (sales, NOPAT, EVA, etc.).

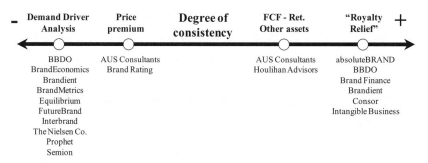

Figure 7.7 The degree of consistency of various techniques used to determine profits or income attributable to brand.
Source: Developed by author

7.1.11 Differences in implementation

Methods that use discounted cash flow/profits must incorporate at least three principal variables: business cash flows or earnings (and the proportion of these cash flows or earnings attributable to brand), the remaining useful life of the brand, and an appropriate discount rate that reflects brand risk.

Among models that use discounted cash flow/profits, the principal difference in application lies in the determination of cash flow or profits (cf. Section 7.1.10). Specifically, these differences in application derive from:

● market research which includes different attributes, variables and indexes derived from them;

● statistical analysis or arbitrary calculations that determine the proportion of earnings or profits attributable to brand;

● different bases for applying the proportion of earnings or profits attributable to brand.

Discount rates are determined much more consistently, and are usually calculated as the weighted average cost of capital with or without minor adjustments.

7.1.12 Diversity and divergence of results yielded by different methods

Figures 7.8 and 7.9 show brand valuations for Microsoft, GE, Toyota Apple and Samsung, performed in 2004 and 2005 by various branding and brand valuation firms. Both figures manifest the variability of the results obtained by the different respective valuers. The great disparity at work here is well exemplified by the fact that the value that Corebrand yielded in its valuation of Microsoft is only half of that estimated by Predictiv. Such divergence results from differences in implementation as well as in methodology (as most methods are based on the subjective analysis of "demand drivers" and brand attributes).

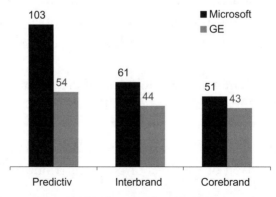

Figure 7.8 Comparison of 2004 brand valuation estimates for Microsoft and GE calculated by Predictiv, Interbrand and Corebrand (in US$ billion).
Source: Corebrand (2004b), *Business Week* (2004), *Forbes Magazine* (2004)

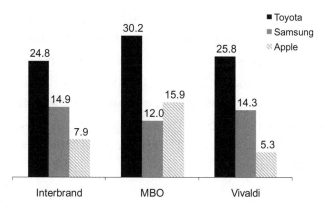

Figure 7.9 Comparison of 2005 brand valuation estimates for Toyota, Samsung and Apple calculated by Interbrand, Millward Brown Optimor and Vivaldi Partners (in US$ billion).
Source: Interbrand (2005), Millward Brown Optimor (2006)[64], Badenhausen and Roney (2005)

7.1.13 Determining useful life

According to Smith (1997), while there is no analytical tool for precisely determining a brand's remaining useful life, some techniques use historical data to forecast tangible and intangible assets' economic useful life. In brand valuation, tools for estimating remaining useful life tend to be subjective. It is widely assumed that a brand's life is indeterminate, unless proven otherwise through an analysis of the following factors (p. 123):

- *Life cycle* of the product or service (typical, truncated, fashions, fads, etc.).

- *Functional obsolescence:* brands do not suffer from functional obsolescence as a result of technological innovation,

[64] Note: The ranking of MBO published by the *Financial Times* on 24 March 2006 used 2005 data.

but rather as a result of style; this factor can heavily influence a brand's useful life. For example, slogans or taglines have finite lives, as they are developed to suit a short-term situation. An umbrella brand tends to have a longer useful life than a specific sub-brand because there is a greater risk of functional obsolescence at a more specific level. Therefore, Shell would have a longer life than V-Power or Apple than iPod.

- *Event obsolescence:* Economic obsolescence may be used "to describe potential trademark value reductions caused by business transactions or events that are outside the course of normal trademark life activities" (Smith, 1997: 113). Enron serves as a good example of this, as its economic life was abruptly truncated by an accounting scandal.

- *Technological obsolescence:* This may occur when a trademark is tied exclusively to a product with a high risk of technological obsolescence. Therefore, the greater the brand's versatility, the longer its life.

- *Cultural obsolescence:* Certain cultural issues may affect a brand's economic life. A brand may become obsolete because it is not politically correct, or because its name is displeasing or offensive to other cultures.

7.1.14 Determining discount rates

In my experience, this aspect has been one of the greatest sources of conflict in the practice of brand valuation. Many of my clients' corporate finance departments prefer to use

WACC to discount cash flow/profits attributable to brand. Other branding professionals argue that the risk for the brand may be lower than that of the sector in which it operates, citing Coca-Cola as an example. Others, such as Gordon Smith (1997) affirm that the risk of intellectual property assets, and among them, brand risk, is often greater than tangible asset risk and average business risk, due to the market risk deriving from the intangibles' illiquidity. In this respect, there is no consensus among valuation practitioners on the nature and behavior of intangible asset risk. This is, in many ways, what leads to the different treatments of the components we observed in Chapters 5 and 6:

- some use WACC to discount cash flows or profits attributable to brand;

- others use adjusted WACC to discount cash flows or profits attributable to brand;

- others reflect risk through multiples calculated in innumerable ways;

- others do not reveal their method of calculating the discount rate.

The diversity of approaches to this valuation component has generated much criticism from scholars. When I spoke with Professor Pablo Fernández on the topic, he asked me to reflect on what a discount rate really is: a reflection of an opinion on company risk at a determined moment in time. This perspective coincides with that of many analysts, such as Jan Hofmann of Deustche Bank, who finds that choosing an appropriate discount rate is more of an art than a science (Hofmann, 2005). Evidently, the vast majority of valuation specialists understand it this way, and therefore use various mechanisms to reflect the brand-specific risk in the discount rate.

7.2   Common errors and misconceptions in brand and intangible asset valuation

As we saw in Section 7.1.1, the growing attention received by brand valuation has generated a multitude of brand and intangible asset valuation proprietary methods, many of which contain fundamental errors and misconceptions.

We shall discuss these errors in accordance with the classification developed by Professor Pablo Fernández (2006):

- conceptual errors

- errors in management

- errors in interpretation.

7.2.1   Conceptual errors

1. *Conflating EVA and "intangible value" or "intangible earnings:"* this error is widespread among "marketing valuers," and made habitually by at least three companies. According to Interbrand Zintzmeyer & Lux (n.d.), "the first step towards isolating brand earnings from other forms of

income is to determine the Economic Value Added (EVA) which tells whether a company is able to generate returns that exceed the costs of capital employed." According to Interbrand, calculating intangible earnings requires that operating costs, taxes and cost of capital (WACC) be deducted from branded business earnings. Clearly, Interbrand is confusing EVA with intangible earnings. But it is not alone in this conflation; the methodology developed by Millward Brown Optimor, developed years later, adopts a strikingly similar approach, and falls into the same conceptual pitfalls. In an article published in the *Financial Times* on 3 April 2006, Millward Brown Optimor's method is described thus: "From [the current earnings of the company], operating costs, relevant taxes and a charge for the capital employed are deducted, which gives a figure for the intangible earnings coming from the branded business." And lastly, Brand Economics also confuses "intangible value" with EVA, upon affirming that "intangible value is equal to the present value of current and expected future EVA, which is mathematically identical to the net present value of forecasted free cash flows" (Ehrbar and Bergesen, 2002: 4). EVA is a registered trademark of Stern Stewart & Co. As Andriessen writes (2004), "there is only an indirect link between EVA and the value of intangible resources" (p. 293). EVA is calculated in the following manner (Fernández, 2001):

$$EVA = NOPAT - (D + Ebv)\,WACC$$

where:

NOPAT or Net Operating Profit After Tax = the after-tax profit of the unlevered firm

D = the firm's debt

Ebv = the book value of equity, and

WACC = the weighted average cost of capital (debt and equity)

Andriessen (2004) notes that EVA was never designed to measure the value of intangible assets. However, EVA appears in many catalogs of methods for measuring intellectual capital (Bontis, 2001; Bontis et al.; 1999; Sveiby, 2002; Van den Berg, 2003; as cited in Andriessen, 2004: 294). What are the origins of this grievous confusion? There are at least two elements that might explain it:

- Strassman (1998) and Bontis et al. (1999) (as cited in Andriessen, 2004: 294–5) correlate efficient knowledge management with rises in EVA. But according to Andriessen (2004), EVA is not produced exclusively by intangibles. Tangible assets also contribute to EVA, producing a NOPAT higher than the cost of capital required to acquire and maintain them. Therefore, a portion of EVA must also be attributed to tangible assets.

- The present value of future EVA discounted at WACC is equivalent to MVA (Market Value Added), which is essentially the difference between the equity's market value and its book value (cf. Fernández, 2001). "The fact that the present value of EVA, discounted at the WACC, matches the Market Value Added leads some to suggest that each period's EVA can be interpreted as an increase in the MVA or shareholder value creation during each period. However, this is a tremendous mistake: it is one thing to say that the present value of the future EVAs matches the MVA but quite a different thing to suggest that each period's EVA represents the value created during that period" (p. 314).

2. *Discounting risky cash flows at the risk-free rate:* Hirose et al. (2002) state that their brand valuation model reflects risks in cash flows. But actually, none of the factors used in the model to estimate the cash flows attributable to the brand (ED, PD, LD) can be interpreted as the risk correction coefficient reflecting the cash flow risk. In this case, discounting at the risk-free rate is erroneous.

3. *Using excess earnings as proportion of earnings attributable to brand:* excess earnings include earnings from all intangible assets.

4. *Designating a fixed return on tangible assets when using excess earnings:* Baruch Lev sets a wholly arbitrary return of 7% on fixed assets.

5. *Deeming the differential between cash flows and return on tangible assets as the return on intangible assets or brand:* this error may be seen in the examples provided by Houlihan Advisors and AUS Consultants (see Section 4.3.9 in Chapter 4 and Table 5.23 in Chapter 5.)

6. *Failing to consider expected growth:* the method proposed by Hirose et al. (2002) does not include any expectations for brand growth; this omission is unsound.

7. *Discounting earnings or cash flows attributable to brand at an inconsistent rate.*

8. *Using branded company sales as the basis for valuation when performing a comparison of price/sales ratios:* this error is evidenced in the method proposed by Damodaran, which multiplies the difference between the unbranded and branded companies' price/sales ratios by the branded company's sales (see Section 5.10 in Chapter 5). However, the sales revenues of the unbranded company could be lower than those of the branded one.

9. *Assuming that higher multiples on the brand strength scale should translate into higher P/E ratios than the average of the sector in which the company operates.*

10. Pablo Fernández (2006) cites *"using strange formulas"* as a general error in intangible asset valuation. As an example, he alludes to a valuation consulting firm that proposes "quantifying the bonds that shareholders deposit in banks" as part of their approach to intangible asset valuation. The firm figures that if the company's financial debt is $20 million, the bank loans without the shareholders' bonds could have an additional cost of 2.5% annually. By quantifying this 2.5% for 10 years, the firm concludes that the additional cost would total $2 million, which it then considers an accurate approximation of the value of the intangibles.

11. *Not clearly defining the concept of "brand" during the initial phases:* "The starting point in any valuation is to carefully define the property being appraised, requiring clear

boundaries and an understanding of the rights included in – and excluded from – the valuation" (Smith and Parr, 2005: 256).

12. *Using factors that are not determinants of the level of the royalty rate in the market as attributes of comparison for determining the appropriate royalty rate within a range of comparables* (Smith and Parr, 2005).

13. *Forgetting that brand value is a value within a business context:* Pablo Fernández (2001) exemplifies this confusion by citing the following statement made by a renowned marketing professor and published in 2000 in a Spanish newspaper: "Brand value can reach up to triple the amount of market capitalization."

14. *Estimating brand value by the brand's replacement cost measured through the present value of historical investment in marketing and promotions:* According to Pablo Fernández (2001), this method is frequently used by Cadbury-Schweppes.

15. *Confusing "product brand" with "corporate brand:"* this error is very common among branding companies and specialists (Pettis, 1995; Corebrand, Predictiv).

16. *Applying a set of methodologies (appropriate or not) for valuing brands and averaging their results to arrive at brand value:* it is advisable to apply the methodology that best suits the valuation's objectives. If it does not make sense to use a certain method, or if various methods produce very different

results, they clearly cannot all be appropriate for the given situation. Why average them and bring the error into the final value?

17. *Affirming that intellectual property assets are not intangible assets.*

18. *Adding earnings from past periods to discounted earnings in order to yield the present value of earnings in the explicit forecast horizon.*

19. *Not defining "for whom the value is being determined," which may lead to "questionable" practices such as estimating the value of a "nation brand:"* A few brand valuation specialists have claimed in the past to have valued country brands. For some, country brand valuation can be used as a means of comparison for measuring progress in areas as diverse as tourism, foreign trade of goods and services, and foreign debt. It seems highly implausible that policy-makers in the fields of tourism, bond placement and foreign trade could accept the nation brand as a measure of their activities; and even if this were somehow accurate, there are much better indicators than the "nation brand value" to guide public policy in these three areas. The problem is that when the intended audience of the brand value is undefined, the boundaries of the definition of income the brand generates become debatable.

7.2.2   Errors in management

1. *Not involving Finance in the process:* many firms have seen brand valuations fail spectacularly because of the

lack of participation of finance departments. In one of the most notorious cases, a specialist firm was forced to work without any form of contact with the finance department, for "internal politics" reasons. The result was hundreds of thousands of euros down the drain in an absolutely futile exercise.

2. *Not involving Marketing in the process:* brand valuation is not unlike firm valuation, in that it involves a host of variables. To really understand these variables, and to produce a sound opinion on brand value, the company's strategy and the brand's legal status and plans for expansion, etc., must all be on the table. Therefore, the participation of the marketing department is key, as well as that of the corporate finance and legal departments. A well-managed valuation should be an interdisciplinary exercise.

3. *Not clearly defining the objectives of the valuation:* an error commonly made by specialists is taking on a valuation project without being familiar with its objectives. Clients often maintain an air of "secrecy" around the objectives of the valuation. This can have severe effects on the process, since the purpose and the method of the valuation ought to inform the definition of brand to be used, and will heavily shape the focus of the final report. If a valuation is performed for a potential buyer who is considering using the brand in new sectors and products, this premise will clearly influence expectations on the earnings that the brand can generate, and therefore, its value.

4. *Not reviewing the client's hypothesis* (Fernández, 2006): particularly when the objective involves the sale of a brand,

clients tend to present "highly optimistic forecasts." Specialists must check that growth in sales corresponds to increased investment, personnel costs, etc.

5. *Selling or trusting "magic software" that claims to be capable of carrying out a valuation on its own:* an error made by both consultants selling brand valuation software, and clients thinking of buying it, is believing that using such software can eliminate the trouble of a periodic valuation exercise.

7.2.3 Errors in interpretation

1. *Asserting that goodwill includes brand value:* according to Pablo Fernández (2006), goodwill is simply the difference between the price paid for shares and their book value, and there may be cases in which the price paid is less than the book value (particularly when interest rates are high).

2. *Asserting that the valuation reflects a scientific value and not an opinion:* in a recent article, Mark Ritson compares Millward Brown Optimor's method with that used by Interbrand, affirming that "Interbrand estimates: Millward Brown Optimor measures."[65] This assertion shows a profound misunderstanding of what an economic valuation represents, regardless of the asset being valued. In an article on Prophet's website, Tim Neale, Boeing's spokesman, is quoted as having said: "We took a hard look at it a couple of years ago … but we haven't been able to make a good case for using [one methodology] over another. It's not a

---

[65] http://www.brandrepublic.com/bulletins/design/article/540167/mark-ritson-branding-getting-bottom-line-brand-equity/.

science."[66] No value yielded by a valuation is any more than an expert opinion. In this sense, as we saw in Chapter 3, brand valuation is no different than valuations of financial assets, real estate, or fine art.

3. *Confusing value with price:* while Pablo Fernández (2006) includes this error among other errors of interpretation within the context of company valuation, it also applies to brand valuation.

7.3 Conclusions

1. *Lack of methodological consensus in theory and practice*

(a) Scholars propose a wide range of valuation methods based on price premiums, stock price movements, conjoint analysis and multiples.

(b) Most practitioners lean towards demand driver analysis or royalty relief; some use price premiums. But there is no consensus on a specific method for determining drivers, royalty rates, or price premiums.

2. *Two worlds: academic vs. professional practice*

(a) While the academic world has harshly criticized the royalty relief method, (Torres Coronas, 2002; Barwise et al., 1989; Sinclair, 2007), in practice, we see a clear preference for models based on brand strength analysis and royalty relief.

---

[66] http://www.prophet.com/newsevents/news/story/20060512story.html.

(b) Although the academic world exhibits a wide range of approaches to calculating appropriate discount rates for brand valuation (Fernández, 2001; Smith and Parr, 2000), in the realm of practitioners, we often see that appraisers make adjustments to WACC to reflect brand-specific risk (Haigh, 2001; Zimmermann et al., 2002; Intangible Business, 2004).

3. *Why royalty relief continues to be the method of choice for large firms and financial entities.* After reading the critiques of the royalty savings method, as summarized in Chapter 4, the reader may ask why so many major financial and audit firms continue to use it as their principal methodology, particularly for technical purposes. Although this method is not perfect, and its application is rather complicated, as many scholars have previously noted (among others, Torres Coronas, 2002), it continues to be a highly popular method for brand valuations with technical objectives, because it combines practicality with reliability better than any other method, which is key for any valuation, whether it is valuing tangible or intangible assets. Furthermore, it is the method with the greatest degree of consistency in its practical application. While imperfect, it is not much more flawed than most company valuations and other financial or economic models, that (like all models) entail a concise oversimplification of reality. Like many other brand valuation specialists, I'd love to find a better model from an econometric perspective, but having exhaustively reviewed the current landscape of models and methodologies, I believe that the royalty savings method is the one that presents the fewest weaknesses relative to others, even though such weaknesses are not small nor minor. Until experts in the field find a better model for technical and

accounting purposes, I'm afraid that many of us will have to continue using this method.

4. *Brand valuation profiles – the good, the bad and the ugly.* The development of the models reviewed in Chapter 5 have undoubtedly contributed to the level of sophistication of brand valuation practices. But the diversity of methods and results has not always been positive; it has also led to uncertainty and lack of credibility on the part of professionals and financial officers, who commonly perceive brand valuation as a highly subjective, unreliable and "unscientific" process. But perhaps more damage still has been done to brand valuation by the few but notorious practitioners who hide behind their poor and wholly defective "black box" methodologies.

5. In practice, *adjustments are made to discount rates,* despite overwhelming criticism from the academic arena. These adjustments are often made on the basis of brand-specific risk factors (brand illiquidity).

8

Is Corporate Brand Valuation Possible?

THERE IS NOT VERY MUCH LITERATURE ON CORPORATE brand valuation. When CoreBrand, Predictiv and several other firms claim that they are equipped to value what they call "corporate brands," they are often referring to product or service brands. The models they employ in corporate brand valuation are very similar to those used in product brand valuation, and involve no corporate-specific variables or procedural elements. While Predictiv's valuation method is rather opaque and its individual components cannot be discussed in depth, the final figures that it has yielded cannot possibly correspond to values generated exclusively by the corporate brand, particularly in the case of companies with "house of brands" architecture, such as P&G.

The models we reviewed in Chapter 5 apply (albeit with varying degrees of reliability) to service or product brand valuation. But, as we saw in Chapter 1, for many brands, such as Sony, Honda, Mitsubishi or Samsung, the corporate brand name is identical to the product brand name, which substantially complicates the distinction and relationship between product and corporate brand value.

The corporate brand may also act as a product brand endorsement; we see this in the cases of Nestlé and Danone. Since Nestlé endorses Kit Kat, the question becomes: How much does Nestlé actually contribute to the brand value of Kit Kat? How much does Danone contribute to Actimel's?

At other times, as in the case of SABMiller and partly due to the acquisition strategy the brand has adopted in recent years, the brand portfolio is composed of independent brands that generate demand and cash flows at the level of a commercial product. What is the corporate brand value in this case? The sum of the values of each product brand and sub-brand? The value that SABMiller brings to them via lobby, negotiation power with distributors, etc.?

In this chapter we will explore the different methods proposed and employed for corporate brand valuation. We will begin by reviewing the concept of "corporate brand," specifically addressing its frequent conflation with the concept of "corporate reputation."

8.1 What is "corporate brand," and is it the same as "corporate reputation?"

In Section 1.1.3.1, we looked at different approaches to and definitions of *brand* and *corporate reputation*. Clearly, the experience that any stakeholder may have with the brand at any touchpoint is a source of reputation. But in my opinion, reputation is ultimately the result of brand management, and is therefore not controllable. One may manage a brand by controlling communications with stakeholders, each touch-point with clients, from call centers and customer service departments, to the store environment itself. But it's another thing altogether to control consumer perception. While brand may be managed and controlled, reputation is simply granted; it is the result of the management of the factors previously mentioned. Furthermore, while the brand is an intangible asset, corporate reputation is not. In strict accounting terms, corporate reputation does not qualify as an intangible asset because it fails to meet the separability criterion; it cannot be bought, sold or transferred (see Chapter 1, Section 1.1.1.1). The fact that corporate reputation does not technically classify as an "intangible asset" severely challenges the legitimacy of the very notion of "corporate brand valuation models." Nonetheless, many view corporate reputation as an intangible asset that "belongs to the company" (Hall, 1992, 1993; Srivastava, McInish, Wood and Capraro, 1997; Tadelis, 1997).

Many marketing and corporate reputation experts feel differently on the subject, and refer to "corporate brand" and "corporate reputation" interchangeably. In light of the nature of this circumstance, this section will address economic valuation models proposed for corporate brands and corporate reputation alike.

8.2 Why value corporate brands?

While in the literature we see various references to corporate brand valuation (Hirose, 2002; Srivastava et al., 1997; Zimmermann et al., 2001), it is not a widely employed practice.

There are no transactional or accounting motives for valuing corporate brands separately from product or service brands.

Some of the reasons for valuing corporate brands' "economic contribution" may include:

- assessing an endorsement of a product brand by a corporate brand, in order to enhance brand architecture decision-making;

- determining the impact of corporate *re-branding*, as in the case of Philip-Morris, when it changed its name to Altria;

- revealing the value added by corporate brand management policies, using the valuation as an internal organization tool.

Beyond these premises, corporate brand valuation has no purpose other than to show the value of its effective management.

Despite the minimal utility of corporate brand valuation, scholars and business executives have shown growing interest in this practice, viewing it as a tool for improving corporate brand management policies and internally reporting the value that they may add.

8.3 Methodological options proposed for corporate brand valuation

The chief difficulty in valuing corporate brands derives from the impossibility of properly allocating a determined cash flow, particularly when the corporate brand is not associated with a particular product. At least four different approaches have been used by practitioners or proposed by scholars for the valuation of corporate brands:

1. *Calculate corporate brand value as the direct sum of the values of the product or service brands whose names are associated with the corporate brand.* For example, under this approach, in the case of Telefónica, the value of the corporate brand would be the value of the product or service brand of the fixed telephony business that also operates under the name Telefónica. The problem with this approach is that it does not isolate the value that the corporate brand adds to the business. This approach considers commercial audiences, but ignores the value that corporate brands add through negotiation power with providers, banks, distribution channels, etc.

2. *Calculate corporate brand value as the value that it "adds" to product or service brands.* This approach merely considers one group of stakeholders: consumers. Two different techniques have been used to estimate the value that the corporate brand adds to product brands:

   a) Determine the degree to which consumers associate the corporate brand with the product or service brand, and evaluate the affinity or favorability that they show towards the corporate brand. The value that the corporate brand brings to the product brand will depend on the level of association between the corporate and product brand, and the target market's affinity for the latter.

b) Examine the corporate brand's impact on demand drivers in each segment/category. The value that the corporate brand brings to the product or service brand will depend on the impact that the corporate brand's support and perception has on the relevant demand drivers in each segment.

3. *Measure how sensitive the company value is to changes in reputation level* (Srivastava et al., 1997). This approach, based on the CAPM, has several methodological drawbacks, which we will examine more closely in Section 8.4.

4. *Measure the percentage of market capitalization attributable to the corporate brand.* This model was proposed by CoreBrand. As we will see later on, the results that it yields are very similar to those obtained through product brand valuation methods; the only difference is that in this case, the surveys are aimed at a different audience.

Any corporate brand valuation model should recognize that corporate brands generate value not only through interaction with the general public, but also through relationships with all stakeholders, including:

- clients

- distributors

- providers

- employees

- shareholders

- investors

- public administration/government

- general public/consumers.

One of the fundamental obstacles in corporate brand valuation is that the information available on these various facets is often insufficient to estimate the value created through (for example):

- improved conditions with providers;

- lower recruitment costs;

- lower cost of capital resulting from excellent corporate reputation among investors;

- better reputation among government administration or regulatory bodies, who can effectively remove commercial restrictions that may provide opportunities for future value creation, although it may not have any immediate effect on cash flow.

8.4 Models based on the concept that "corporate brand or reputation" adds value to product brands

8.4.1 Association-Affinity Model

In this model, used predominantly by practitioners, the value of the corporate brand or corporate reputation is understood

Table 8.1 Corporate brand contribution and association

Corporate brand–product brand relationship	Corporate brand contribution	Product brand contribution
The name of the corporate brand coincides with that of the product brand, as in the case of Vodafone	100%	0%
The corporate brand explicitly endorses the product brand, as in the case of Danone and Daníssimo	X%	Y%
The corporate brand weakly endorses the product brand, as in the case of Unilever and Dove	X%	Y%
There is no relationship between the corporate brand and the product brand, as in the case of L'Oréal and Lancôme	X%	Y%

as the contribution that the corporate brand makes to the total value of the product brand, as shown in Table 8.1. This contribution depends on the nature of the extant relationship between the corporate and product brand:

- The name of the corporate brand may coincide with that of the product brand, as in the case of Vodafone.

- The corporate brand may explicitly endorse the product brand, as in the case of Danone and Daníssimo.

- The corporate brand may weakly endorse the product brand, as in the case of Unilever and Dove.

- There may be no relationship between the corporate brand and the product brand, as in the case of L'Oréal and Lancôme.

Still, the contribution of the corporate brand will in turn depend on the degree to which final consumers appreciate it; the greater the consumer affinity for the corporate brand, the greater will be its contribution.

The two variables this model uses to determine corporate brand value may be obtained relatively simply through consumer surveys:

1. *"Association" or degree of affiliation between the product and corporate brand, among those interviewed.*

- The corporate brand cannot contribute to demand unless consumers know that the product brand is owned by the corporation.

- The degree of this "association" is likely to be higher when the corporate brand's endorsement is explicit, and lower when it is weak.

2. *"Affinity" or degree of positive attitude towards the corporate brand.*

- The corporate brand cannot contribute to demand unless consumers show a positive attitude towards it.

- Affinity may be measured on the basis of confidence, sympathy, consideration, etc.

To value corporate brand or reputation contribution, the values of the two abovementioned variables are inserted into the following equation:

$$\begin{pmatrix} \% \text{ Corporate} \\ \text{Affinity} \end{pmatrix} \times \begin{pmatrix} \% \text{ Corporate brand} - \\ \text{product brand} \\ \text{association} \end{pmatrix} = \begin{matrix} \% \text{ Corporate} \\ \text{Reputation value} \\ \text{contribution} \end{matrix}$$

$$(8.1)$$

- If Association = 0%, the corporate brand contribution is 0%

- If Affinity = 0%, the corporate brand contribution is 0%

- If Association and Affinity are positive values, we may assume that the corporate brand contribution directly correlates with such values

- The highest possible brand contribution level is 100% (when market research indicates that Association = 100% and Affinity = 100%).

Therefore, if a corporate brand that explicitly endorses a product brand earns an association score of 75% and an affinity score of 50% through consumer surveys, the corporate brand contributes 37.50% to the total brand value estimated, and the product brand contributes 62.50%. Corporate brand contribution may then be used to allocate total brand value among the corporate brand and various product brands. If the brand value is €5000 million, and the corporate brand contribution is 37.50%, the value generated by the product brand would be €3125 million, and the value added by the corporate brand would be €1875 million.

8.4.2 Critique

- This corporate brand valuation model is based on the role that the corporate brand plays for consumers and the general public.

- The model allocates a proportion of total brand value to the corporate brand that reflects the perceived strength of the role it plays in each segment.

- This model gives an indication of the corporate brand value; in other words, a partial estimation of "the economic contribution of a good reputation."

- The estimation is only partial because the corporate brand plays a major role for audiences beyond the consumers (affecting providers, employees, the financial community, society, etc.), and relationships in these environments can also shape corporate reputation.

8.4.3 Model based on demand analysis

This model is based on the demand driver analysis discussed in Chapter 5 – see Figure 8.1.

Based on these demand drivers, the model calculates the proportion of brand contribution generated by the corporate brand and the product brand respectively. To do so, it determines brand contribution by driver, and "estimates" how much the corporate brand contributes to the generation of income for each particular attribute. For example, in Table 8.2, reputation and image contribute 6.74% to income generation. Because the corporate brand generates 80% of perception in this driver, corporate brand contribution here is 5.39%. The individual corporate brand contributions in each of the brand variables that contribute to demand are then added to yield the total corporate brand contribution to value; in this case, 16%.

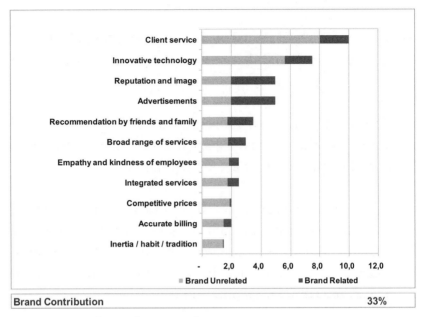

Figure 8.1 Brand contribution analysis.
Source: Based on Marketing Leadership Council (2003: 8) and Binar (2005)

The 33% of the brand contribution index is then sub-divided as:

- 16% corporate brand contribution

- 17% product brand contribution.

8.4.4 Critique

This technique is only applicable for final customers; it does not take corporate audiences into account. In optimal circumstances, if product brand contribution is estimated through trade-off or conjoint analysis, and if the names of the corporate and product brands coincide, there is no way of statistically determining corporate brand contribution.

Table 8.2 Corporate brand contribution calculation

#	Drivers	Importance	Brand contribution	Individual brand contribution	Corporate brand contribution	Corporate brand contribution to product brand value
1	Client service	10.0	20.0%	4.49%	50.00%	2.25%
2	Innovative technology	7.5	25.0%	4.21%	20.00%	0.84%
3	Advertisements	5.0	60.0%	6.74%	80.00%	5.39%
4	Reputation and image	5.0	60.0%	6.74%	80.00%	5.39%
5	Recommendation by friends and family	3.5	50.0%	3.93%	0.00%	0.00%
6	Broad range of services	3.0	40.0%	2.70%	20.00%	0.54%
7	Integrated services	2.5	30.0%	1.69%	80.00%	1.35%
8	Empathy and kindness of employees	2.5	25.0%	1.40%	5.00%	0.07%
9	Accurate billing	2.0	25.0%	1.12%	30.00%	0.34%
10	Competitive prices	2.0	5.0%	0.22%	20.00%	0.04%
11	Inertia/habit/tradition	1.5	5.0%	0.17%	0.00%	0.00%
	Corporate / product brand contribution			33%		16%

Source: Developed by author based on drivers shown in Figure 8.1

In cases of strong, weak or non-existent corporate brand endorsement, this method does not address whether the corporate brand would be presented as another attribute in a trade-off analysis, or as an additional attribute in a series of attributes valued by the final customer.

8.5 Model based on the company value's sensitivity to variations in "corporate brand or reputation" value

This model, developed by Srivastava et al. (1997), is based on the relationship between corporate reputation and market value.

8.5.1 Assumptions

1a. *Definition of reputation*: Reputation is measured through variables established by Fortune magazine for the survey it has published since 1983. This reputation index is based on a survey administered to 12000 managers and analysts who evaluated 1000 firms on the basis of eight dimensions of reputation, through Likert's 11-point scale. The eight dimensions are:

- wise use of corporate assets

- quality of management

- social responsibility

- financial soundness

- quality of products or services

- innovativeness

- ability to attract, keep and develop talent

- long-term investment value.

1b. *Corporate brand is synonymous with corporate reputation.* As this model is based on the notion that corporate reputation and corporate brand are synonymous, its authors provide evidence of the impact on the value of reputation. They cite Ohmae, who in 1989 noted that banks had loaned large sums of money to companies, taking their "good name" as security.

1c. *A strong reputation can affect market valuation through its impact on operating results.* A strong reputation reinforces messages of product quality and allows a company to charge higher price premiums. The authors studied the relationship between the strength of reputation and return on sales.

1d. *CAPM betas reflect "objective risk," but not "perceived risk" or reputation.* According to the authors of this model, a strong reputation improves investors' risk perception: "If a firm's positive reputation enhances operational performance, increases the likelihood of maintaining superior performance over time, and induces a positive frame for interpreting events related to the firm, it seems likely also to reduce the degree to which shareholders perceive the firm as being risky" (p. 63). This suggests that:

> 1d.1. Investors will accept higher risk (measured through the CAPM beta) when there is a better reputation.

> 1d.2. Investors will accept lower returns given a steady level of financial risk (measured through the CAPM beta) when there is a better reputation.

According to the authors, markets express the objective risk associated with an investment through the beta (CAPM model). Therefore, the required return on investment (R_p) will be determined by the characteristics of objective risk of the investment portfolio (β_p) – see equation (8.2). However, if the investor were to consider the company's reputation upon evaluating the investment risk (i.e., if the investment were made on the basis of perceived risk), the required return would not be calculable through the beta. If a strong reputation leads investors to perceive the firm as less risky, they will be more willing to accept a lower return than that which the objective risk (beta) would indicate alone. Were this not the case, and if the required returns were constant, companies with higher reputations would be able to maintain higher betas.

$$R_p = R_f + \beta_p(R_m - R_f) \tag{8.2}$$

where:

R_p = the required return on investment

R_m = the return on the market portfolio

R_f = the risk-free rate

β_p = the beta associated with the investment portfolio.

Table 8.3 Selected portfolios

Portfolio	Average reputation	Portfolio beta
1	7.39029	1.47771
2	7.19667	1.39239
3	7.00305	1.38292
4	6.80947	1.37577
5	6.61589	1.42148
6	6.43248	1.37202
7	6.24125	1.28862
8	6.04725	1.32386
9	5.85328	1.35697
10	5.65944	1.34928

Source: Srivastava et al. (1997)

8.5.2 Empirical development

This model was developed based on the analysis of 10 portfolios of companies listed in Fortune's 1990 ranking. Portfolio selections were made such that levels of expected return were virtually equivalent, but levels of reputation varied widely (see Table 8.3).

To prove the model's hypothesis, the authors carried out reputation and beta regressions for the set of portfolios selected. Because they were chosen such that their returns were identical, according to the CAPM theory, their betas should have been the same. The authors' hypothesis was that reputation influences risk perception beyond the beta. Therefore, they expected the "more reputable" portfolios to have higher betas.

The model assumes a linear relationship between the reputation variable (REP_i) and the investment portfolio beta (β_i). A linear regression (Beta, β_i vs. Reputation, REP_i) is used to prove the model's hypothesis (the better the reputation, the higher the beta):

$$\beta_1 = X_0 + X_1 * REP_i + \varepsilon_i \qquad (8.3)$$

where:

β_i = the investment portfolio beta

X_0 and X_1 = the parameters to be estimated

ε_i = a random error term.

Thus, the beta is a function of the reputation index (see Figure 8.2).

The coefficient X_1, or the "reputation coefficient" reflects the extent to which investors are willing to accept a higher beta for a better reputation. A positive value for X_1 indicates that the stronger the reputation, the greater the risk investors are willing to take for a given return; in the words of Srivastava et al. (1997), "investors value reputation" (p. 64).

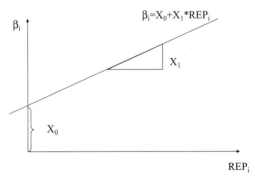

Figure 8.2 Reputation-beta relationship.
Source: Developed by author

Table 8.4 Results of the beta vs. reputation regression

Constant (X_0)	0.9606
t-statistic	24.8563*
Coefficient (X_1)	0.0634
t-statistic	2.8573*
R^2	0.5051
Sample	10
Degrees of freedom	8

* Significant at an interval of 0.05
Source: Srivastava et al. (1997)

The results of the regression are shown in Table 8.4.

According to the authors, the fact that the reputation coefficient (X_1) is positive at 0.0634 and significant at t = 2.87 with p < 0.05 proves that the higher the reputation index, the more inclined investors are to accept greater risk (measured through the beta). In other words, with each unit that the reputation index (REP_i) increases, investors are willing to accept a beta increase of 0.0634 without demanding an increase in the required return.

R^2 is 0.5051, indicating that reputation can account for more than half of the portfolio variations.

8.5.3 Theoretical model

Based on the empirical results, Srivastava et al. (1997) constructed a model in which higher reputation can lead to lower required returns.

Figure 8.3 shows two firms with the same market value and required return, but different beta and reputation levels. In the example, the beta for Firm 1 is higher than the beta for

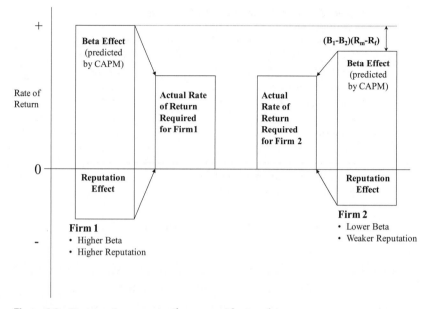

Figure 8.3 Reputation-required return relationship.
Source: Srivastava et al. (1997). Reproduced by permission of Palgrave Macmillan

Firm 2. Based exclusively on the CAPM, investors would require a higher return for Firm 1. That is, the beta effect would be higher for Firm 1 than for Firm 2. According to the CAPM, the difference in the two required returns yielded by the beta effect would be:

$$R_1 - R_2 = \lfloor R_f + B_1 (R_m - R_f) \rfloor - \lfloor R_f + B_2 (R_m - R_f) \rfloor = (B_1 - B_2)(R_m - R_f)$$
(8.4)

In other words, the prediction of the CAPM is that the higher the risk investors will have to bear, the higher the return they will demand from the firm securities – what Srivastava et al. (1997) call the "beta effect"– and this relationship is linear (cf. equation (8.2)).

But Srivastava et al. (1997) propose that reputation has an effect on the return investors require a firm to pay them. Reputation effectively reduces the required return that a company with a given beta must "pay" to investors as predicted by the CAPM. This reduction in the required return is known as the "reputation effect." In Figure 8.3, Firm 1 has a higher reputation, and therefore, a greater reputation effect. According to the authors, the actual rate of return that a firm has to pay to investors is interpreted as a combination of the "beta effect" compensated by the "reputation effect."

Equation (8.4) estimates the incremental required return that a firm with a higher beta must pay in accordance with the CAPM. But, when this is due to a better reputation, the firm with the higher beta (Firm 1) does not need to pay this incremental required return, and so the value of the better reputation is equal to the incremental required return that the firm is able to circumvent:

$$R_1 - R_2 = (B_1 - B_2)(R_m - R_f) \qquad (8.5)$$

Equation (8.5) shows an expression of the monetary value generated by a strong reputation, in terms of differential return. But there is another, more functional equation based on reputation score differentials. If we take a look at the beta-reputation relationship estimated in equation (8.3), we see that the coefficient X_1 describes the magnitude of the change in reputation that counterbalances the change in required return, when the beta varies by one unit. By combining equations (8.3) and (8.5), we may express the value of the difference in reputation (ΔREP) as follows:

$$Value\ of\ a\ Reputation\ Difference = (X_1)(\Delta REP)(R_m - R_f)$$

$$(8.6)$$

According to the authors, if a firm can improve its reputation, it can also benefit from the risk-reduction effects of equation (8.6), which is then used to measure this effect within a range of changes in reputation:

$$Value\ of\ a\ Change\ in\ Reputation = (X_1)(\Delta REP)(R_m - R_f)$$

$$(8.7)$$

An application presented by the authors
Table 8.5 shows the case of a company whose reputation has improved by 1 point. In this case, the reduction in annual required return Rp would be 0.00317. If its reputation improved by 3 points, i.e., if it rose from 5 to 8, the reduction in the annual cost of equity capital would be (3*0.00317), or close to 1% (if the authors' regression estimates hold over this range of changes in reputation).

Variations in reputation and corporation value
Variations in the cost of equity capital (such as those we observed in the previous example) may also affect a firm's value. Assuming a level of perpetual earnings D, the firm's value could be calculated as a perpetuity:

Table 8.5 Simulation for a hypothetical case

$(R_m - R_f)$	5%
X_1	0.0634
$\Delta R_p / \Delta REP$	(5%*0.0634) = 0.00317

$$V = \frac{D}{k}$$

where k = the firm's equity discount rate.

According to the authors, the firm's value is sensitive to the cost of capital, which is related to the required return. Assuming that a 3-unit change in reputation would allow the company to reduce its required return (and cost of capital) to 1%, the authors state that the ratio between the firm's value and this new rate (V_N) relative to its original value ($V_{original}$) may be expressed as:

$$\frac{V_N}{V_{original}} = \frac{k_{original}}{(k_N - 1)}$$

This formulation is erroneous; if the original value is

$$V_{original} = \frac{D_{original}}{k_{original}}$$

and the firm's value with the new reduced required return is

$$V_N = \frac{D_N}{k_N}$$

then the new value–old value ratio would be:

$$\frac{V_N}{V_{original}} = \frac{D_N / k_N}{D_{original} / k_{original}} = \frac{D_N}{k_N} * \frac{k_{original}}{D_{original}}$$

Because the authors' model establishes that original earnings would not be affected by variations in reputation, but only risk perception, it follows that:

$$\frac{V_N}{V_{original}} = \frac{D_N\big/k_N}{D_{original}\big/k_{original}} = \frac{D}{k_N} * \frac{k_{original}}{D} = \frac{k_{original}}{k_N}$$

Nonetheless, the authors alter this relationship by subtracting 1 from the denominator of one of the equation's expressions, which appears to be an error:

$$\frac{V_N}{V_{original}} = \frac{k_{original}}{(k_N - 1)}$$

The authors cite an example in which a 3-point change in reputation would generate a 15% or 14% reduction in 1% of equity capital costs, resulting in a 7.1% increase in company value. Because the average value of the firms included in this sample is $3 billion, the increase in value would represent $200 million. According to the authors, while large increases in value may be difficult to attain, even smaller changes in reputation can have a significant impact on firm value, especially for firms with higher market capitalization.

8.5.4 Critique

Conceptual problems

This model is based on a financial asset valuation model (the CAPM, or Capital Asset Pricing Model) which, in turn, is based on a set of rather restrictive assumptions. Because the authors do not directly confront these assumptions, their own become rather wobbly.

- For example, why assume that the beta has nothing to do with investor perception, or that it is only a measure of objective risk? Historical betas for an asset or portfolio actually reflect all its movements relative to the market portfolio; and many of these movements can be produced by different risk perceptions on the part of investors. In fact, corporate press releases, and the way in which they are received by the market, can have a tremendous impact on stock prices, and therefore, on the company's beta.

- It is unreasonable to assume that companies with better reputations (i.e., with higher perceptions of product or service quality, financial soundness or innovativeness) can sustain higher betas for the same returns. Why would an investor be willing to invest in a security whose "better reputation" increases the risk of his portfolio and reduces his expected return?

- The CAPM assumes the same time horizon for all investors. But what happens when investors have short time horizons? Does reputation have the same importance then?

Problems in procedural design

- *The procedure does not consider that cost of capital or required return is an "expected" concept*: The authors regress betas and reputations observed in portfolios with identical returns, and suggest that according to the CAPM, these portfolios should also have the same betas. However, the CAPM was developed to estimate expected yield, and historical yields very rarely coincide with what investors can expect for the future. A stock's yield reflects expectations, as well as the disappointments or surprises that lead them to deviate from forecasted values.

- *The method does not take into account all relevant stakeholders:* The survey was administered to 12 000 equity analysts and executives, and therefore ignores a rather important audience: the general public.

- *The method does not consider the relative importance of the variables that define reputation are not ordered:* For the general public, the quality of products and services criterion may be much more important than that of financial soundness.

- *The regression's R2 is low (.5051):* This points to the absence of variable that would explain the risk within the segments surveyed (executives and equity analysts). These would most likely represent objective variables.

8.6 CoreBrand's model for measuring the percentage of market capitalization attributable to corporate brand

This model, developed by James Gregory in the USA, was designed to illustrate the relationship between changes in brand investment and financial returns. The data used derives from CoreBrand's Corporate Branding Index® (CBI), made up of financial, advertising and reputation data on 1000 companies that CoreBrand has monitored for almost 20 years. CoreBrand's analysis involves four principal components:

- Brand Power™ Analysis (BPA)

- Return-on-Investment Analysis

- Brand Equity Valuation Model

- Stock performance forecast.

8.6.1 Brand Power™ Analysis

CoreBrand's website states: *"Brand Power Analysis determines the size and quality of a company's brand vs. peers."* To calculate Brand Power,™ CoreBrand carries out a study among 10 000 high-level executives who assess corporate brand strength on the basis of different "familiarity" and "favorability" determinants for the most important listed companies in the United States. The goal is to determine levels of brand awareness and affinity among senior business managers holding decision-making positions at the North American companies with the highest earnings. The surveys are designed to determine:

- *Familiarity*, a measure of the firm's visibility, i.e. brand awareness.

- *Favorability*, a reflection of perceived quality, i.e. brand reputation or affinity.

Brand Power™ is expressed as a single figure and may be monitored throughout time in order to identify historical trends. CoreBrand also compares their clients' Brand Power™ relative to the average performance of similar companies.

Based on a statistical analysis of the data contained in the Corporate Branding Index® (CBI), CoreBrand asserts that while stock price and market value depend fundamentally on financial factors, Brand Power™ can account for around 5% or 7% of changes in a company's stock price.

8.6.2 ROI Analysis

This analysis allows CoreBrand to determine the degree to which market cap or revenues are impacted by changes in controllable inputs such as investment on advertising and communications.

Through a regression analysis applied to its 1000-company database, CoreBrand identifies the impact that various levels of brand investment have on the Brand Power™ Index. Once the firm's Brand Power™ has been determined for the base case, CoreBrand uses the database to estimate the effect that additional investments would have on the index.

8.6.3 Brand Equity Valuation Model

This component quantifies the brand's economic value by estimating the difference between the actual market capitalization value and what the actual capitalization value would be if the brand did not exist. The brand value is expressed as the brand's contribution to market capitalization. The corporate Brand Power™ estimated on the basis of surveys (cf. 8.6.1) is combined with financial data on the relevant listed companies in a statistical model that allows for the percentage of market capitalization attributable to the corporate brand. An economic value for the corporate brand is then designated from this percentage. CoreBrand claims that it statistically determines the brand value by estimating the impact of

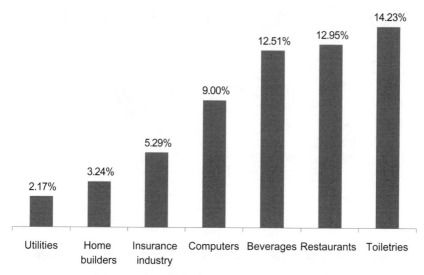

Figure 8.4 Impact of corporate brand by industry.
Source: CoreBrand (2004). Reproduced by permission of CoreBrand (www. corebrand.com)

familiarity and favorability on market value, but does not explain in detail how it calculates the Brand Power's™ impact on market value.

Figure 8.4 shows how greatly Brand Equity calculated in this manner will vary by industry, and indicates that the corporate brand's financial impact will depend heavily on the segment in which it operates.

8.6.4 Stock performance forecast

Using a quantitative hierarchy system, CoreBrand produces 90-day stock price forecasts for over 500 "large cap" American companies within its database.

Figure 8.5 illustrates the principal components of the Core-Brand model.

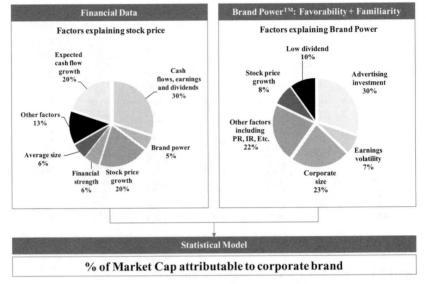

Figure 8.5 CoreBrand corporate brand valuation model.
Source: Developed by author

Table 8.6 shows a brand ranking produced by CoreBrand and published in *BtoB* magazine on 15 July 2002.

8.6.5 Critique

This model has various conceptual and structural flaws:

1. *Vague definition of "corporate brand."* Is "corporate brand" interpreted as a brand aimed exclusively at a business audience, i.e., a B2B business? Or does it instead refer to brands whose ownership and visual identity are identical on both the corporate and commercial levels, such that corporate brand value necessarily encompasses product brand value?

2. *The single clear element in the definition of "corporate brand" is that the only relevant audience for this model are*

Table 8.6   CoreBrand's estimation of "Brand Equity Values"

		Estimation of value of "Brand Equity"	
Rank	Company	Brand equity value (in millions)	Brand equity as % of market capitalization
1	General Electric	61 246	16.4
2	Microsoft	59 588	18.3
3	IBM	27 140	16.7
4	Intel	26 194	13.2
5	Pfizer	25 384	9.9
6	AOL Time Warner	14 458	13.7
7	Cisco Systems	10 965	9.5
8	Merck	10 627	7.8
9	Citigroup	10 441	4.8
10	Nokia	10 399	11.2
11	Bristol-Myers Squibb	10 116	11.4
12	Wells Fargo	9 467	12.1
13	Bank of America	9 466	10.1
14	Dell Computer	8 860	14.3
15	AT&T	7 971	15.2
16	American Express	7 748	17.4
17	GlaxoSmithKline	7 431	4.9
18	Du Pont	7 371	15.5
19	Eli Lilly	7 371	8.6
20	Texas Instruments	7 300	14.1

Source: Callahan (2002). Reproduced by permission of CoreBrand (www.corebrand.com)

top managers and decision-makers for other corporations. Therefore, the model does not consider the value that the corporate brand may add by influencing the perception of audiences other than the top management of other firms, such as equity analysts, public administrations, consumers and the general public.

3. *The participants involved in the market research studies on which this model is based make it quite different from*

most product brand valuation models. While models proposed by Interbrand, The Nielsen Company and other firms are framed by marketing research based on consumer surveys, this model is based on surveys administered to high-level decision-makers in other corporations.

4. *The relationship between the variables that influence Brand Power*™ *and Familiarity/Favorability is not explained.* CoreBrand's explanation of the relationship between Brand Power™ and Familiarity/Favorability, and their respective determinants (dividend level, advertising investment, volatility, etc.) is vague and scanty.

5. *The method's results demonstrate the laxity of the definition of "corporate brand."* If we compare the values of the top "corporate brands" in CoreBrand's ranking (based on corporate manager surveys) with those published by Interbrand in 2002[67] (based on information from consumer-oriented market research), we may infer that CoreBrand's corporate brand concept may be confused with product brand value. Although CoreBrand's corporate brand valuation model is based on top-level manager surveys, it yields values very similar to those obtained through methodologies based on consumer-oriented market research. CoreBrand's and Interbrand's brand value rankings are shown together in Figure 8.6. The corporate brand values for Microsoft and Dell Computers estimated by CoreBrand are practically identical to those of

---

[67] This does not imply that the Interbrand method is suitable for estimating the fair value of a product brand or any other type of support for this method. The rankings are compared simply to determine if the results indicate any type of functional relationship that might allow us to properly interpret the scope of CoreBrand's corporate brand definition.

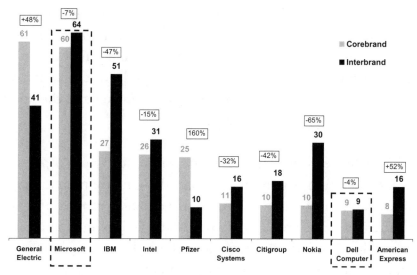

Figure 8.6 Comparison of CoreBrand's corporate brand value estimates and Interbrand's product brand value estimates.
Source: Developed by author based on rankings published by CoreBrand and Interbrand in *B2B* and *Business Week*, 2002. Reproduced by permission of CoreBrand (www.corebrand.com)

their respective product brands (or product brand portfolio) estimated by Interbrand. With other brands, such as GE and Pfizer, the corporate brand values calculated by CoreBrand are much higher than the brand values estimated by Interbrand. The rest of the time, the corporate brand value estimated by CoreBrand is noticeably lower than the brand value estimated by Interbrand.

8.7 Conclusions

Each of the four approaches that have been used to value corporate brands contain major procedural or conceptual flaws; consequently, the results they yield represent no more than rough approximations.

A fundamental difficulty in the analysis and comparison of these models derives from the utter lack of consensus on the definitions of "corporate brand" and "corporate reputation." Certain models, such as that of CoreBrand, never explicitly define these terms, leading to general confusion and the possible misinterpretation of results.

Although the commercial and economic utility of corporate brand valuation is nominal, we are likely to see more corporate brand or corporate reputation valuation models in the future, given the growing interest that scholars and managers have shown in this subject as a tool that may somehow enhance internal corporate management policy.

9

The Future of Brand Valuation

T HE VAST MYRIAD OF BOTH CURRENT AND FUTURE applications of brand valuation is absolutely indisputable, and the practice is sure to grow in light of recent changes in the economic relevance of intangible assets, and the tax and accounting standards that regulate them. But the future of brand valuation may look very different depending on the actions of its key players: providers, scholars, regulators and users.

9.1 The prospect of methodological consensus: Standardization vs. affinity of applications and methods

As we saw in Chapter 1, numerous initiatives undertaken all over the globe are working towards a "practical" consensus on the valuation and reporting of intangible assets. While these projects suggest good prospects for the sophistication and depth of intangible asset valuation tools, the diversity of opinion among different consultancies, auditors and valuation specialists will make achieving full and unanimous consensus quite difficult.

In light of this, and with respect to the concepts we discussed in Chapter 3, no single method can viably suit all our purposes:

- Some methods are more appropriate for technical valuations (for example, royalty savings).

- Other methods (or at least some of their modules, such as the demand driver analysis, or competitive benchmarking components of some proprietary brand valuation methods) may be used for marketing purposes. Recall that, as shown in Chapter 3, brand managers do not need to know the value of a brand to manage it effectively; rather, they need to understand the reasons behind its variations.

- Lastly, different methods may be adapted to espouse various hypotheses for legal purposes, or to resolve judicial conflicts, depending on the country at hand and its relevant legislation.

No single model can simultaneously satisfy accounting, management and legal objectives, and it is unlikely that one will be able to do so in the future. If we cannot even agree on a definition for "brand," how could we expect to use a uniform valuation model that meets all our needs? It is this central problem that will most likely spur different methodological approaches in the future, designed to suit different kinds of purposes.

9.2 Future trends in the supply and demand of brand valuation services

Three major trends will shape long-term supply and demand in this industry, and make winners and losers of its key players.

- *From sector dispersion to concentration around a small group of technically solvent independent providers.*

We have recently witnessed a widespread "brand valuation ranking fever." *Forbes*, *Business Week*, the *Financial Times* and other renowned publications have published rankings of product brand values and even "celebrity" brand values; rankings estimated by Interbrand, Vivaldi Partners, Predictiv, CoreBrand, Brand Finance, Future-Brand, BBDO, Landor and Millward Brown Optimor, among others. This array of findings manifests the sector's current state of dispersal and the vast proliferation of brand valuation providers.

As we noted in Chapter 7, methodological differences will often lead to very disparate value estimations that ultimately hurt the sector's credibility. And because so many of these new providers depend on leading corporate groups (such as FutureBrand, which is a division of IPG, Interbrand, a division of Omnicom, or Millward Brown Optimor, part of the WPP group), there is a slight lack of neutrality in the valuation of assets that are too often valued and managed by firms belonging to the same holding group. While such factors may work well for these divisions today, I believe that they will ultimately represent obstacles to long-term growth in the field. Financial executives who oversee technical valuations (particularly those in accounting departments) deserve and should demand independent estimates provided by audit or valuation firms wholly unaffiliated with advertising groups. This will put the concentration of the technical supply in the hands of the "Big 4" and the independent companies specializing in the economic valuation of intangible assets.

But, as is often the case, things must get worse before they get better; and the field is bound to see further dispersion before ultimate consolidation. Partly encouraged by the growing interest that the media and clients have shown in this new, appealing topic, many market research companies, IP lawyers and scholars have begun to offer brand valuation services (not always supported by the expert knowledge of the right team). These practices also work to hurt the credibility of this budding industry; while they may be very short-lived themselves, their contributions to valuation users' skepticism may be lasting.

- *Growing convergence among marketing and finance specialists.*

Some providers have recognized the need for interdisciplinary teams that combine various skill sets to provide proper brand valuation practices. Two of the principal audit firms currently taking this approach are located in Germany:

- E&Y AG collaborated with BBDO to develop their model, BEVA (Brand Equity Valuation for Accounting) in 2004.

- – PWC uses Sattler's Advanced Brand Valuation (ABV) model.

- – BrandEconomics uses a model developed jointly by Stern Stewart & Co. and Young & Rubicam.

- *Increasingly sophisticated valuation techniques.*

  Even if the same basic valuation methods continue to be employed, the current situation suggests that they will involve increasingly sophisticated techniques. For example, valuation specialists have recently begun to use various statistical methods in order to enhance the objectivity of their results.

These trends will determine clear winners and losers in the field. The *winners* will include:

- providers or users of financially sound royalty relief models (in the technical valuation sector);

- providers or users of models that close the breach between marketing and finance and are intelligible to both sectors;

- providers in clearly independent positions.

The *losers* will include:

- brand valuation providers affiliated with advertising groups who attempt to justify the value of their communication proposals through spurious exercises;

- providers who are not specialists and whose methods do not involve financial or marketing expertise.

9.3 Accounting users: financial officers' discomfort

The two trends that are most likely to shape the future of the brand valuation industry, and to affect the degree to which "technical" users are willing to accept one method over another, can be characterized by the following expressions:

- "Let's all do everything:" the proliferation of brand valuation providers with highly diverse origins and specializations.

- "Everything is valid:" the vast divergence of their methods and results.

These two factors have already contributed to the widespread distrust of the brand valuation industry and the uneasiness felt by financial officers. Rankings, in my opinion, act and are treated as "buzz marketing" tools, when really they should be used more prudently. It comes as no surprise that valuation service users approach providers with skepticism; within a period of just six months, rankings will rate the same brands 30% or even 50% higher or lower. And who is one to believe? Can we trust the methodology? Is the difference in value arising from the analyst's judgment?

The lack of methodological consensus, together with the novelty of the subject, is one of the principal sources of financial officers' discomfort with valuation projects. Most likely, advances in research in the field will bring more unanimous voices on valuation methods suitable for technical applications and lead to the eventual dissipation of skepticism and distrust in the field.

Similarly, as the voluntary reporting of intangible assets becomes more widespread, and the level of education among users improves, more financial users will feel encouraged to report indicators and values of intangible assets and brands.

9.4 Marketing specialists: using valuation prudently and founding a new language compatible with finance

Many times, and often because of the way in which valuation projects are offered and sold, marketing specialists try to use brand valuation projects to control the performance of brand managers. But when misinterpreted, the valuation tool can quickly create internal conflict. Because brand value often fluctuates for reasons beyond the control of the marketing team, using brand valuation as a "control tool based on a number" leads to problems. In these cases, as we indicated in Chapter 3, it is advisable to use other types of indicators, and to *evaluate*, not *value*, the brand.

Marketing users also contribute to the gap between marketing and financial departments by using terminology imprecisely or inconsistently; for example, by referring to "brand equity" as:

- description of brand image or personality;

- measure of "brand strength" or loyalty rate;

- concept of economic value.

These concepts must be refined and treated cautiously, particularly during the initial phases of a brand valuation project that will invariably involve financial components. In this context, brand equity may be defined as certain audiences' propensity to choose freely and express preferences that are financially favorable for the firm. Measuring brand equity represents the key arena in which marketing departments can contribute to calculating brand value, allowing them to isolate and analyze the attributes that explain the changes in these propensities and indicate trends in future behavior.

9.5 Regulators: behind the scenes, but with great confidence

In the intangible valuation sector, legal and regulatory initiatives tend to conform to general industry practices, partly because regulators share the same sense of distrust as users in the financial and accounting segments. But changes in the treatment of intangible assets are largely due to developments embodied in new IFRS accounting standards.

In the future, we will see not only more refined valuation models, but also more sophisticated applications that use brands as collateral in securitization and other credit operations. When brand valuation becomes a key component in credit analysis, credit analysts will need more consistent parameters. It is therefore likely that valuation standards in the future will be designed to meet the needs of certain sectors, such as risk analysis. Similarly, users are showing great interest in building guidelines specific to the financial sector, which will lead to new valuation and/or sectorial reporting guidelines designed to reflect the specific relevance of intangible assets in the financial industry.

Numerous government bodies have promoted initiatives to advance the development of unanimous and objective standards for valuing and reporting intangible assets and brands. Though far from perfect, one of the most impactful government initiatives has been that endorsed by Japan's Ministry of Economy, Trade and Industry; in 2002, the Hirose Committee introduced an "objective" brand valuation model that met the requirements of Japan's Commercial Code and tax legislation. The establishment of other government-backed initiatives that work towards sound valuation model proposals will lead the way towards a practical consensus.

The standardization of such guidelines must be sought prudently, and must involve the participation of all market players: users, providers, scholars, auditors as well as the investment community.

References

Aaker, D.A. (1991) *Managing Brand Equity: Capitalizing on the value of a brand name*, The Free Press, New York.

Aaker, D.A. (1996) *Building Strong Brands*, The Free Press, New York.

Aaker, D.A. and Keller, K.L. (1990) Consumer Evaluations of Brand Extensions. *Journal of Marketing*, 54(1 January), 27–41.

AASB (2001) Accounting for Intangible Assets. December 2001, Agenda paper 9.4.

A.C. Nielsen GMBH (2006) AC Nielsen Brand Performance. Germany, presentation prepared by M.G. Schilken from A.C. Nielsen and O. Franzen from Konzept & Markt GmbH. Available at: http://www.konzept-und-markt.com/Docs/ACNBrandPerformance_kurz-Engl_1.pdf (accessed 18 June 2006).

Accenture (2003) Intangible assets and future value. Accenture survey conducted by the Economist Intelligence Unit, August and September 2003. Available at: http://down.ciw.com.cn/ShowSoftDown.asp?UrlID=1&SoftID=18890 (accessed 18 October 2008).

Andriessen, D. and Tiessen, R. (2000) *Weightless Weight – Find your Real Value in the Future of Intangible Assets*, Pearson Education, London.

Andriessen, D. (2004) *Making Sense of Intellectual Capital: Designing a Method for the Valuation of Intangibles*, Elsevier, Oxford.

Angberg, A. (n.d.) "What You Should Know About Branding and Brand Value," Houlihan Valuation Advisors, http://www.houlihan.com/research/what_you_should_know_about_branding.pdf (downloaded 29 November 2004).

Anson, W. (2005) *Fundamentals of Intellectual Property Valuation: A Primer for Identifying and Determining Value*, American Bar Association, Chicago, Il.

Anson, W. and Martin, D. (2004) Accurate IP Valuations in Multiple Environments. *Intellectual Asset Management*, February/March, pp. 7–10. Available at: http://www.consor.com/editor/docs/Accurate%20IP%20Valuation%20in%20Multiple%20Environments1.pdf (accessed 17 May 2006).

Badenhausen, K. and Roney, M. (2005) Next Generation. Methodological Explanation of the Forbes-Vivaldi Partners Ranking published by Forbes. Available at: http://www.forbes.com/forbes/2005/0620/115tab.html (accessed 25 January 2006).

Barwise, P., Higson, C., Likierman, A. and Marsh, P. (1989) *Accounting for Brands*, London Business School/The Institute of Chartered Accountants in England and Wales, pp. 1–84.

BBDO Consulting (2004) Brand Valuation has established itself on top management agendas. Point of View 5, March 2004, Germany. Available at: http://www.markenlexikon.com/d_texte/verfahren_bbdo_beva.pdf (accessed 17 October 2008).

Beccacece, F., Borgonovo, E. and Reggiani, F. (2006) Risk Analysis in Brand Valuation. (July). Bocconi University, Milan, Italy. Available at SSRN: http://ssrn.com/abstract=931023 (accessed 10 October 2006).

Biesalski, A. and Sokolowski, T. (2008) IP Manager: Value-oriented management of the asset brand. Documentation provided by Alexander Biesalski.

Binar, J. (2005) *The value of brands ... A view from an advertising agency*. Presentation prepared by Jan Binar of McCann WorldGroup in June 2005. Available at: http://www.marketingmanagement.cz/home/sessions/summit/2005/download/C/7_MM%2005%20Binar.pdf (accessed 21 September 2008).

Boos, M. (2003) *International Transfer Pricing: The Valuation of Intangible Assets*, Kluwer Law International, The Hague.

BrandEconomics (2002) Bringing new clarity to brand management and strategy, New York. Available at: http://www.brandecon.com/docs/WhitePaper20pp.pdf (accessed 13 August 2005).

BrandEconomics (2003) *Enhancing the Value Contribution of Brand Strategy.* Available at: http://www.brandecon.com/docs/BEIntro.pdf (accessed 13 August 2005).

Brandient (2006) Top 50 most valuable Romanian brands: A premiere in Romania: Brandient realized for BusinessWeek Romania the first ranking of Romanian brands value, Bucharest, 12 December. Available at: http://www.brandient.com/downloads/brandient_top50_2006_en.pdf (accessed 30 June 2008).

Brand Finance (2000) Current Practice in Brand Valuation, A Gee Bulletin, June 2000, London, United Kingdom. Available at: http://www.brandfinance.com/Uploads/pdfs/CurrentPracticein_Brand_Valuation. pdf (accessed 30 June 2001).

Brand Finance (2002) Brand Valuation Workshop, presented at DIRCOM, Spain, April 2002.

Brand Metrics (n.d.) *Graphical depictions of the model*, downloaded from http://www.brandmetrics.com/outline1.htm (accessed 12 September 2004).

Brand Rating (2008) Monetary Brand Evaluation with BRAND RATING Background: Approaches, Philosophy, Services. Munich, September. Presentation provided by Alexander Biesalski.

Brealey, R. and Myers, S. (1993) *Fundamentos de Financiación Empresarial*, McGraw-Hill Interamericana de España, 4th edn, Madrid, Spain.

Burgman, R., Roos, G., Ballow, J. and Thomas, J. (2005) No Longer 'Out of Sight, Out of Mind': Intellectual Capital Approach in AssetEconomics LLP & Accenture Inc. Working Paper.

Business Week (2004) Brand Values Surge, 18–24 November 2004.

Business Wire (1998), Licensing Industry Leader Reorganizes for Greater Leverage; TLA Changes Name to Consor, New York, June 10. Available at: http://findarticles.com/p/articles/mi_m0EIN/ is_1998_June_10/ai_n27534661/pg_1?tag=artBody;col1 (accessed 24 June 2004).

Callahan, S. (2002) Firm devises equation to quantify brand value. *BtoB Magazine*, 15 July.

Carrier, J. (2008) Personal communication, 24 November 2008.

Castanheira, J. (2008) As marcas mais valiosas do Brasil. Istoé Dinheiro, 11 June. http://www.brandanalytics.com.br/pdf/istoedinheiro-marcas_maisvaliosas_062008.pdf (downloaded 5 January 2009).

Clarke, K. (2001) What price on loyalty when a brand switch is just a click away? *Qualitative Market Research*, 4(3), 160–168.

Cohen, J. (2005) *Intangible Assets: Valuation and Economic Benefit*, John Wiley & Sons, Inc., Hoboken, NJ.

Copeland, T., Koller, T. and Murrin, J. (2000) *Valuation: Measuring and Managing the Value of Companies*, John Wiley & Sons, Inc., New York.

CoreBrand (2004) How Branding Works and Creates Value. Presentation at the National Association of Water Companies, 11 October.

Corebrand (2004b) Directory of Brand Equity™: Quarterly Report, SAMPLE. Available at: www.corebrand.com (accessed 9 January 2005).

Cravens, K.S. and Guilding, C. (1999) Strategic brand valuation: a cross-functional perspective, *Business Horizons*, 42(4), July–August.

Damodaran, A. (1996) *Investment Valuation: Tools and Techniques for Determining the Value of Any Asset*, John Wiley & Sons, Inc., New York.

Ehrbar, A. and Bergesen, M. (2002) A New Approach to Managing Brand and Business Value. *Strategic Investor Relations*, Winter 2002, United States of America, 1–7.

Eisbruck, J. (2007) Royal(ty) succession: the evolution of IP-backed securitization. Introduction to *Building and enforcing intellectual property value 2007*, Moody's investor service, 17–21. Available at: http://www.buildingipvalue.com/07intro/p.17-21%20Intro,%20Moody.pdf (accessed 19 October 2008).

Farr, A. (2006) How the BrandZ Top 100 Global Ranking was created. *Financial Times*, United Kingdom, 3 April.

Feldwick, P. (1996) Do we really need 'brand equity'? *The Journal of Brand Management*, 4(1), 9–28.

Fernández, P. (2001) Valoración de empresas: Cómo medir y gestionar la creación de valor. *Gestión 2000*, Barcelona, Spain.

Fernández, P. (2006) 102 errores en valoraciones de empresas, Research Paper No 631, May, IESE Business School – Universidad de Navarra, Barcelona, Spain.

Fischer, M. (2007) Valuing brands: A Cost-Effective and Easy-to-Implement Measurement Approach, Marketing Science Institute, Report #07-107, Cambridge, Mass.

Fombrun, C.J. (1996) *Reputation: Realizing Value from the Corporate Image*, Boston: Harvard Business School Press.

Forbes Magazine (2004) What's In A Name? 19 April.

Frampton, J. (2008) The Red Thread: Creating and Managing Brand Value. Available at: www.ana.net/michome2/getfile/14819 (accessed 3 November 2008).

Günther, T. and Kriegbaum-Kling, C. (2001), Brand Valuation and Control: An Empirical Study, *Schmalenbach Business Review (sbr)*, 53(4), pp. 263–294. Available at SSRN: http://ssrn.com/abstract=304447 (accessed 20 June 2008).

Haigh, D. (1994) *Strategic Control of Marketing Finance*, Financial Times Pitman Publishing, London.

Haigh, D. (1999) Understanding the Financial Value of Brands, A report prepared for and published in conjunction with the European Association of Advertising Agencies, June 1999, London. Available at: http://www.brandfinance.com/Uploads/pdfs/EAAA_Underst_FinValueofBrands.pdf (accessed 19 July 2001).

Haigh, D. (2000), Brand Valuation: Measuring and Leveraging your Brand, a report prepared for the Institute of Canadian Advertising, May 2000, Toronto, Canada. Available at: http://www.markenlexikon.com/texte/brandfinance_brand_valuation_leverage_may_2000.pdf (accessed 15 August 2008).

Haigh, D. (2001) Make brands make their mark, *International Tax Review*, London, 12(2 February), pp. 40–43.

Haigh, D. and Chng, D. (2005) Singapore Firms' Intangible Assets are Grossly Undervalued, A Study of Intangible Value by Brand Finance, Nanyang Business Review, 4(1). Available at: http://www.brandfinance.com/Uploads/pdfs/NBR_Intangibles_Study.pdf (accessed 21 July 2006).

Haigh, D. and Knowles, J. (2004) How to define your brand and determine its value, *Marketing Management*, ISSN: 1061-3846, 13(3), pp. 24–28. Available at: http://www.brandfinance.com/Uploads/pdfs/How%20to%20define%20your%20brand%20and%20determine%20its%20value.pdf (accessed 21 July 2006).

Haigh, D. and Knowles, J. (2004b) Don't Waste Your Time With Brand Valuation, Marketing NPV, 1(6 October), pp. 17–19. Available at: http://www.howbigisbrand.com/articles/2004%2010%20Brand%20Valuation%20-%20MNPV.pdf (accessed 17 October 2008).

Hall, R. (1992) The strategic analysis of intangible resources, *Strategic Management Journal*, 13(2 February), pp. 135–144.

Hall, R. (1993) A framework linking intangible resources and capabilities to sustainable competitive advantage, *Strategic Management Journal*, 14(8), pp. 607–618.

Hannington, T. (2006) *Cómo Medir y Gestionar la Reputación de su Empresa*, Ediciones Deusto, Barcelona, Spain.

Harms, T. (2008) Consumer products IFRS financial statements survey, November 2008. Available at: http://www.ey.com/Global/assets.nsf/International/Consumer_products_IFRS_survey/$file/Consumer_products_IFRS_financial_statements_survey_25.11.08.pdf.

Henry C. Co. (n.d.). The Growth Curve. Available at: www.csupomona.edu/~hco/MoT/03bGrowthCurve.ppt. Downloaded 16 April 2009.

Hillery, J. (2004) Securitization of Intellectual Property: Recent Trends from the United States. Available at: http://www.iip.or.jp/summary/pdf/WCORE2004s.pdf (accessed 31 October 2007).

Hirose, Y. et al. (2002) The Report of the Committee on Brand Valuation, The Ministry of Economy, Trade and Industry, The Government of Japan, 24 June 2002. Available at: http://www.meti.go.jp/english/information/downloadfiles/cbrandvalue.pdf (accessed 25 August 2004).

Hofmann, J. (2005) Value intangibles! Intangible capital can and must be valued – owners and valuers alike will benefit, 19 October 2005, Deutsche Bank Research, Frankfurt am Main, Germany.

Howrey (2002) A Survey of Investor Attitudes on IP, London, Howrey Europe, www.howrey.com/docs/UK_IP_Survey0102.pdf (accessed 14 October 2006).

Intangible Business (2004) On Brand Valuation and Brand Management. Available at: http://www.intangiblebusiness.com/store/data/files/129-IB_Viewpoint_On_brand_valuation_and_management.pdf (accessed 30 November 2005).

Interbrand (2001) Global Brands: Annual Report, published by *Business Week*, July 2001. Available at: http://www.interbrand.com/images/bgb_BW/BGB_Business-Week_2001.pdf (accessed 13 April 2009).

Interbrand (2001b) World's Most Valuable Brands Ranked by Interbrand 2001. Available at: http://www.brandchannel.com/images/home/ranking_methodology.pdf (accessed 13 April 2009).

Interbrand (2002) The Best Global Brands: Special Report, published by *Business Week*, 5 August 2009. Available at: http://www.interbrand.com/images/bgb_BW/BGB_BusinessWeek_2002.pdf (accessed 13 April 2009).

Interbrand (2003) The Best Global Brands: Annual Ranking of the Top 100, published by *Business Week*, 4 August 2003. Available at: http://www.interbrand.com/images/bgb_BW/BGB_BusinessWeek_2003.pdf (accessed 13 April 2009).

Interbrand (2004) The Best Global Brands: Our Annual Ranking of the Top 100, published by *Business Week*, 9–16 August 2004. Available at: http://www.interbrand.com/images/bgb_BW/BGB_BusinessWeek_2004.pdf (accessed 13 April 2009).

Interbrand (2005) Global Brands: Annual Report, published by *Business Week*, 1 August 2005.

Interbrand (2006) Best Global Brands 2006: A Ranking by Brand Value, published by *Business Week*, 1 August 2006. Available at: http://www.interbrand.com/images/studies/BGB06Report_072706.pdf (accessed 15 August 2006).

Interbrand (2007) All Brands are not Created Equal: Best Global Brands 2007. Available at: http://www.interbrand.com/images/BGB_reports/BGB_2007.pdf (accessed 21 September 2007).

Interbrand (2008) Best Global Brands 2008. Available at: http://www.interbrand.com/images/BGB_reports/BGB_2008_EURO_Format.pdf (accessed 12 March 2009).

Interbrand (2008b) Top Taiwan Global Brands 2008: A Ranking by Brand Value. Available at: http://www.interbrand.com.sg/images/studies/Taiwan_Bro_2008.pdf (accessed 12 March 2009).

Interbrand (2008c) Competing in the Global Economy: Best Canadian Brands 2008. Available at: http://www.ourfishbowl.com/images/surveys/BestCanadianBrands2008.pdf (accessed 12 March 2009).

Interbrand (2009) Best Retail Brands 2009: Global Perspectives on a Changing Marketplace. Available at: http://www.interbrand.com/images/studies/85_Interbrand_Best_Retail_2009.pdf (accessed 12 March 2009).

Interbrand Design Forum (2009) The Most Valuable US Retail Brands 2009. Available at: http://d.scribd.com/docs/1l4q0ir62gfef90svquw.pdf (accessed 12 March 2009).

Interbrand Zintzmeyer&Lux (2003) The Value of the Brand. Fundamentals of an economic evaluation, 03000700, 5 December 2003. Available at: http://www.ram.ru/outbound/2003/BrandValuation.pdf (accessed 25 November 2004).

Interbrand Zintzmeyer&Lux (n.d.) Brand Valuation. The key to unlock the Benefits from your Brand Assets. Available at: http://www.interbrand.ch/e/pdf/IBZL_Brand_Valuation_e.pdf (accessed 15 August 2006).

Interbrand Zintzmeyer&Lux (2007) If you can't measure it, you can't manage it. Analysing the brand's strategic drivers. Conference presentation. Available at: http://bestbrand.by/download_files/interbrand_brandconference_070924.pdf (accessed 1 March 2009).

International Valuation Standards Committee (2003) *International Valuation Standards*, 6th edn, London.

International Valuation Standards Committee (2007) Determination of Fair Value of Intangible Assets for IFRS Reporting Purposes, Discussion Paper, July. Available at: http://www.ivsc.org/pubs/comment/intangibleassets.pdf (accessed 10 September 2007).

Jourdan, P. (2001) Le capital marque: proposition d'une mesure individuelle et essai de validation, *Recherche et Applications en Marketing*, 16(4), pp. 3–24

Kahle, L. and Kim, C. (2006) *Creating Images and the Psychology of Marketing Communication*, Routledge.

Kam, S. and Angberg, A. (n.d.) *The Creation, Maintenance and Valuation of Brands*, HVA, San Francisco, United States of America. Available at: www.houlihanadvisors.com (accessed 7 August 2004).

Keller, K.L. (1991) Conceptualizing, Measuring and Managing Customer-based Brand Equity, Marketing Science Institute, Working Paper, Report No. 91-123, Cambridge, MA.

Keller, K.L. (2008) *Building, Measuring and Managing Brand Equity*, 3rd edn, Pearson Prentice Hall, Upper Saddle River, NJ.

Kendrick, John W. (1994) Total Capital and Economic Growth, *Atlantic Economic Journal*, 22(1 March), pp. 1–18.

Kerin, R. and Sethuraman, R. (1998) Exploring the brand value-shareholder value nexus for consumer goods companies, *Journal of the Academy of Marketing Science*, 26(4), pp. 260–273.

Kumar, S. and Hansted Blomqvist, K. (2004) Mergers and acquisitions: Making brand equity a key factor in M&A decision making, *Journal of Strategy & Leadership*, 32(2), pp. 20–27. Available at: http://www.prophet.com/downloads/articles/SL32(2)05-Kumar.pdf (accessed 17 August 2005).

Lamb, R. (2002) "The Role of Intellectual Property and Intangible Assets in Mergers and Acquisitions," in *Intellectual Property Assets in Mergers and Acquisitions*, ed. L. Bryer and M. Simensky, John Wiley & Sons, Inc., New York, chapter II.

Lasinski, M. (2002) "Valuation of Intellectual Property Assets in Mergers and Acquisitions," in *Intellectual Property Assets in Mergers and Acquisitions*, ed. L. Bryer and M. Simensky, John Wiley & Sons, Inc., New York, chapter IV.

Leuthesser, L. (1988) Defining, measuring and managing brand equity: A conference summary, Report #88-104, Marketing Science Institute, Cambridge MA.

Lev, B. (1999) Seeing is believing: A better approach to estimating knowledge capital, *CFO Asia Magazine*. Available at: http://pages.stern.nyu.edu/~blev/cfoarticle.html.

Lindemann, J. (2003) "Brand Valuation," in *Brands and Branding* ed. R. Clifton and J. Simmons, The Economist Series, Profile Books, London, chapter II.

Lindemann, J. (2004) Serving self or serving society? Influencing external stakeholders: a presentation to The Council on Foundation, 18 June 2004. Available at: http://int2.cof.org/conferences/presentations/2004corporatesummit/lindemann.pdf (accessed 13 April 2009).

Lonergan, W. (1998) *The Valuation of Businesses, Shares and Other Equity*, 3rd edn, Business and Professional Publishing.

Mard, M., Hitchner, J., Hyden, S. and Zyla, M. (2002) *Valuation for Financial Reporting: Intangible Assets, Goodwill and Impairment Analysis, SFAS 141 and 142*, John Wiley & Sons, Inc., New York.

Marketing Leadership Council (2003) Measuring the impact of brand-building investments: An overview of measurement approaches and vendors, April, Corporate Executive Board.

Martin, G. and Brown, T. (1991) In Search of Brand Equity: The Conceptualization and Measurement of the Brand Impression Construct, Proceedings of the American Marketing Association 1991 Winter Educators Conference, Orlando, FL, February, pp. 431–438.

McAuley, T. (2003) Brand Family Values, *CFO Europe*, 31 December. Available at: http://www.cfo.com/article.cfm/3011151/4/c_2984368?f=related (accessed 4 October 2004).

Millward Brown (n.d.) Brochure on BrandDynamics. Available at: http://www.millwardbrown.com/sites/millwardbrown/Media/Pdfs/en/Services/BrandDynamics.pdf (accessed 27 October 2007).

Millward Brown Optimor (2006) BRANDZTMTOP 100 Power Brands, 24 March 2006. Available at: http://www.ft.com/cms/4683957a-c0a7-11da-9419-0000779e2340.pdf (accessed 15 October 2006).

Millward Brown Optimor (2007) BrandZ™ Top 100 Most Powerful Brands. Available at: http://www.millwardbrown.com/Sites/optimor/Media/Pdfs/en/BrandZ/BrandZ-2007-RankingReport.pdf (accessed 1 October 2007).

Mintz, S. (1999) Seeing is believing: A Better Approach to Estimating Knowledge Capital, *CFO Magazine*, February 1999. Available at: http://pages.stern.nyu.edu/~blev/cfoarticle.html (accessed 15 August 2008).

Motameni, R. and Shahrokhi, M. (1998) Brand equity valuation: a global perspective, *The Journal of Product and Brand Management*, 7(4), pp. 275–290.

Mussler, S., Hupp, O. and Powaga, K. (2004) *Evaluation of the Financial Value of Brands*, GfK Custom Research Inc., Minneapolis.

Myers, C. (2003) Managing brand equity: A look at the impact of attributes, *The Journal of Product and Brand Management*, 12(1), pp. 39–51.

Nakamura, L. (2001) Investing in Intangibles: Is a Trillion Dollars Missing from GDP? *Business Review*, Q4 2001. (www.phil.frb.org/files/br/brq401ln.pdf (accessed 7 October 2007).)

Obae, P. and Barbu, P. (2004) Capital is a valuable brand, *Capital*, Issue 40, Romania, 30 September 2004. Available at: http://www.brandient.com/en/news_and_viewpoints/interviews_articles/capital_is_a_valuable_brand.html (accessed 15 September 2008).

Park, C. and Srinivasan, V. (1994) A survey-based method for measuring and understanding brand equity and its extendibility, *Journal of Marketing Research*, 31(2 May), pp. 271–288.

Pavri, Z. (1999) Valuation of Intellectual Property Assets: The Foundation for Risk Management and Financing, Price Waterhouse Coopers. Available at: www.sristi.org/material/11.1valuation%20%20of%20intellectual%20property%20assets.pdf (accessed 15 October 2004).

Pettis, C. (1995) *The Relationship of Corporate Brand Strategy and Stock Price*, Morgan Stanley, U.S. Investment Research, pp. 20–27.

Pike, S. and Roos, G. (2004) Mathematics and modern business management, *Journal of Intellectual Capital*, 5(2), pp. 243–256.

Pratt, S. (2002) *Cost of Capital: Estimation and Applications*, 2nd edn, John Wiley & Sons, Inc., Hoboken, NJ.

Raboy, D. and Wiggins, S. (1997) Intangible capital, hedonic pricing and international transfer prices, *Public Finance Quarterly*, 25(4), pp. 347–365.

Reilly, R. and Schweihs, R. (1999) *Valuing Intangible Assets*, McGrawHill, New York.

Rivilla, I. (2005) El Valor Económico de las Marcas, *Manual de la empresa responsable*, Vol. 2, p. 47.

Roos, G. (2005) Valuing Brands: A Presentation to The Brand Finance Forum, London, 19 August 2005.

Roos, J., Roos, G., Dragonetti, N. and Edvinsson, L. (2001) *Capital Intelectual: El valor intangible de la empresa*, Paidós Empresa, Barcelona, Spain.

Salinas, G. (2008) Valoración económica de marcos: ¿ dexiste un método óptimo para valorar marcas? In *La Comunicación Empresarial y la Gestión de los Intangibles en España y Latinoamérica*, Pearson Educación, Madrid.

Salinas, G. and Ambler, T. (2008) A Taxonomy of Brand Valuation Methodologies: How Different Types of Methodologies Can Help to Answer Different Types of Questions, Marketing Science Institute, Special Report No. 08-204, Cambridge, MA.

Sattler, H., Högl, S. and Hupp, O. (2002) Evaluation of the Financial Value of Brands, Research Papers on Marketing and Retailing, 7 August 2002, Hamburg University, Germany.

Seetharaman, A., Nadzir, Z. and Gunalan, S. (2001) A conceptual study on brand valuation, *The Journal of Product and Brand Management*, 10(4), pp. 243–256.

Simon, C. and Sullivan, M. (1993) The measurement and determinants of brand equity: a financial approach, *Marketing Science*, 12(1 Winter), pp. 28–52.

Sinclair, R. (2007) The Relief from Royalty Enigma, Newsletter May 2007. Available at: http://www.brandmetrics.com/cgi-bin/brandmetrics/brand-displayarticle.pl? 20070530_1180539060 (accessed 10 October 2008).

Smith, G. (1997) *Trademark Valuation*, John Wiley & Sons, Inc., New York.

Smith, G. and Parr, R. (2000) *Valuation of Intellectual Property and Intangible Assets*, 3rd edn, John Wiley & Sons, Inc., New York.

Smith, G. and Parr, R. (2005) *Intellectual Property: Valuation, Exploitation and Infringement Damages*, John Wiley & Sons, Inc., Hoboken, NJ.

Srivastava, R., McInish, T., Wood, R.A. and Capraro, A.J. (1997) The value of corporate reputation: Evidence from the equity markets, *Corporate Reputation Review*, 1(1 July), pp. 62–68.

Srivastava, R. and Shocker, A. (1991) Brand equity: a perspective on its meaning and measurement, Marketing Science Institute, Working Paper, Report No. 91-124, Cambridge, MA.

Tadelis, S. (1997) What's in a Name? Reputation as a Tradeable Asset, Department of Economics, Stanford University. Available at: http://www-econ.stanford.edu/faculty/workp/swp97033.pdf (accessed 1 March 2007).

Tollington, T. (1999) The brand accounting side-show, *The Journal of Product and Brand Management*, 8(3), pp. 204–217.

Torres, F. (2006) Establishing Royalty Rates Through Options. Available at SSRN: http://ssrn.com/abstract=1014743 (accessed 10 May 2008).

Torres Coronas, T. (2002) *La Valoración de Marcas*, Gestión 2000, Barcelona, Spain.

Walker, C. (1995), How strong is your brand? *American Demographics*, January, pp. 46–53.

Whitwell, S. (2005) Brand Valuation: Why and How. Available at: http://www.intangiblebusiness.com/store/data/files/216-Viewpoint_Brand_Valuation_whyandhow.pdf (accessed 30 November 2005).

Winters, L. (1991) Brand equity measures: Some recent advances, *Marketing Research*, 3(3), pp. 70–73.

Wood, L. (1999) Market power and its measurement, *European Journal of Marketing*, 33(5), p. 612.

Woodward, C. (2003) Valuing intangible assets and impairment testing in the pharmaceuticals industry, Price Waterhouse Coopers. Available at: www.pwcglobal.com/images/gx/eng/about/ind/pharma/woodward_workshop.pdf (accessed 11 June 2006).

Yoo, B. and Donthu, N. (2001) Developing and validating a multidimensional consumer brand equity scale, *Journal of Business Research*, 52(1 April), pp. 1–14.

Zimmermann, R., Klein-Bölting, U., Sander, B. and Murad-Aga, T. (2001) Brand Equity Review©, Brand Equity Excellence©, Volume 1, BBDO Group Germany, Düsseldorf, Germany.

Zimmermann, R., Klein-Bölting, U., Sander, B. and Murad-Aga, T. (2002) Brand Equity Evaluator©, Brand Equity Excellence©, Volume 2, BBDO Group Germany, Düsseldorf, Germany.

Index

Note: Page numbers in *italics* refer to figures and tables

AbsoluteBrand 110–12, *315*
academic courses 30–1
academic models 301–2
  in Anglo-Saxon countries 337–8
  versus professional practice 359–60
  vs. practitioners' methods 343
accounting data, equations based on 321,
    322
  see also Hirose model (2002)
accounting perspective
  brand as an intangible asset 2–3
  conflict generated by brand
      capitalization 36–7
  discomfort over lack of consensus
      402–3
  internally generated brands 4–5
  trademark, brand and branded
      business 5–7
accounting standards 24–6, 52, 404
acquisitions
  of brands in the 1980s 33–4
  external transactions 53–4, *52*
Advanced Brand Valuation (ABV) model
    183–4
  brand earnings forecast 187
  brand potential index 184–5
  brand-specific earnings 185–6
  brand-specific risk 187–9

brand value 189–91
  critique of model 191–2
"annuity" model, Interbrand 216–22
Association-Affinity Model 369–73
AUS Consultants 112–17, *313*, *314*, *318*,
    320, *323*
  trademark valuation 114, *115–16*

Baruch Lev's Intangible Scoreboard 100,
    234–6
BAV (Brand Asset® Valuator) model
    133–43
BBDO valuation models 117–18
  Brand Equity Evaluation System
      (BEES) 118–21
  Brand Equity Evaluator® (BEE) 121–6
  Brand Equity Valuation for Accounting®
      (BEVA) 126–9
  classification 297–8
binomial valuation model, real options
    105–7
"black box" methods 86, 343–4
Black-Scholes model 107–8
brand allegiance *see* loyalty
Brand Asset® Valuator (BAV) model,
    Young & Rubicam 132–44
Brand Balance Sheet, Nielsen Company
    274–7

"brand contribution" calculation, MBO
model 240–3, 249
BrandDynamics™ Pyramid, Millward
Brown 245–7
brand earnings
ABV model 185–7
"earnings split" method, Brand
Finance 147–50
Interbrand 216–17
"Role of Brand Index (RBI)" 225–7
MBO model 235, 237–40, *312*
methods of calculating 162, 175
compared to theoretical earnings *317*
through royalty relief *315*
variations of excess earnings
method *314*
multiple applicable to 175–7, 218
Nielsen Company 278–9
BrandEconomics® model 132–3, 143
critique of model 143–4, 143–4
phases in application of method 133–4
brand strength 137–8
brand value, calculation of 140–2
intangible value multiple 139–40
role of brand, determining 136–7
separation of total market value
134–5
brand equity 12–14
"brand evaluation" models 18–19,
299–300
CoreBrand's estimation of value of *393*,
390–1
GfK-PwC-Sattler model *191*
imprecise terminology of marketing
users 403–4
Motameni and Shahrokhi's model
250–7
see also brand value
Brand Equity Evaluation System®
(BEES) 118–21
Brand Equity Evaluator® (BEE) 121–2
determinants of brand equity 122–4
discount rate calculation 124–5
model critique 125–6
net present value of cash flow 125
Brand Equity Valuation for Accounting®
(BEVA) 126–9
Brand Equity Valuation Model,
CoreBrand 390–1
brand expected life, determination of
155–6
Brand Finance 144–5
critique of models 150–1

earnings split method 147–50
royalty savings method 145–7
see also FutureBrand
brand health
measurement of 137–8
and relative impact of economic
performance 136–7
brand iconography 159–60
Brandient models 129
based on demand driver analysis 129–30
based on royalty savings 131
critique of models 132
Brand knowledge structure (BKS)
analysis 155–6
brand loyalty *see* loyalty
BrandMetrics 151–8
"Brand Momentum", Millward Brown
Optimor 243–4
"Brand Performance" model, Nielsen
Company 277–80
Brand Potential Index (BPI®), ABV model
184–5
Brand Power™ analysis (BPA),
CoreBrand 389–90
brand premium profits (BPP), expert
workshops 153–4
brand presence 244
"Brand Rating" model 158–64
"brand risk"
analysis of, FutureBrand 181–2
calculations, AUS Consultants 323
calculations, Brand Finance 146
classification of risk-based models 322,
327
comparison of models using *321, 323–6*
determination of, ABV model 187–9
brand role determination 136–7
Brand Stamina™, Brandient 130, 132
brand strength
BBDO models 117–29
Motameni & Shahrokhi's GBE model
251–5
and multiple applicable to brand
earnings 175–7
Young & Rubicam's Brand Asset
Valuator 137–8
see also demand drivers/brand strength
analysis
brand valuation process 47–8
brand league tables 48–9
defining scope of valuation and concept
of brand 54
definition of brand valuation 48

purpose of brand valuation 50–4
questioning necessity of brand
   valuation 49–50
selection of appropriate methodology
   54–6
brand value 18–20
   BrandEconomics 140–3
   Brandient 130
   BrandMetrics 156
   Brand Rating 162
   Consor 165–7
   Hirose 194, 199–201
   Interbrand 220, 229
   Kern 233
   Nielsen 269
   Sander's Hedonic model 264
   Sattler 266
   Semion 269
   Villafañe & Associates 284
brand value added
   BVA® or "earnings split" method
      147–50
   calculation of 160–1
   forecast 161
brand value criteria, determination of 275,
   276
Brand Voltage™, Millward Brown 247–8
"Bundle of Brand Rights" theory 76–7
business initiatives 20–2
BVA® (brand value added) model 147–50
BVE$_Q$™ model 168–70

Capital Asset Pricing Model (CAPM) 124
   and assessing brand risk 149–50
   and corporate reputation 377–8
   methods using 322–7
classification of methods *see* taxonomy of
   methods
cluster analysis, royalty rates 80–2
Coca-Cola brand, valuation of 170
commercial methods 301–2
   in Anglo-Saxon countries 337–8
   approaches used 305, 306
company valuation less value of net
   tangible assets 102–3
competitive equilibrium analysis,
   Villafañe & Associates model
   283–289, 319, 321
concepts of brand 1–2, 54
   accounting perspective 2–7
   brand equity 12–14
   economic perspective 7–8
   intellectual capital 14–18

management perspective 8–12
   conceptual errors 350–6
conjoint analysis 67–8
   Herp's model 192–3
Conjoint Value Hierarchy (CVH) 318–19
Consor 164–5
   BVE$_Q$™ model 168–70
   residual approach 170–1
   royalty savings model based on
      Valmatrix® analysis 165–7
   ValCALC® model (excess earnings)
      167–8
constant coefficient method, "Repenn
   Factor" 260–1, 319, *320*
corporate brand valuation 363–4
   CoreBrand's model 388–9
      Brand Equity Valuation Model 390–1
      Brand Power™ analysis 389–90
      critique 392–5
      ROI analysis 390
      stock performance forecast 391–2
   and corporate reputation 364–5
      adding value to product brands
         Association-Affinity Model 369–73
         demand driver analysis 373–6
      link to market value
         assumptions 376–9
         critique 386–8
         empirical development 379–81
         theoretical model 381–6
   methodological options proposed for
      366–9
   reasons for valuing corporate brands
      365–6
corporate reputation 364–5
   Association-Affinity Model 369–73
   and CAPM betas objective risk 377–8
   and corporate value 384–6
   demand driver analysis 373–6
   dimensions of 376–7
   link to higher risk taking 379–81
   and lower required returns 381–4
   theoretical model 381–6
cost approach 58–61, 305–6
courses on intangible assets 30–1
customer loyalty *see* brand loyalty
CVH (Conjoint Value Hierarchy) 318–19

Damodaran's valuation model 171–4, *318*
demand drivers/brand strength
   analysis 82, 309
   absolute approach 83
   BBDO's models 117–29

BrandEconomics model 132–44
Brand Finance model 149, 150
Brandient's model 129–30, 132
BrandMetrics model 151–8
corporate brand model 373–6
disadvantages of 86–8
FutureBrand model 179–83
GfK-PwC-Sattler: ABV model 183–92
inconsistency in application of 344–5
Interbrand's DCF model 215, 222–3,
   230–2
Interbrand's multiplier approach
   217–19, 227–9
methods for determining brand
   profits *310–11*
Nielsen Company models 274–80
Prophet Influence model 257–60
relative approach 83–5
Sattler's model 265–7
Semion's model 267–70
"discounted cash flow" (DCF) methods 63
Brand Finance 144
differences in implementation 345–6
FutureBrand 179, 183
Interbrand 215, 222–3, 230–2
discount rate
calculations 124–5, 149–50, 161–2,
   227–9
methodologies using as a risk factor
   322–7
methods of determining 279, 348–50
"Don't Waste Your Time with Brand
   Valuation" (Haigh & Knowles
   article) 49

earnings *see* brand earnings
EBIT (operating profit) 91–4
economic profit, BrandMetrics' financial
   analysis 152–3
Economic Value Added (EVA)® model
   132–44
"economies of scale method" 89–91, 316
errors and misconceptions 350
conceptual errors 350–6
errors in interpretation 358–9
management errors 356–8
EVA® (Economic Value Added) model
   132–44
excess earnings technique 96–7
Baruch Lev's Intangible Scoreboard 100
ROI analysis 100–2
U.S. Revenue Ruling 68-609 97–100
VALCALC® model 167–8

Expansion Driver (ED), Hirose's model
   198–9, 206
external transactions 53–4

Financial World (FW) 174–5
brand-related earnings 175
   compared with theoretical *317*
brand strength multiple 175–7
critique of model 177
Gillette case study 177, *178*
"Formula Approach" 97–100
free cash flow (FCF) less return on assets
   other than brand 96, 319, *320*
AUS Consultants model 112–17
Houlihan Advisors model 207–8
FutureBrand 179–83

GfK-PwC-Sattler model *see* Advanced
   Brand Valuation (ABV) model
Gillette case study 177, *178*
Global Brand Equity (GBE) model 250–1
brand net earnings 255–6
brand strength 251–5
critique of model 256–7
Global Reporting Initiative (GRI) 21
goodwill
categories of assets allocated to 25–6
as percentage of acquisition price
   33–4
gross margin
comparison with that of competitors
   89–91
differential, royalty rates 78–9
group analysis, royalty rates 80–2
guidelines, future standardization of
   404–5

hedonic analysis 68–9
Herp's valuation model 192–3
Hirose model (2002) 193–4, *322*
application of model 201–3
brand valuation model 199–201
critique of model 203–6
expansion driver (ED) 198–9
loyalty driver (LD) 197–8
prestige director (PD) 195–7
Houlihan Valuation Advisors (HVA)
   207–9, *208*
brand profit calculation *320*
human capital 16

"icon iceberg model" 159–60
ICS (Intellectual Capital Services) 318

income approach 63–4, 303–7
  company valuation less value of net
    tangible assets 102–3
  demand drivers/brand strength
    analysis 82–8
  excess earnings 96–102
  free cash flow (FCF) 96
  gross margin comparisons 89–91
  operating profit comparisons 91–2
  price premium 65–7
    conjoint analysis 67–8
    hedonic analysis 68–9
  real options 103–8
  royalty savings 70–8
    cluster or group analysis 80–2
    gross margin differential 78–9
    Knoppe formula 79–80
  "subtraction approach" 94–5
  theoretical profits of generic product
    comparison 92–4
  value of business with and without
    brand 95–6
Institute for the Analysis of Intangible
  Assets 21
intangible assets
  accounting standards recognition of
    24–6
  and brand equity 12–14
  definition and examples of 2–3
  economic vs. accounting criteria 7–8
  growth of investment in 24, 25
  importance of in business 20–2
  increasing economic relevance 22–4
  initiatives promoting reporting of 26–9
  and intellectual capital 14–18
  non-recognizable 4–5
Intangible Business Ltd 210–14
"intangible earnings"
  conflation with EVA 248, 350–1
  Interbrand's estimation of 224–5
  MBO model 235, 237–40, 312
intangible value
  confusion with EVA 350–1
  definition of 135
intangible value multiple,
  BrandEconomics 139–40, 143–4
intellectual capital 14–18
Interbrand 214–16
  brand vs. theoretical earnings
    calculation 317
  discounted cash flow model 222–32
    critique of model 230–2
    stage 1: segmentation 223

stage 2: financial analysis 224–5
stage 3: role brand index (RBI) 225–7
stage 4: brand strength analysis 227–9
stage 5: calculation of brand value
  229–30
multiplier ("annuity") model 216–22
  brand strength indicator 217–18, 219
  calculation of brand value 220
  critique of model 220–2
  determination of the multiplier
    218–20
  earnings attributable to brand
    216–17
internally generated brands 4–5
internal transactions 53
International Valuation Standards
  Committee (IVSC) 26–7
interpretation, errors in 358–9
intrinsic value of brand, BrandEconomics
  model 140–2, 143
investors, factors preventing adoption of
  valuation methods 42–3

Kern's x-times model 232–4
Knoppe formula, royalty rates 79–80
Knowledge Capital Scoreboard 100, 234

Lev's Intangibles Scoreboard 100, 234–6
loyalty
  and BPI index 184–5
  Brand Rating's model 159–60
  Hirose's model 197–8, 206
  methods of measuring 252
  Millward Brown Optimor model 245–7

management errors 356–8
management perspective
  brand and corporate reputation 8–11
  brand equity and intangible assets
    12–14
  brand, intangible assets and intellectual
    capital 14–18
  brand and visual identity 11–12
market analysis, Intangible Business
  model 213
market approach 61–2, 303–7
market capitalization (market cap) 14–15,
  23
  CoreBrand's model 388–95
  macro-analysis 271–3
  residual approach to valuation 170–1
marketing specialists, terminology issues
  403–4

market share (MS) calculation, Villafañe
  & Associates 286–8
Millward Brown Optimor 236–8
  application of 244
  "brand contribution" calculation 240–2
  brand multiple calculation 243–4
  critique of model 248–50
  general overview 245–8
  "intangible earnings" calculation
    238–40
monetary value of brand see brand
  earnings
Motameni and Shahrokhi's Global Brand
  Equity Valuation model 250–7

Nielsen Company
  Brand Balance Sheet 274–7
  Brand Performance model 277–80
non-recognizable intangible assets 4–5

obsolescence of trademark, determining
  347–8
operating profit comparisons 91–2, 312

Prestige Director (PD), Hirose's model
  195–7, 206
price premium-oriented methods 65–7,
  299, 313
  "Brand Rating" model 158–64
  conjoint analysis 67–8
  Herp's model 192–3
  hedonic analysis 68–9
  Sander's model 261–5
  Trout & Partners model 280–3
price-to-sales ratio difference,
  Damodaran's model 171–2
Prophet valuation model 257–60
purpose of brand valuation 50–4

Rank Hovis McDougall 35–6
real option models 103–5
  binomial method 105–7
  Black-Scholes model 107–8
"reasons-to-buy" analysis 82–8
regulations, future trends 404–5
Repenn's model 260–1
reputation see corporate reputation
residual return, excess earnings technique
  100–2
"Resource Recognition Procedure" (RRP)
  153–5
Return-on-Investment (ROI) analysis,
  CoreBrand 390

risk drivers see "brand risk"
royalty relief/savings methodology
  55–6, 61–2, 71–3
  advantages and disadvantages 74
  based on Valmatrix® analysis 165–7
  BEVA financial model 127–8
  Brand Finance "Royalty Relief" model
    144–7
  Brandient Model 131, 132
  for calculating brand earnings 315
  cluster or group analysis 80–2
  disadvantages of 74–8
  gross margin differential 78–9
  Intangible Business Model 210
  Knoppe formula 79–80
  RR 68-609 see U.S. Revenue Ruling
    68-609
Rubicam & Young's model, brand
  health 137–8

Sander's Hedonic brand valuation
  method 261–5
Sattler's brand valuation model 265–7
Semion® Brand-Broker GmbH 267–70
Shahrokhi and Motameni's Global Brand
  Equity Valuation model 250–7
Simon & Sullivan's stock price
  movements model 270–4
Skandia, intellectual capital model 16–17
S&P 500 book-to-market ratio 23–4
Srivastava's model 376–83
standardization of methods 397–8, 404–5
Stern Stewart & Co see BrandEconomics
stock performance forecast,
  CoreBrand 391–2
stock price movements model, Simon and
  Sullivan 270–4
structural capital 16
"subtraction approach" 94–5
supply and demand, future trends in
  399–402
System Repenn 260–1

taxonomy of methods 295
  academic vs. commercial origin 301–2
  by application or possible objectives
    296–7
  by approach employed (cost, market and
    income) 303–7
  brand contribution to income/revenues
    307–21
  brand's growth and useful life 327–30
  classification proposed by BBDO 297–8

classifications based on mixed criteria
299–300
by intended universality of calculated
value 300–1
by method of "representing brand risk"
321–7
using financial or non-financial
indicators 295–6
theoretical profits comparison 92–4, 316,
317
trademarks 5–6, 7
securitization using 53
valuation of using royalty savings
method 71–2
trends in brand valuation 331–3
industry trends
academic vs. practitioner world 343
concentration in Anglo-Saxon
countries 337–8
convergence between marketing and
finance 338–9
detrimental "black box" methods
343–4
financial validity vs. usage of models
341–3
professionalism and sophistication
338
proliferation of methods and firms
333–5
users' lack of credibility/
understanding 335–6
widespread use of certain models
339–41
methodological trends
differences in usage of income-based
models 345–6
divergence of results from different
methods 346–7
income-based models and useful life
347–8
inconsistency in application/use of
techniques 344–5
risk models with WACC
adjustments 348–50

Trout & Partners 281–4
trusted institutions 22

useful life of brand
Brandmetrics analyses 155–6
factors determining 347–8
methods/companies using 327–30
users, lack of understanding 335–6
U.S. Revenue Ruling 68-609 97–100

ValCALC® model (excess earnings)
167–8
valuation of brand 20
academic evidence 30–1
business evidence 20–2
economic evidence 22–4
normative and institutional evidence
24–9
social evidence 22
see also brand value
valuation methods 33
accounting conflict 36–7
corporations' use of 40–1
current brand valuation services
38–40
first brand valuation 35–6
investment analysts' use of 41–3
origins of 33–4
players' use of 43–5
rapid development and applications
37–8
taxonomy of 295–330
valuation providers 289–93
future trends in supply and demand
399–402
proliferation of 333–5
Villafañe & Associates' Competitive
Equilibrium Model 283–9

weighted average cost of capital (WACC)
161, 239, 348–50

Young & Rubicam's Brand Asset Valuator
137–8